SOME ASPECTS OF THE STUDIES OF DHARMA-ŚĀSTRA

BY
DR. S. G. MOGHE

BHARATIYA KALA PRAKASHAN
DELHI (INDIA)

First Published : 2003

Published by **C.P. Gautam**
BHARATIYA KALA PRAKASHAN
3421-A, IInd Floor, Narang Colony, Tri Nagar,
Delhi-110035. Phone : (O) 27153083,

ISBN : 81-8090-019-3

Laser Type Setting by
A-ONE GRAPHICS
X-4, Street No. 2, Brahmapuri, Delhi-110053
Phone : 2218 3470

Printed at
Santosh Offset Press
Delhi

DECICATED

THIS WORK

TO

MY PROFESSORS

1. The Late. Dr. S.N. Gajendragadkar.
2. The Late. Dr. P.S. Sane.
3. Dr. M.D. Paradkar.
4. Dr. G.H. Godbole.

Who impressed me by their good teaching.

CONTENTS

PREFACE

It is a matter of pleasure to me to present my book 'some aspects of the studies of Dharma-Śāstra' to the sincere lovers of Dharma-Śāstra.

In this book, I have included the papers already published in the research journals and the papers sent for the felicitation volumes of scholars like Dr. Satya Vrata Sastri, Dr. M.D. Paradkar and others.

In this book, am attempt is also made to evluate the works of the modern scholars like Gode, Mandalik and Gharpure. It may by, incidentally noted here, that these papers will form the part of my lengthy article on 'Contribution of Dharma-Śāstra to Indian Culture.'

Two special papers are also written on the basis of the Descriptive catalogues of a the Sanskrit Manuscripts for showing the contribution of Maharashatra authors to the domain of Dharma-Śāstra.

Two papers in this bunch take the survey of the research work done in the twentieth century A.D.

Some papers deal with the intersting topics of Holidays, theft and the importance of association with the aged persons.

In other two papers, I have included my note on the article of a scholar and also review on the Dharma-Śāstra Smṛti.

I only hope that this variety of articles will surely interest the lovers of Dharma-Śāstra and also will be of some use to the young scholars of Dharma-Śāstra.

I take this opportunity to thank my publisher Shri. C.P. Gautam, for Bharatiya Kala Prakashan, Delhi-35 for the good printing and excellent get up of the work and also his keen interest in my work.

Ananta Caturdaśī i.e. **S.G. Moghe**
20-9-2002
Mumbai.

I
THE VYĀGHRASMṚTI

The Vyāghrasmṛti appears to have been neglected my M.M. Dr. P.V. Kane, in his monumental History of Dharma-Śāstra Vol.I, Part-I, possibly due to the fact that this Smṛti was not published in the year 1930 and at the time of the revision of this Volume, Dr. Kane's attention was not drawn to the 'volumes of Smṛti Sandarbha published by Mansukhalal Mor, from Calcutta.

The present author is happy to mention here that he has recently prepared a critical edition on the Vyāghra Smṛti in the light of the two manuscripts. The Manuscript No. 163 of 1884-1886 from the Bhandarkar Oriental Research Institute, Poona and the one published in the fourth volume of the Smṛti Sandarbha—are utilised for the critical edition of the Vyāghra Smṛti.

The critical edition of the Vyāghra Smṛti prepared by the present author is published by the Bhandarkar Oriental Research Institute, Poona. In this critical edition, there are 382 stanzas; the stanzes that are uncommon to both the manuscripts are noted below in the foot-notes. The major part of the Vyāghrasmṛti deals with the Śrāddha resptect of Dharma-Śāstra, though the other aspects of Dharma-Śāstra like *Ācāra*, Prāyaśacitta and Śuddhi are given very meagre treatment in this work. In addition to this, the present author has collected about 144 stanzes on the name of Vyāghra quoted in the vast Dharma-Sāstra literature right from the 11th[1] century up to the 19th century A.D. Here it may be added, in passing that even on the Śrāddha aspect of Dharma-Śāstra, the present critically edited Vyāghrasmṛti cannot be said to be complete; for I have collected about 39 stanzas on the name of Vyāghra on the Śrāddha aspect of Dharma-Śāstra . Moreover, I have also collected about 32 stanzas in Śuddhi section, 4 stanzas in the Vyavahāra, 36 stanzas in the prāyaścitta, 30 stanzas in the Ācāra section, and one stanza in the Samaya section. From this collection of stanzas on the name of Vyāghra in the vast Dharma-Śāstra literature, it would be fair to conclude that the present critically edited Vyāghrāsmṛti cannot be said to be a complete text available to us. In fact, it will have to be regarded as a part of the vast bulk of the Vyāghrasmṛti which was available to the scholars and which is not now available to us. If, however, it is brought to light it may help us to know more peculiar views of Vyāghra in the Dharma-Śāsṭra literature.

The name Vyāghra enjoys a great antiquity. We find a reference to the name of Vyāghra in the Sarvānukramaṇi of the the ṚV, IX, 87-19-21. Besides, in the Mahābhārata IV. 7.12, Yudhiṣṭhira refers to himself as 'Vaiyāghrapadya'. Nīlakaṇṭha, the commentator of the Mahābhārata, explains, this as the name of Yama from whom Yudhiṣṭhira is born. The commentator Caturbhuja explains this expression as 'Kulīno gotreṇa.'[2] From the commentary Lakṣaṇābharaṇa, 30 It is further evident that Vyāghra was the originator of the Soma Vaṁśa and the name of the sage. The [3]Mahābhārata XIV. III refers to Vyāghrapāda as one who belonged to the Kṛta age. He was well versed in the Veda along with six

Dhaumya. he managed to feed Upamanyu at a sacrifice with the mixture of rice and milk.

In the Dharma-Śāstra literature, there are three names associated with Vyāghra such as Vyāghra, Vyāghrapāda, and Vaiyaghrapadya. The quesiton often arises whether there are three different authors or one and the same author bears three different names. The present author here draws the attention of the readers to the remarks of Dr. Kane that probably these three names refer to one and the same person. The identry of these three names can be established by drawing the attention of the readers to the following discussion.

Nandapanḍita[4] in his commentary Śuddhcandrikā on saḍaśīti quotes a stanza from the text of Vaiyāghrapāda. The same stanza is also found quoted by Haradatta in his commentary on the Gautam Dharma-Sāstra XIV, 42 from the text of Vyāghra, Devaṇṇabhaṭṭa, the author of the Smṛticandrikā has quoted the same stanza in his Āśauca Kāṇḍa from the text of Vyāghra. From this, it is evident that Vyāghra is also called by the other writers as Vaiyāghrapāda.

Vijṅāneśvara[5] in his commentary Mitākṣarā on the Yājnavalkya smṛti 111. 30 quoted from the text of Vyāghrapada and the same by Haradatta in his commentary on the Gautam-Dharma Sūtra XXII. 5, from the text of Vyāghra. Maskari also on the Gautama Dharma-Śāstra XXII.4 quotes the same stanza from the smṛti of Vyāghra. This discussion establishes the identity between Vyāghrapada and Vyāghra since one and the same stanza in quoted by these auothors from the text of one author whose name is written differently.

Vijñāneśvara[6] in his Mitākṣarā on the Yājñvalkya Smṛti III.17 quotes a stanza from the text of Vaiyāghrapāda. It may be pointed out here that the same stanza is also quoted by

Nandapaṇḍta in his commentary Keśava-Vaijayantī on the Viṣṇusmṛti P. 356 from the text of Vyāghrapada. This illustration is sufficient to establish the identity between the two names Vyāghrapada and Vaiyāghrapada.

As regards the exact date of the Vyāghra-smṛti, it may be stated that the internal evidence is not of any use to us. As regards the external evidence to be considered in this respect, it may be pointed out that both Viśvarūpa (between 750 and 1000 A.D.) and Medhātithi (825-900 A.D.) do not quote the text of the Vyāghra-smṛti. It is further interesting to note that right from the 11th century A.D. onwards the text ot the Vyāghra-smṛti is quoted in the vast Dharam-Śāstra literature. Vijñāneśvara (1100-1120 A.D.). Aparāka (1125 A.D.) Devaṇṇabhaṭṭa (1225 A.D.) Mādhavācārya (between 1300 to 1380 A.D.) Raghunandana (1520-1580 A.D.) Vaidyanātha Dīkṣita (between 1650-1700 A.D., Nīlakaṇṭha (1600 A.D.) Kamalākarabhaṭṭa (1612 A.D.), Mitramiśra (1615-1645 A.D.) and Bālaṁbhaṭṭa Pāyaguṇḍe (1750-1820 A.D.) have profusely quoted the text of the Vyāghra Smṛti. Besides, some of the stanzas from the Vyāghra Smṛti could be traced in the Matsya Purāṇa (4th and 6th century A.D.), Bhaviṣyat (later thatn 9th century A.D. but earlier than 15th century A.D.) If the Paurāṇnic evidence is considered along with the fact that Vyāghra is quoted from the 11th century A.D. onwards upto the 19th century A.D., it would be reasonble on our part to fix the date of the Vyāghra Smṛti as the 10th century A.D.

As regards the other works of Vyāghra or ascribed to Vyāghra, it may be pointed out that he seems to have written Daśaka Vyākaraṇa, This is further evident from the Mahābhāraṣya[7], and Kāśikā on Pāṇini's Aṣṭādhyāyi. IV. 2.65. Even Pāṇini refers to Vyāghrapada in the Gargādi Gaṇa on IV.1. 105. From this, it is quite evident that the Vyākaraṇa consisting of ten chapters is ascribed to Vyāghra.

Attention may be drawn to some other work ascribed to Vyāghra. The work named-Aṅkaṇa-Śāstra published by the Kerala University as No. 222 is ascribed to Vyāghrapāda[8]. It must be stated here that this workd is based on Astrology.

Some of the peculiar views of Vyāghra deserve special mention here. Vyāghra points out that when the Gotra of any dead person or living person is not known, one should utter the name of Kaśyapa.[9] This view is ascribed to Vyāghra in several texts of Dharma-Śāstra. Whenever the death of any person falls in the intercalary month, in the opinion of Vyāghra, the Śrāddha of such a person may be performed within two months on the completion of the intercalary month.[10] He also avers that the feeding of the brahmins well versed in the three Vedas brings inexhaustible fruit. Vyāghra also specifically holds that at the time of offering the rice balls in the Śrāddha ceremony, one should declare one's own relationship with the dead person and mention one's own Gotra.[11] It is further evident that Vyāghra does not appear to be in favour of eating a betel leaf at the time of Darśa Śrāddha, Gayā Śrāddha and the Śrāddha that is performed in the dark fortnight of the month.[12] That a brahmacārī should perfom the srāddha of a Vānaprastha person and even an ascetic appears to be a pecliar view of Vyāghra.[13] It is rather interesting to note that Vyāghra permits a man to speak the untruth, if one is mentally harassed or troubled in[14] words (by anybody). The most interesting aspect of the peculiar view of Vyāghra is that he has clearly pointed out the sizes[15] of the morsels of food, one should take at the time of the expiations like Cānadrāyaṇa and others.

Finally a word more about the position of Vyāghra in the Dharma-Śāstra literature. In the first place, there is no commentary, so far available, on the text of Vyāghra. Secondly, whatever position is enjoyed by the Manu Smṛti literature, the same cannot be said be to be enjoyed by the Vyāghra Smṛti. Perhaps the possible reason at the back of this may be the time factor responsible for the composition of this Smṛti. However, it must be stated without any fear of contradiction that the Vyāghra Smṛti is quoted bythe writers on Dharma-Śāstra right from the 11th century A.D. upto the 19th century A.D. This is the independent sufficient evidence to show that in the domain of Dharma-Śāstra the Vyāghra Smṛti has some place, though in the History of Dharma-Śāstra, M.M. Dr. P.V. Kane has not assigned any position to this work. In conclusion, one will be right in holding that on the point of popularity, the Vyāghra Smṛti occupies or holds the place of second magnitude.

FOOT NOTES

1. व्याघ्रपाद्वासिष्ठः। R.V IX. 6.1.
2. वैयाघ्रपद्यगोत्रायेति भीष्मस्य कथनात् सोमवंशप्रवर्तकः व्याघ्रपादिति कश्चिदस्ति ऋषिरिति बाह्यो भावः। लाक्षाभरण on विराटपर्व P. 30 (Gujarati Printing Press edition, Bombay 1915).
3. पुरा कृतयुगे तात ऋषिरासीन्महायशाः।
   व्याघ्रपाद इति ख्यातो वेदवेदाङ्गपारगः।। महाभारत XIII. 14 111a-112b (Chitrashala Press edition Poona, 1933).
4. जाते मृते सपिण्डानां सद्यश्शौचं विधीयते।
   दशाहेनैव दम्पत्योस्सोदराणां तथैव च।। हरदत्त on गौतम धर्मसूत्र P. 156.
5. चण्डालं पतितं चैव, दूरतः परिवर्जयेत्।
   गोवालव्यजनादर्वाक्सबासा जलमाविशेत्।। याज्ञवल्क्यस्मृतिः। P. 352.
6. स्मार्तकर्मपरित्यागो राहोरन्यत्र सूतके।
   श्रौते कर्मणि तत्कालं स्नातः शुद्धिमवाप्नुयात्।। Ibid. P. 333.
7. दशकाः वैयाघ्रपदीयाः। Quoted in महाभाष्य पृ० १३४
8. व्याघ्रपादमहं वन्दे शेषांशेन समुद्भवम्।
   पुण्डरीकपुरीशस्य पदपङ्कजसंश्रयः। अंकणशास्त्र P. 1
9. गोत्रनाशे तु कश्यप.......स्मृतिचंद्रिका-श्राद्धकाण्ड P. 388.
10. मासद्वयगतं श्राद्धं मलमासेऽपि शस्यते। वर्षे वर्षे च यच्छ्राद्धं मातापित्रोर्मृतेऽहनि।।

मासद्वयेऽपि तत् कार्यं व्याघ्रस्य वचनं यथा। स्मृतिचंद्रिका श्राद्धकाण्ड, p. 114 (Mysore edition).

11. संबंध प्रथमं ब्रूयात् गोत्रं नाम ततः परम्।
पश्चाद्रूपं विजानीयात् व्याघ्रस्य वचनं यथा।। व्याघ्रस्मृति-St. 249.

12. दर्शश्राद्धे गयाश्राद्धे श्राद्धे चापरपक्षके।
ताम्बूलचर्वणे दोषो व्याघ्रस्य वचनं यथा। व्याघ्रस्मृति-St. 62.

13. वानप्रस्थयतीनां च ब्रह्मचारिस्तथैव च।
कुर्याच्छ्राद्धादिकं तस्य व्याघ्रस्य वचनं यथा।। Ibid. St. 70.

14. यस्योक्तौ वाङ्मनः पीडा नित्यं भवति चेत्ततः।
तत्र वक्तव्यमनृतं व्याघ्रस्य वचनं यथा।। मस्करि on गौतमधर्मसूत्र-XIX. 3. P. 304 (Mysore edition 1917)

15. चतुरंगुलमुत्सेधं चतुरंगुलमायतम्।
एतद् ग्रासप्रमाणं तु व्याघ्रेण परिभाषितम्।। स्मृतिमुक्ताफलम् P. 203 (Gharpure's edition).

II

KĀŚINĀTHA UPĀDHYĀYA

Kāśinātha Upādhyāya. alias Bābā Pādhye is the famous author of the Dharma-Sindhu, the leading work in the matter of religious obserance in the Deccan. His family hailed from Goḷavalī, a village in the Ratnāgiri Disctrict. He was a Karhaḍā Brāhmaṇa and had the Joshi and Upadhye Vṛtti of the 72 villages, in the Sangameśvara Taluka of the Ratnagiri District. He was the son of Ananta.

Though the title of the work is called as 'Dharmasindhu' it is described as Dharma-Sindhu-Sāra at the end of the several sections of the work. Hence it would be but proper to accept the title 'Dharma-Sindhu Sāra'. if this this title is accepted, then it would mean that this work gives 'Essence of the ocean of Dharma (Śāstra). This would be in keeping with the treatment of the topics.

It must be admitted that the Dharma-Sindhu Śara is a digest of a very different nature. In the Dharma-Śāstra, we have the Smṛti, Dharma-Sūtras, commentaries on the Smṛtis and the Dharma-Sūtras and the independent digest works. The commentators of the smṛtis or the Dharma-Sūtras try to explain the text in their own way. But the digest authors bring together the contradictory passages by quoting several Smṛti passages and try to resolve the conflict by resorting to the Mīmāṁsā rules of Interpretation or determining the scope of the particular text.

In the Dharma-Sindhu-Sāra, one finds that the treatment given to the topics is totally different. Here one will not find several texts quoted by the author. But whatever are the established conclusions on the particulary discussed topics, are stated by consulting the previously published digest works of Nirṇaya-Sindhu of Kamalākara-bhaṭṭa, Mayūkhs of Nīla-kaṇṭha, Mādhavācārya's commentary on the Pārāśara Smṛti and several other works. Hence it would be more correct to say that the present work is an abridged work of the larger digests on the Dharma-Śāstra. Kāśīnātha Upādhyāya states the conclusions either in his own language or sometimes as noted by Kane, the conclusion by quoting the lines from the Nirṇaya-Sindhu. As this work gives us the essence of the conclusions of the larger digest works, it would be apt to describe it as 'Dharma-Sindhu-Sāra.

Kāśīnātha Upādhyāya is also the author of the Prāyaś-cittenduśekhar, Vedastuti in the Bhāgawata Purāna, and Viṭṭhala-ṛṇamantrasāra-bhāṣya. As noted by Kane in his History of Dharma-Śāstra Vol.-I/II P.77, Kāśīnatha seems to be the devotee of Viṭṭhala at Pandharapur in the Sholapur Disctrict. He takes freely that in the Ṛg-Vedic mantras, there is the description of the god Viṭhabā or Viṭṭhala.

Recently Dr. Miss. Usha R. Bhise contributed a paper on 'some unknown works of Kāśīnatha Upadhyāya' to the MM. Dr. P.V. Kane Centenary Volume brought out by the Asiatic Society of Bombay in the year 1980. In this article, Bhise points out that there are three works—Bodhadvirada-padyāvalī, Viṭṭhala-dhyāna-Mānasa-pūjā and Śayanotsava-krama. In the Moropant Paradkar Collection of Manuscripts presented to the University of Bombay, these works are available in the Manuscript form. Thanks to Usha Bhise for publishing these works in the journal of the Asiatic society of Bombay Vol. Nos. 52-53 for 1977-78 covering pages 55 to 74. Here it must be mentioned that the first one i.e. Bodhadviadapadyāvalī is the typical Bhūpālī in the Marāthī language. Dr. S.Y. Wakenkar has already pointed out the Bhūpālī of Shri Acutarai Modaka and Vāsudevānanda (1854-1914) has also written 'Datta-Prabodha-Bhūpālī to arouse god Datta from the sleep. Attention of the readers is further drawn to the article of Usha Bhise, for details in the works of Kāśinātha Upādhayāya. In passing, it may be noted that in Kane's History of Dharma-Śāstra, there is no mention of these works because the Catalogue of the Moropanta Collection of of manuscripts prepared by Dr. Usha Bhise was published after the revision of the first volume of the History of Dharma-Śāstra by Kane.

On behalf of the Ānandāśrama Sanskrit Series, Poona, the Prāyaścittendu-śekhara originally written by Nāgoji-bhaṭ ṭa but revised and enlarged by Kāśinātha Upādhayāya is published in the year 1931 as the series No. 100. This work covers printed 88 pages. This is further followed by a small chapter written by Kāśinātha Upādhayāya. This is technically known as the 'Sarva-prāyaścitta-Prayoga'. The procedural details of this prayoga covers printed 88-95 pages. These two important works of Kāśinātha Upādhayāya, have escaped the eagle eye of Kane. Though the work was published in the year 1931, Kane's attention was not drawn to this work at the time of the revision of the first Volume of the History of Dharma-Śāstra.

In his Dharma-Sindhu-Sāra, Kāśinātha Upādhayāya has quoted the works or authors such as Smṛtyartha-Sāra, p. 236, Vijeṅāneśvara, p. 452, Heṃādari pp. 26, 27, 101, 508, 534, 545, 456 etc. Mādhavācārya pp. 437, 539, 566, Kamalākara-bhaṭṭa, the author of Nirṇaya-Sindhu, pp. 259,

288, 290, 362, 363, 456 etc. Medhātithi on the Manu-Smṛti p. 581, Nīlakaṇṭha bhaṭṭa or the author of the Mayūkhas-260, 363 etc. Smṛtikaustubha pp. 140, 145, 152, 154, 240, 286, 288, 313, 316, 360, 511, etc. Mātṛdatta p. 284 Puruṣārtha-Cintāmāni, p. 36, 56, etc. Manu-Smṛti pp. 238, 290, Rājmārtanda of Bhoja p. 298 etc.

Generally it is the style of the digest authors to introduce Mīmāmāsā rules of interpretation for resolving the conflicts of the contradictory texts of Dharma-Śāstra. Though Kāśinātha Upādhayāya has not personally introduced the Mīmāṁśa rules of interpretation, yet whaever Mīṁāmśa doctrines are utilised by the other digest authors are used by him in the course of his discussion. This can be illustrated by referring to the terms such as Tantra, p. 548, Vidhi-Niṣedha, pp. 451-52, Pratipradhānam Guṇāvṛttiḥ, p. 221, Pratinidhi nyāya, p. 239, Upalakṣaṇam, p. 46, Punarvacana p. 545, Kāṇḍānusamaya, p. 566, Padārthānusamya, p. 570 etc.

As regards the topics discussed in the Dharma-Sindhu Sāra, it may be noted that the author has dealt with several aspects of Dharma-Śāstra such as Ācāra, Prāyaścitta, Samaya, Saṁskāra, Śrāddha, Dāna, Śuddhi, Utsarga, Pratiṣṭha, Śānti-very briefly. He has slightly touched the Vyavahāra aspect of the Dharma-Śāstra with a particular reference to the Dattaka son, his varieties, marriage in respect of the position of the dattaka son etc. Possibly the author might not have thought it proper to deal with the Vyavahāra aspect of Dharma-Śāstra, indicating the nature of the suits, petitioners, Respondents, Written Statement, witness, validity of the documents etc, for the internal reason that Padhye family lost a case in the Darbar of Peshwas, on the point of the Joshi and Upādhye-vṛtti.

Kāśinātha Upādhayāya has also clarified his stand point in writing this work. This work is written to satisfy the needs of the common people in respect of the debatable matters of daily observances. He has particularly avoided hairsplitting discussion and the use of the Pūrva-Mīṁāsā doctrines as this work is already done by the giants in the field of Dharma-Śāstra like Kamalākarabhṭṭha, Nīlakaṇṭha, Hemādri and others. It is true that Kane[2] has made the abundant use of the views of the Dharma-Sindhu, in his History of Dharma-Śāstra for allowing a wife to use vedic mantras for the funeral ceremony of a husband, Samānodakas to observe impurity for three days and sagotra to observe for one day. When there is the absence of āśuca i.e. impurity, for the soldier died on the battle-field, Saṁkalpa for the Mahālaya-Śrāddha, great merit arises when one takes bath in the waters of the river Godāvarī when the Jupiter enters in to the sign of Leo, the Sapiṇḍa ralationship arises like the leap of a frog, for the marriage with a maternal uncle's daughter is supported by the vedic authority, and if the person has many wives, then all the wives will be the mothers of his sons, the brothers of their wives will be the mothers sisters for the sons etc. and the importance of the Svastivācana, pūnyāhavācana and the Mātṛkāpūjana are necessary for the Jātkarma-saṁskāra, etc.

Now I take this opportunity to highlight some of the special views of Dharma-Sindhu-Sārā as his contribution to the thought development in the domain of Dharma-Śāstra.

He specially held[3] that a son deserves to be called a good son, if he obeys his father during his life-time, performs his Śrāddha every year and also makes the donation of ample food to the brāhmaṇas apart from the meagre food that is distributed at the time of the Śrāddha ceremony.

He further pointed[4] out that at times, the Madhuparka[5] is given to a person about to die. This view has escaped the eye of Kane.

Though it is not binding on a person to perform the

Śrāddha ceremony of his grand-father (whose son is not alive) if he performs it, it will bring excessive[5] fruit for him.

If at the time of the Śrāddha ceremony, inquiry is made about the distribution of salt, then it is said that the dead[6] ancestors go away from that place.

When the gotra of a person is not known, it is said that Kaśyapa is the gotra of such a person. This is the accepted view in the Dharms-Śāstra literature. But Kāśīṅatha Upādhyāya specially held the view[7] that kaśyaya is said to be the gotra[8] of all the Śāstra.

Now a days, there is a practice of performing the Grahayajna for any pacificatory rite and when the house is newly built. But Kāśīṅatha Upādhyāya specifically held[8] the view that the graha-makha is absolutely necessary when the pacificatory rite is performed on the constellations. In the case of other Śāntis, it naturally follows that the performance of the graha-makha is not, at all, necessary.

As regards the holiday in the Vedic study, he was of the view[9] that this applies to the teaching of the vedic portion and committing the vedic portion to memory. This rule is not to be applied to the study of six auxiliary sciences like śikṣā, kalpa, vyākaraṇa etc., for reading of the Mahābhārata and Purāṇa, or for the nitya muttering of the mantras and Kāmya acts and for the pārāyaṇa of a particular book.

He was of the opinion that though the marriage of the eldest son has not taken place, yet a younger daughter may be married. But when the thread ceremony or the Upayana of the eldest son has not taken place, the younger daughter is not to be married.

For the adoption of a son, he was of the view that a son should either be of same varṇa or of the same Gotra. In this respect, he has not given any consideration to the view of

Medhātithi on the Manu-Smṛti that a brāhmaṇa can adopt a Kṣatriya boy.

He further held that when a sagotra or sapinda dattka son is not available, then a person whose intiation ceremony has taken place and has married, can be adopted as a dattaka son.

He personally held[11] the view that even a married person can be adopted, provided there is no son born to him.

When any wife prefers immolation on the death of her husband, the question arises whether the Śrāddha ceremony of such a woman is to be performed on the same tithi on which a husband died or on other tithi. Kāśīnātha Upādhyāya refers to the view of some who held that it should be performed on the same tithi. But Kāśīnātha Upādhyāya points[12] out that this is possible only if there is a short intereval between the death of a husband a wife. But if, however, there is the interval of two or three days, then the Śrāddha of both of them cannot be performed on the same tithi. As the question of immolation of a Satī is out of consideration for the modern people, this view that is expressed by him has naturally become time-barred. However, for the thought development of the Dharma-Śāstra aspects, its importance can hardly be gainsaid.

In conclusion, Kāśīnatha Upādhyāya is the author of some other works other than the Dharma-Sindhu-Sāra, his work gives us the essence of the Dharma-Śātra digests, he has consulted good many digest works and smṛtis for giving the essence of Dharma-Śāstra, he has dealt with almost all the aspects of Dharma-Śātra except vyavahāra, Kane has consulted this digest abundantly for the monumental work 'History of Dharma-Śātra, he has also contributed some special views on some important aspects of Dharma-Śāstra, as noted above by the author of this note against the background of the vast Dharma-Śātra works.

FOOT NOTES

* References are to the edition of the Dharma-Sindu with Hindi Translation published by the Venkateshvara Press. Bombay, in the year 1961.

1. Dharma-Sindhu-Sāra stanzas 6 and 8 on page 709.
2. P.V. Kane- History of Dharma-Śāstra Vol. IV, pp. 236, 245, 249 275, 288, 299, 319, 502, 353, 536 etc. and fifth Volume.
3. Dharma-Sindhu Sāra P. 675.
   क्वचिन्मुमूर्षोर्मधुपर्कदानमुक्तम्।
4. Ibid. p. 647.
5. Ibid. p. 676.
6. Ibid. p. 577.
7. Ibid. p. 457, reads
   केचित् सर्वप्रजानां काश्यपत्वात् सर्वशूद्राणां काश्यपगोत्रम्।
8. Ibid. p. 264, reads
   इतरशांतिषु ग्रहमखो नावश्यकः।
9. Ibid. p.323.
10. Ibid. p.315.
11. Ibid. p. 241.
12. Ibid. p. 597.
    न तु द्वित्र्यादितिथिव्यवधाने।

III

THE VIEWS OF THE DHARMAVID IN THE MAHABHARATA AS THE SOURCE OF DHARMA

Dr. P.V. Kane in his History of Dharmaśāastra Vol. I/1, pp. 6-12 has discussed the sources of Dharma such as Veda, Smṛti, usages of the virtuous men and self-satisfaction and practice of those that know the Veda.

Elsewhere, Dr. Kane has also shown[1] that when the Śruits and Smṛtis are silent on some religious aspect, the opinion of the old ladies is considered as the source of Dharma and this view is based on the Āpastamba Dharmasūtṛa II. 2.29.15.

On carefully reading the critical edition of Mahābhārata published by the Bhandarkar Oriental Research Insititue, Pune, with the serious but studious efforts of several scholars, one comes to know the importance of the views of the Knowers of Dharma incidentally or casually referred to in body of the text of the Mahābhārata.

Here it should be noticed that the views of the knowers of Dharma are stated at some places by the general expression dharma-vid, at other places by making specific references to the persons who are treated as the knowers of Dharma and at still some places by the expressions such as brahmavādibhiḥ, dharmavādinaḥ, dharmaśastravidaḥ, and the characteristics of the best of the dharma-vid are also noted. In the light of this background an attempt is made in this paper to present some peculiar views expressed in the Mahābhārata and particularly those views which have not become the centre of attraction of the scholars.

At 1.94.59, Śantanu refers to the view of the speakers[2] of Dharma that the possession of one son is treated as a case of childlessness. This view is expressed by Śantanu when he asks the hand of Gaṅgā for the continuity of the family tradition.

At I.113.27, Vaiśampāyana puts in the mouth of Dharmarāja the view of the Knowers[3] of Dharma that whatever is said by a husband to a wife, whether it is in keeping with Dharma or not in consonance with dharma, the same is to be followed by a wife. This is addressed to Draupadī.

At another place in the Mahābhārata I. 149.11, in a conversation between Kuntī and Brāhmaṇa, the latter has expressed the view of the knowers[4] of Dharma in respect of difficulty or distress that one should not practise any censurable (most preferably censured) deed or wicked deed at any point of time.

In the Mahābhārata I 78.33, it is said that one who does not approach a woman desirous of sexual intercourse, is trearted as Bhrūṇahā by the wise. Here this view put in the mouth of the wise persons[5] who are called here as 'budhaiḥ'. At Mahābhārata I. 78. 32, it is said that when a person, particularly selected by a woman, does not approach her for sexual intercourse at the right time, he is treated as Bhūṇahā by the exponents[6] of Brahma (brahmavādibhiḥ) Roughly speaking, this expression comes near to the expression 'dharma-vid.'

It must be noted here that the Udyogaparvan of the Mahābhārata has also contributed some important views of the Dharma-Vid. Here at 5.63.13, Dhṛtarāṣṭra names the persons who are knowers of Dharma suh as Droṇa, Kṛpa, Vikarṇa, the king of Bālhika country, and he expects that Duryodhana should honour these persons like his own father.

On the point of sin, Kṛṣṇa has noted the view of knowers[7] of Dharma in the Mahābhārata 5-91.7. The Knowers of Dharma hold that one who mentally thinks of a sinful act but in practice in does not like it, never gets the fruit of the same. What he means to say is that such a person is not affected by any fruit as such.

In the Mahābhārata at 5.80.18, Vaiśampāyana puts into mouth of Draupadī the view of the knowers[8] of Dharma that just as there is a fault in killing a person who does not deserve to be killed, in the similar manner, there is also a fault in not killing a person who deserves to be killed. What Draupadī means to say is that in the opinion of the knowers of Dharma, the Kauravas deserve to be killed by the Pāṇḍvas.

In the Mahābhārata at 5.139.7, Karṇa in his conversation with Kṛṣṇa, admits his indebtedness to Rādha (his mother) and describes himself as always engaged[9] in hearing the view of the knowers of Dharma in the matter of Dharmaśāstra.

In the Mahābhārata 8.49.29-30, Kṛṣṇa points out the charateristic of the knower of Dharma. He states that when there is a danger to one's life, one may speak the untruth. In such a case the untruth becomes truth and truth becomes untruth. Here Kṛṣṇa adds that by deciding or distinguishing between the truth and untruth, one becomes the knower of Dharma.

In the Śalyaparvan of the Mahābhārata at 9.64.39, Sañjaya refers to the view point of the knowers of Dharma that at the command of a king, a brahmaṇa should specially engage himself in a fight. This behaviour on the part of brāhmaṇa, leading the life of a kṣatriya is treated as the proper dharma by the knowers[10] of Dharma.

In the Sauptikaparvan of the Mahābhārata at 10.1.50-52, Sañjaya refers to the view of the thinkers of Dharma that one should attack the army of the enemy particularly when the army is asleep, at mid-night, and one should act in such a way that the army becomes divided at that time. This kind of thinking on the part of Aśvatthāman, the son of Droṇa, is expressed by referring to the view of the knowers of Dharma.

The Śantiparvan of the Mahābhārata has recorded a view of the knowers of Dharma. At 12.134.7, Bhīṣma states that it is the view of the knowers of Dharma that one who, having snatched the things from the bad people, gives the same to the good and thus exhibits the revolution in himself, is to be known as the best knower of Dharma.

In the Śantiparvan of the Mahābhārata, there is a dialogue between Janaka and Parāśara at 12.285.5 where it is stated that the knowers of Dharma hold that Prajāpati created this world from his mouth, from his arms, from his thighs and from the feet. This is certainly based on the ṚV. X.90.

At 12.73.10 Bhīṣma refers to a dialogue between Alia and Vāyu and states the view of Vāyu that whaterver is produced in the world, the same belongs to the brāhmaṇas, because the brāmaṇas are treated as the senior most.

In the Anuśāsanaparvan of the Mahābhārata, Bhīṣma refers to the view[11] of the knowers of Dharma that who, after promising a gift, does not give it, becomes free from it (the sin) by making the gift of one thousand Śyāmakarṇa horses. Briefly it means that such a person, who is breaking the promise of giving, can become free from sin by making the above gift.

In the Anuśāsanaparvan of the Mahābhārata, Bhīṣma considers Śāṇḍilya as the knower of the Dharma and qoutes his view[12] that the gift of a chariot excels all other gifts.

In the Mahābhārata Anuśāsanparvan 13.129.55, the characteristics of the best knowers[13] of Dharma are stated. Such a person is not adamant, not proud, never fails in his duties, is never wonderstruck by any happening in the world and one who is a friend to both the friends and enemy. Such a kind a person alone is to be regarded as the best of the knowers of Dharma.

In the Mahābhārata, particularly in Anuśāsanparvan, when Kuntī refers to the birth of Karṇa in her maidenhood as a sin, Vyāsa replies[14] that whatever is done by the mightly is wholesome, pure, and dharma. Here the expression balavatām referes to the persons who are spitritually advanced like Durvāsas and others. By the side of this view, one many quote the view[15] casually expressed by Bhīṣma by way of a reply to Draupadī that whatever is declared by the mighty persons, the same is looked upon as a Dharma. Here the expression 'balavatām' naturally refers to the strong politically in a particular situation.

In conclusion, one may state that the views of knowers of Dharma expressed in the Mahābhārata particularly in different parvans, either in a general tone or by referring to some specifice persons or by the general expression budha, dharma-vid, dharma-vādin, brahma-vādin can also be considered as the valid source of Dharma, an aspect which is not given any place by MM. Dr. P.V. Kane in his discussion on the sources of Dharma.

FOOT NOTES

References are to the critical edition of the Mahābhārata published by B.O.R.I. Pune.

1. P.V. Kane—History of Dharmaśāstra-Vol.III, P.856.
2. अनपत्यता एकपुत्रत्वमित्याहुर्धर्म्वादिनः। महाभारत I. 94.596.
3. भर्ता भार्यां राजपुत्रि धर्म्यं वाधर्म्यमेव वा।
यद् ब्रूयात्तत्तथा कार्यमिति धर्मविदो विदुः।। Ibid. I. 113.27.
4. कुर्यान्न निन्दितं कर्म न नृशंसं कदाचन।
इति पूर्वे महात्मान आपद्धर्मविदो विदुः।। Ibid I.149.11
5. अभिकामां स्त्रियं यस्तु गम्यां रहसि याचितः।
नोपैति स च धर्मेषु भ्रूणहेत्युच्यते बुधैः।। Ibid. I. 78.33 For a note on भ्रूणहा, Vide S.G. Moghe—A peep at Indology - pp. 31-32 (D.K. Printworld Publication, Delhi. 1994.).
6. भ्रूणहेत्युच्यते ब्रह्मन् स इह ब्रह्मवादिभिः। Ibid. I 78. 32b.
7. मनसा चिन्तयन् पापं कर्मणा नाभिरोचयन्।
न प्राप्नोति फलं तस्य एवं धर्मविदो विदुः।। Ibid. 5.91.7.
8. यथावध्ये भवेद्दोषो वध्यमाने जनार्दन।
स वध्यस्यावधे दृष्ट इति धर्मविदो विदुः।। Ibid. 5.80.18.
9. तस्याः पिण्डव्यपनयं कुर्यादस्मद्विधः कथम्।
धर्मविद् धर्मशास्त्राणां श्रवणे सततं रतः।। Ibid. 5.139. 7.
10. It may be noted here that Dr. Kane has drawn attention for this view to the Mahābhārata शल्यपर्व 64.39 and शान्तिपर्व 78.18 Vide History of Dharma-Śāstra Vol. II./I, p. 123, also read -राज्ञो नियोगाद् योद्धव्यं ब्राह्मणेन विशेषतः। वर्तता क्षत्रधर्मेण ह्येवं धर्मविदो विदुः।। महाभारत–शल्पयपर्व -64.39.
11. अपि चोदाहरन्तीमं धर्मशास्त्रविदो जनाः।
अश्वानां श्यामकर्णानां सहस्रेण स मुच्यते।। महाभारत- XIII.139.6.
12. प्रदानं सर्वदानानां शकटस्य विशिष्यते।
एवमाह महाभागः शाण्डिल्यो भगवानृषिः।। Ibid. 13.64.19.
13. न स्तम्भी न च मानी यो न प्रमत्तो न विस्मितः।
मित्रामित्रसमो मैत्रो यः स धर्मविदुत्तमः।। Ibid. 13. 129. 55.
14. सर्वं बलवतां पथ्यं सर्वं बलवतां शुचिः।
सर्वं बलवतां धर्मः सर्वं बलवतां स्वकम्। Ibid. 15.38. 23.
15. बलवांस्तु यथा धर्मं लोके पश्यति पूरुषः।
स धर्मो धर्मवेलायां भवत्यभिहितः परैः।। Ibid. 2. 62.15.

\+ This paper is published in Dr. M.V. Joshi Felicitation Volume, Rajkot-2000.

IV

THEFT IN ACNCIENT INDIA

In this paper, attampt is made to present different aspects of theft, particularly with reference to the thieves, nature of guilt in this matter, classifiation of theft and thives, abettors in the matter of theft, the proper punishments given to the thieves, the person who is held as qualified to punish thieves, position of a thief in the society, references to thieves in the classical sanskrit literature, circumstantial evidence to be considered on the point of theft, casteism in the matter of theft, purposes at the back of the punishment to the thieves, time factor responsible for the charge of theft, proper time for theft and the acts that are also treated as akin to theft. Even though there are many crimes and punishments laid down in the Dharma Śāstra, yet in the interest of the paper that is concentrated on theft, the other crimes are not given any scope or place in the present paper.

As regards the nature of theft and the behaviour of a thief, a few observations will not be out of place. The question arises as to what kind of act constitues a theft in this respect, we have a good passage from the Mahābhārata[1] Śānti Parvan which clearly goes to prove that a thing in possession of another person, when taken by another person, though it is not given to him, constitutes the act of a theft. In the context, the expressions adatta, 'adānam or anisṛṣṭāni bhaksitāni' employed in the story of Śānskha and Likhita, are quite clear particularly in respect of the fruits eaten by Likhita, the younger brother of Śāṅkha, in the hermitage of the latter.

The Āpastamba[2] Dharma Sūtra I. 28.1 refers to the views of Kautsa, Hārīta and Kaṇva and Puśkarādi that he who under any condidtions whatsoever, covets (takes) another man's possession, as his own, is held as a thief. Haradatta[3] in his comments on this sūtra states that whatever the object or the material that is taken by another person may be of small quantity or large quantity, it constitutes a theft. From this explanation, it becomes clear that the quantity of the theft is immaterial. He further adds that the theft may be with reference to the time of distress or absence of distress. It is further interesting to add that Maskari in his commnts[4] on the Gautama Dharma Sūtra points out that the act of theft is always intentional or purposeful. He further adds that when the act is not done intentionally, it does not become a case of theft.

Here the view point of the Manu[5] Smṛti VIII.332 is particularly noteworthy. This smṛtikāra holds that when the taking away of the article or object of another persons takes place in the absence of the owner, it becomes a case of theft. Hence the force need not be utilised. The commentataor [6]Medhātithi points out on this portion of the Manu Smṛti that it becomes a case of theft when the deposit or the loan of another person is taken away. 'Medhatithi[7] also adds that taking away the object of the another person amounts to a theft and the person who thus takes it way, becomes a thief, Kullūka[8], however, adds that not only taking away but stealing away the object of another person also amounts to a theft. This discussion in the above direction clearly explains the position of the smṛtikāras on act of theft and the theif who thus becomes guilty of it.

Before proceeding further with the discussion on another aspect, it is also the view of the Manu[9] Smṛti that when the theft is committed by using physical force, it becomes a case of robbery. But when the taking away of the possession of another person takes place in the absence of the owner, it become a case of theft.

The writers on Dharma-Śāstra have gone to the extent of proposing the gradations of thefts and also of the thieves. It is held that the theft of gold, silver, jewel etc., is held as the theft of the first grade. In the second grade of theft, there is the inclusion of the garments, beasts, iron, vrīhi, yava, corn. etc. In the third rate of theft, there is the inclusion of the theft of soil, vessel, wood, grass, corn, skin etc. It is but natural to hold the gradations of the thives as per the objects stolen by them and the nature of the stolen things. Hence the thives are also of the three types-first grade thief, second grade thief and third grade thief.

As regards the types of thieves, we have a good quotation in the Vyavahāra[10] Mayūkha which enumerates nine types of thieves such as one stealing a garment, a housebreaker, a highway robber, cut-purse, and one who steals women, men, cow, horse and beasts. It is further added that utkṣepaka is one who quitely steals money and clothes lying with the owner when the latter is rather inattentive.

In addition to this, the Dharma Śāstra[13] authors make proper the classification of open thieves and secret thieves. In the category of open thieves, there is the inclusion of merchants using false weights, doctors, gamblers, assessors, a partner deceiving another coparceners, those who foretell portend fortunes, the persons selling imitations, the persons acting as arbitrators in a conflict between the two persons, some persons cheating the persons by using magic such as magicians. It may be significantly added that according to Bṛhaspati[14], there are thousands of thieves depending upon thier intellectual capacity and the employment of magic.

But the smṛtikāras Bṛhaspati and Vyāsa suggest the category of crypto-thives[15]. Vyāsa points out that the persons who move about in the night with good equipments and whose whereabouts are not known, they are to be known as pracchanna thieves. The Nārada Smṛti adds that these are also known as apracchanna thieves who overcome the persons who are asleep, intoxicated highly and rob them of thier possessions. Bṛhaspati includes among the pracchanna thieves the persons who are house-breakers, who rob the persons on the high-way, who steal away the animals that are two footed or four footed, who steal the corn and the persons when appointed on some responsible posts take bribes. But the Manu Smṛti IX.292 is very specific in pointing out the best of thieves. It states that of all the most sinful sinners it is the gold smith who is regarded as the best secret[16] thief who cheats the persons to his face. Such a sinner when found doing injustice to the public, or behaving dishonestly, should be cut to pieces with razors. It must be noted that the manu smṛti employs the expression 'sarvakaṇṭaka-pāpiṣṭham' with referene to a gold-smith. It must be stated in passing that in the Vivāda- Ratnākara, Kaṇṭaka is explained as praśasta-taskara. In the context of thieves and ideal king and kingdom, Āpastaṁba[17] has expressed the view that that is to be regarded as a king bringing out the welfare of the public or subjects, in whose kingdom, either in the village or in the forest, there is no danger from the thieves of any type. The Manu Smṛti[18] VII. 143 is important on this point. It states that a monarch whose subjects are carried off by robbers from his kingdom, while are quitely looking on that act, is a dead person and not a living person at all. Hārīta[19] gives a warning that in a kingdom, when the sinner robbers increase, the sin of a king also increases and that sin ultimately cuts off his root.

It should not go neglected that the principle of casteism always and also plays very important part on the Dharam-Śāstra in respects not only one and in this respect, the aspect of theft cannot be treated as an exception. It is said that when the thief belongs to the higher caste, he is treated as the best thief. It is further said that if a Śūdra thief commits a theft, his sin becomes 32 eight-fold, in the case of a Kṣatriya theft, the sin becomes fold and in the case of a Vaiśya thief, his sin becomes 16 fold and the sin of a brahmana becomes 64 fold or a hundred fold. Thus, the casteism has a part to play and purpose to serve in the matter of deciding the nature of a guilt of a thief. This is the position taken by the Manu-Smṛti VIII. 336-337. It is further held that as regards the Śūdra thief of a brāhmana's property, it is said that he should be made blind by tying a cloth over his eyes. He should be kept blind-fold, according to Haradatta. It is further held that he should be orally reprimanded for the intentional act of theft on his part and his garment shall be taken away.

It also important to point out that at the back of a theft, the intention of a thief should also be taken into consideration. The point is whether the theft is intentional or unintentional. For the unintentional theft of fodder, vegetables, he should be reprimanded. If, however, the theft is committed intentionally, he should be punished by asking him to see a king with a club.

It is held by the Manu Smṛit IX. 235 that the theft of the gold of a brāhmaṇa is a case of great sin. Here the word theft is connected with gold by Medhātithi and this lead of Medhātithi is followed by the other commentators of the Manu Smṛti. But in order to constitute the theft of gold as a great sin, the Mitāksara[20] points out that there should be the theft of 16 māṣas of gold. But if the theft is of the māsas below 16, then it cannot be treated as a case of great sin. In fact, such a case of the theft of gold below 16 masas is held as a case of Upapātaka. Some writers have also gone to the extent of holding that even the stealing away of the deposit of a person is equal to the theft of the gold of a person. This kind of sin is tṛeated as a mortal sin.

The question also arises as to who is better qualified to give punishment to a thief. It is further clear from the story of Śaṅkha and Likhita, that it is not the duty of an individual to punish a thief. In such a case, a thief is supposed to approach a king and declare his sin before a king and request him to punish him as per the nature of the theft. Secondly, in the matter of theft, it is further held[21] that when a sinner is thus properly punished by a king, he becomes purified and becomes qualified to go to heaven. Thirdly, it is also further held that when a thief is forgiven by a king, then the sin of the theft falls on the forgiver. It is also further held[22] that a thief should approach a king with a club and request him to strike him with a club. If he survives, then it is held that he has free become from a sin. If, however, a thief dies, then his sin is treated as expiated. This will have to be regarded as a direct case of justice given by a king. It must be noted here that Likhita was punished by a king by cutting off his arms which were later on restored to him by Śaṅkha by the power of his penance. Dr. Kane[23] points out that when the expression 'Rājan' occurs in the context of a thief and when the matter is referred to him, this does not necessarily refer to a king in all the cases but this refers to the subordinate officers appointed by a king to punish the persons. This is the view specifically expressed in the Vivāda-Ratnākara and the Daṇda-Viveka of Vardhamāna Upādhyāya. Incidentally, it may be remarked that in the Andhra, the word Rājan is applied to those Kṣariya persons who are not the protectors of people from the calamities, as indicated by Śabara[24] in his bhāṣya on the Pūrva-Mīmāṁsā Sūtra II. 3.3.

It is also further held that it is the duty of a king to see that the property stolen by the thieves should be restored to the original owner. If he fails in his duties, he should compensate from his treasury and if he retains such a stolen property with him, he does incur sin for the same. It is the special view of the Viṣṇu Dharma Sūtra that if a person is robbed by his own servants, then the king is not bound to compensate him from his treasury. The Yājñavalkya Smṛti goes one step further and takes the view[25] that a thief should be made to return the stolen property to its original owner and if he cannot return the stolen property, he should pay the price of it. In the matter of responsibility of the officers, the administration of the village also has a part to play. It is held that if a theft takes place in a village, the headmen of, a village should pay for it. In case, he is unable to recover the stolen property and the theft takes place in a pasture, it was held that the owner of the field should pay for it. If, however, the theft takes place in the limits of village, the whole village is bound to pay for it. In this context, it is equally important to remember that when the thief is caught red-handed with a part of the stolen property, a thief should be made to return the whole property to the owner. Incidentally, it may be noted here that we mostly come across the expressions such as Cauroddharaṇika for the officer who catches the thief. Kauṭilya has used the expression Cora-Rajjuka. There are also other officers like Koṭṭpāla akin to Kotawāl in Marathi whose duty was to catch the thief. In the inscriptional[26] record, we also come across some other words.

In the context of the theft, it would be worth nothing the view point of the Smṛtikāra Saṁvarta[27] that it is the duty of a king to take action against the ten faults, though not referred to him and in which there is the danger from thieves.

As regards the evidence to be considered for imposing any punishment, the Dharma Śāstra authors have pointed out that the judges should take into account the age of a thief, the nature of the stolen property, circumstances under which he committed a theft. In this context, the case of the sage of the Mbh. Aṇi Māṇḍvya referred to in the Ādi parvan chapter 101 and the Kauṭilīya Arthaśāstra IV. 8.11 should not be neglected. In the Mahābhārata, it is said that the robbers created the atmoshere that the sage Aṇi-Māṇḍvya is a thief and kept the stolen goods in his hermitage. When however, the goods were found in the hermitage of the sage Aṇi-Māṇḍvya, he was observing the vow of complete silence. As he did not make his position quite clear in the matter, he was treated by a kind as a thief. But in the Kauṭiliya[28] Arthaśāstra IV. 8.11, it is stated that the sage Aṇi-Māṇḍvya admitted himself to be a thief for the fear of physical torture. These two versions of the sage Aṇi-Maṇḍvya as presented in the Mahābhārataand the Kauṭilīya Arthaśāstra give different grounds for the behaviour of the sage Aṇi-Māṇḍvya,. In this respect, Dr. Kane passes an important observation[29] that the circumstantial evidence is not always to be accepted as reliable, since the dangerous persons create the atmosphere congenial to a particular crime and they take pleasure in transferring their guilt to the innocent persons. Hence in deciding any case the proper care should be taken by an offcicer who has to decide the merits of the case.

In the Dharma-Śāstra, the question also arises whether concealement of a part of the joint family property by any coparcener is a case of theft or not. In this respect, Nīlakaṇṭha[30] and other writers treat that this is a case of theft and such a coparcener deserves good punishment. But some other writers[31] like Jīmūtavāhana and others take that this is not a case of theft, since the coparcener who conceals the part of the joint family property is also an owner of that property. Hence he should not be treated as a thief in the strict sense of the term. This discussion goes to show that on this point the opinions among the Dharma-Śāstra authors are divided.

It deserves to be specifically noted that the time factor is also held as responsible for the false charge of a theft on a person. It is said that if one looks at the moon on the fourth day of the bright fortnight of the month of Bhādrapada, one is alleged with the false charge of a theft. To justify this statement or event, it is further shown that the lord Kṛṣṇa cleared himself of the false charge of the theft of the syamantaka jewel when he fought with Jāmbuvata and defeated him and married his daughter Jāṁbuvatī and got Syamantaka jewel as a dowry and gave it to the brother Satrajit of Prasens. This incident is specially described in the Harivaṁśa of the Mahābhārata.[32]

On the aspect of theft, we get quite an interesting matter in the science of Astrology. In the Jyotiṣa Maṇimāla an interesting classificaion[33] of the constellations is suggested. Here the constellations into the four groups is recommended and each group is accordingly called as Andhākṣa, Mandākṣa, Mādhyākṣa and Svākṣa. In the Jyotiṣa Ratnamālā, it is further stated[34] that the theft committed on the Andhākṣa constellation may be recoverd quickly. On the Mandākṣa constellation, or nakṣatra, there is no possibility of any recovery, but it is simply heard that it is taken to a distant place. But on the Svākṣa or sulocana nakṣatra, there is no recovery of the stolen good, though the wherebouts are known.

It is of great interest to note that in the Muhūrta[35] Muktāvalī verse 42, the proper time for the theft is also recommended. It is said that theft succeeds when committed on the constellations such as Āśleṣā, Mṛgaśiras, Bharaṇi Svāti, Dhaniṣṭhā, Citrā and Anurādhā. As regards the days, it is said that if the theft is committed on the days Saturday and Tuesday, it is said to turn out to be successful. As regards the tithi, it is said that the theft committed on the Riktā tithi (which occurs on the fourth, ninth and 14th tithis of the fornight) is a good time for success. Thus, it will have to be admitted that the Muhūrta Astrology throws light on the time factor responsible for committing a theft for success.

Before coming to the punishment for a thief, it is necessary to note the position of a thief in the society. It is said that no impurity is to be observed for a thief who dies as a thief, in the opinion of the Yājñvalkya-Smṛti. It is further held that a person whose charge of theft is proved, is not to be accepted as a witness in the court matter, though the Manu Smṛti VIII. 72 states that the competence of a witness is not to be examined. In addition to this, a brāhmaṇa thief is not to be invited for the Śrāddha. This becomes clear from the brāhmaṇas to be completely avoided for the Śrāddha ceremony. There is also one rule of morality to be observed by a brāhmṇa performing the śrāddha of his dead ancestor. It is held that he should not commit any kind of theft for the purpose of Śrāddha on that day. This discussion leads one to the conclusion that the theft is a crime which disqualifies a person from any religious ceremony or degrades him in the eyes of the society.

It would not be out of place, if the evidence of the classical Sanskrit literature is taken into account for the aspect of theft. In the sixth act of the Śākuntalam, the policemen of Duṣyanta describe the fisherman as kuṁbhīlaka, pāṭaccara and granthibhedaka. The word kūmbīlaka or kuṁbhīlaka is explained[36] as one who fills up the small pitcher with wealth. It is thus referring to the act of theft. Alternatively, it is also suggested that kumbhī means an elephan and irayati means taking away or catching and it thus means a crocodile. It is further suggested that ku + bhid means one who breaks the earth i.e. the wall built of earth. Ultimately this has a reference to the act of burglary. The policemen of Duṣyanta also employ the word 'pāṭaccara' which means one who moves about breaking walls i.e. robber. Another expression 'granthibhedaka' used with reference to a fisherman is important. It mans one who breaks the knot of the purse with a view to stealing the articles; thus secretly kept. It thus means a cut-purse. These three expressions used by Kālidāsa refer to the act of theft and robbery. From the speeches of the policemen it can be inferred that such robbers or thieves were executed at the time of Kālidāsa or their bodies were handed over to the dogs and vultures to satisfy their hunger.

In the Vikramorvaśiyam[37] Act IV, we get a good reference to the responsibility of a thief. Here it is mentioned that when a thief is caught with the part of the stolen property, he should be made to return the entire stolen property to the owner of the stolen property.

Still at another place in the Vikramorvaśīyam, the king Purūravasa is described as corānuśāsī i.e. chastiser of thives.

It may be noted here that in the second Act of the Vikramorvaśīyam, the Vidūṣaka says that when the thief is caught red-handed, can he give any reply? Here the expression 'Lotreṇa gṛhītasya' used by Kālidāsa seems to have been taken from the Yājñavalkya Smṛti II. 137-138. Here the Vidūṣaka describes the position of the hero Purūravas caught red-handed in the matter of love affair with Urvāśī. But incidentally it throws light on the position of a thief who cannot justify his act particularly when he is caught red-handed.

In the Mālavikāgnimtram, the Vidūsaka's criticism of the king Agnimitra is humorous. He says[38] that the moon light is to be specially avoided by the thieves and lovers. This remark implies that the thieves have full scope particularly at night and they should engage in burglary rather in dark and not in the moon light.

In the third act of the Mṛcchakaṭika, verses 9, 10 and 11 and some prose passages are very important for the point of theft. From the speech Śarvilaka, it is evident that theft was treated as a regular science. It had the benefit of the sound knowledge of the teachers like Kumārakārtikeya (though this reference is not quite clear) and Kanakaśakti and Yogācārya. The differennt ways of making the breaches in the house are expressly stated in the Act II. One also comes to know from the view of Śarvilaka that the act of theft is really no bravery but it is knavery. This is so because the persons who are robbed have not the slightest idea of the cavil of doubt about the skill on the act of theft. It is further to be noted that Śarvilaka treats that the act of theft is better than the act of servitude, though the former is a mean act.

In passing, a reference can also made to the third act of the Cārudattam of Bhāsa, in which we have more or less the same ideas of the Mṛcchakaṭika. But the thief here expresses his desire that one should not murder any respectable person for one's livelihood. He further states that he is doing the terrible act of burglary and also at the same time censuring the same act.

Before discussing the nature of punishment imposed upon the thieves, it is necessary to note soem points of different purpose at the back of the punishment. It is held that the punishments were deterrent and preventive because the provision of expiation for a thief leads to the inference of the theory of reformative punishment used by the writers on Dharma-Śāstra. It must be admitted that the atonements test the purification of the inner conscience of the offender by means of self-control and self-education. This theory of punishment further indicates that the Dharma-Śāstra authors belived in the goodness and sociability of human nature and condemnation is given less scope. The main intenion at the back of punishment is to improve the offenders and not to convert them into the habitual criminal which shows the anti-social element. The Dharma Śāstra authors tend to elevate man from heavy animality to perfect humanity and is thus an ethical process to bring the guilty person to the path of right and duty.

As regards the nature of punishment, it may be noted that the Manu[39] Smṛti IX. 270 provides for the execution of thieves, if caught red-handed with stolen goods. This punishment has its indication in the sixth act of the Śākuntalam.

Another methd of Punishment is the prescription of penance for a thief. The Āpastamba[40] Dharma Sūtra I. 25. 6 states that a thief should throw himself into the fire or perform severe penance. The same Dharma-Sūtra further states that a thief may kill himself by diminishing the quantity of food. A thief is also asked to penance—'a Krcchra penance' for one complete year. It is also further said that for removing the guilt of theft, a thief should take bath thrice a day, standing by the day time and sitting by the night time and leading the life of this kind he becomes free from the guilt after three years. The Gautama[41] Dharma-Sūtra XXIV. 12 prescribes prāṇāyāma for a thief for purification and repeating the Aghamarṣaṇa mantra. In support of this view, Maskari quotes a stanza from the Manu Smṛti. XII 260. The Vasiṣṭha Dharma Sūtra XXVI.6 prescribes the muttering of the Asya Vāmīya Sūkta of the Ṛg-Veda. I.164 and the Śivasaṁkalpa. This view of Vasiṣṭha is identical with the Manu Smṛti XI. 251. But Manu Smṛti adds the repetition of the Puruṣa Sūkta of the Ṛg.Veda X.90 one thousand times. A thief is also asked to repeat the Gāyatrī mantra one thousand times for becoming free from the guilt. The Vasiṣṭha Dharma Sūtra XX.42 prescribes that a thief should have cut off all his hair and anoint his body with clarified butter, and cause himself tobe burnt from the feet upwards, in a fire of dry cowdung. It may be further added that the Manu Smṛti IX. 240 expects the persons belonging to all the varṇas to perform expiation and if this is not done, then the thieves should be branded.

Banishment is another method of punishment that is sanctioned by the Dharma-Śāstra authors. The Manu Smṛti IX.274 prescribes the banishment of the thieves along with thier paraphernalia. The Baudhāyana[42] Dharma-Sūtra I.19. 18. states that a brahmaṇa thief is to be branded of a tavern on the forehead and banished from his realm.

The cutting of the parts of the body is also another mode of punishment. Here the attempts of the theft are also taken into account. It is said in the Manu Smṛti IX. 277 that for the first attempt of a theft, the two fingers are to be cut off. For the Second attempt, however, one hand and one foot are to be cut off. But for the third attempt, the death punishment is the only punishment for such a thief.

The death punishment is also another important punishment prescribed by the Manu Smṛti IX. 280 particularly in case of those who steal the elephant, horse, chariot and the wealth from the treasury house, breaking an armoury, or a temple etc. and they should be killed without any hesitation. This view of the manu Smṛti agrees with the Yājñavalkya Smṛti II. 273. The same punishment is given to those abettors who help the thieves in different capacities such as providing them with food, fire, shelter, receiving the stolen property or goods. This is also the view of the Yājñavalkya Smṛti II.276. The Manu Smṛti IX. 269 states that if the thief is caught with the stolen goods, he should be killed without a moment's thought along with the material that is used by him for the purpose of theft.

Reprimanding is another mode of punishment. When the theft of the small things such as fodder, vegetables etc. takes place, a thief should be reprimanded and his garment should be taken away.

The casteism has a part to play in the matter of punishment. It is said that in the case of Śūdra person stealing the property of a brāhmaṇa, there should be the consiscation of the property of a Śūdra.

The concession is given to a brāhmaṇa who is very hungry for three days. Such a poor brāhmaṇa is allowed to rob the corn in a field, or vegetables and such other grains as rice, yava etc. But this concession is not given to all the other castes.

It is the special view of Śaṅkha-Lakhita Dharma Sūtra that when there is a theft of a brāhmaṇa by a brāhmaṇa there should be no corporal punishment.

Fine[43] is another method of punishing a thief. The Manu Smṛti points out that there should be the fine of 11 times of the price of the stolen property. This fine is to be paid by a thief. But fur the good of a small value, there should be the fine of five times of the value of the good.

Dr. Kane pointed out in his Dharma-Śāstra that later on the punishment became symbolic. When a thief approached an officer for the theft he has committed, the officers would beat him smoolically with the club. This naturally tends to produce the atmophere which is less serious for such a crime.

In prescribing the punishment it was thought proper to consider the caste of a robber and the person robbed. In addition to this, the qulalities of both the persons are also taken into consideration.

Later on, however, more important change[44] was introduced in the society. This becomes particularly evident from the writings of the 12th century A.D. onwards. It was decided that no death punishment nor the corporal punishment was imposed upon a thief. The drastic change was intoduced by suggesting the gift of some things, recitation of the mantras, feeding the brāhmaṇas, going to a sacred place and also taking bath in the waters of the sacred river, to purity such a sinner. If, However, the objects of the gift like a cow or a bull are not available, it was recommended[45] that one should pay the price that is fixed for the gifts. Such prices of the things were also fixed in order to enable a thief to become free from the sin.

Oaths and ordeals are also recognised as the modes of punishment for proving the purity of a person. We find a reference to the fire ordeal in the Chāndogyopaniṣad[46] and there is also a reference to the Phāla divya[47] laid down for a thief taking away the cattles.

For the ḥouse-burglary, the Manu Smṛti IX. 276 recommends the cutting of both the hands of a burglar and then he should be hanged.

In conclusion, the topic of theft in ancient India is very comprehensive and deals with the nature of theft, types of thieves, punishments for the thieves, burglars fine, atonement, banishment, cutting of the limbs of the body, hanging the person, compelling him to take oaths and undergoing ordeals, concessions in some cases, and the drastic change by symbolic punishment and later on the recommendation of the gift of animals and the price for the same, and visiting the sacred place, taking bath in it and observing fast, prāṇāyāma, recitation of the vedic mantras etc. We get some glimpses of theft in the classical literature and inscriptional records and purpose at the back of the punishment. Any way, one will have to admit the fact that in the matter of imposing punishment on the thieves, some definite evolution has taken place.

FOOT NOTES

1. Mahābhārata-Śānti parvan-122-99, 10 and 15 may be read. (B.O.R.I. edition Poona).
2. यथा कथा च परपरिग्रहमभिमन्यते स्तेनो ह भवतीति कौत्सहारीतौ तथा कण्व पुष्करसादी। आपस्तम्ब-धर्मसूत्र। 1.28.1 (Bühler's edition 1932).
3. यथा कथा चापद्यनापदि वा भूयांसमल्पं वा परपरिग्रहं ममेदमस्त्विति बुद्धौ कुरुते बुद्धौ कृत्वा कृत्वादत्त इत्यर्थः। हरदत्त on आपस्तम्ब-धर्मसूत्र p. 147.
4. बुद्धिपूर्वविषय एवेदम्। अबुद्धिपूर्वकं स्तेयं नोपपद्यन इति। मस्करि on गौतम धर्मसूत्र XII. 40, P. 209 (Mysore edition, 1917).
5. स्यात्साहसं त्वन्वयवत्प्रसभं कर्म यत्कृतम्। मनुस्मृति VIII. 332; but it further states that 'निरन्वयं भवेत् स्तेयं हृत्वापव्ययते च नत्।
6. ऋणादाननिक्षेपादिष्वपि स्तेय दण्डप्रसङ्गात्। मेधातिथि on मनुस्मृति VIII. 332 (Bhārtīya Vidya series, 1990) Page. 506.
7. परद्रव्यापहरणं स्तेयमुच्यते। धात्वर्थप्रसिद्धया चास्यैव कर्ता 'स्तेनः'। Ibid, p. 506.
8. यच्च हृत्वाऽपह्नुते तदपि स्तेयमेव। कुल्लूक on मनस्मृति VIII. 332, p. 507.
9. द्रव्यं स्वामिसमक्षं बलाद् हृतं तत्साहसं स्थात्। सहो बलं तद्भवं साहसम्। यत्पुनः स्वामि परोक्षापहृतं तत् स्तेयं भवेत्। Ibid, p. 507.
10. नारदस्मृति XVIII. 14-16 is quoted by Nīlakaṇṭha in his व्यवहारमयूख pp. 235-236 (Kane's edition, 1926).

11. उत्क्षेपक: सन्धिभेत्ता पान्थमुड् ग्रन्थिमोचक:।
स्त्रीपुंगोऽश्वपशुस्तेयी चौरो नवविध: स्मृत:।। व्यासस्मृति is quoted in व्यवहार मयूख p. 235.
12. उत्क्षेपक: वस्त्रापहारक:। मिताक्षरा on याहावस्वन्यस्मृति II. 274.
13. व्यासस्मृति is quoted in कृत्यकल्पतरु व्यवहाराकाण्ड p. 512 (Baroda edition-1953).
14. प्रज्ञासामर्थ्यमायाभि: प्राभिन्नास्ते सहस्त्रधा। Ibid. p. 507.
15. For अप्रकाशतस्कर's व्यवहारमयूख, p. 235 and मित्रामिश्र's व्यवहारप्रकाश p. 387. Both quote व्यासस्मृति।
16. सर्वकण्टकपापिष्ठं हेमकारं तु पार्थिव।
प्रवर्तमानमन्याये छेदयेल्लवश: क्षुरै:।। मनुस्मृति IX. 292.
17. क्षेमकृद्राजा यस्य विषये ग्रामेऽरण्ये वा तस्करभयं न विद्यते। आपस्तम्ब धर्मसूत्रं II. 25.15.
18. विक्रोशन्त्यो यस्य राष्ट्राद् ह्रियन्ते दस्युभि: प्रजा:।
संपश्यत: सभृत्यस्य मृत: स न तु जीवति।। मनुस्मृति VII. 143.
19. पापास्तु यस्य राष्ट्राद्वै वर्धन्ते दस्यव सदा।
तत्पापमतिवृद्धं हि राज्ञो मूलं निकृन्तति।। हारीत स्मृति quoted in कृत्यकल्पतरु व्यवहारकाण्ड P.512.
20. मिताक्षरा on याज्ञवल्क्यस्मृति III.257. Also see Kane's History of Dharma-Śāstra Vol. IV. P.23. Foot note, No. 55.
21. राजभि: कृतदण्डास्तु कृत्वा पापानि मानवा:।
निर्मला: स्वर्गमायान्ति सन्त: सुकृतिनो यथा। मनुस्मृति VIII.318.
22. बौधायन धर्मसूत्र II. 1.16.
23. Kane's History of Dharma-Śāstra Vol. III 176.
24. शबर on जैमिनिऽ पूर्वमीमांसा II-3.3.
25. विभावितैकदेशेन देयं यदभियुज्यते। विक्रमोर्वशीदम् Act. IV.
26. Kane's History of Dharma-Śāstra-Vol. III. P. 984 for चोरग्राहं, चोररज्जुक, चौरोद्धरणिक and P. 981 for कोट्टपाल।
27. संवर्तस्मृति is quoted in स्मृतिचंद्रिका व्यवहार काण्ड P. 28 (Gharpure's edition) and History of Dharma-Śāstra Vol. I/I P. 542.
28. R.P. Kangle's edition of Kauṭilīya Arthaśāstra part II P. 275.
29. Kane's History of Dharma-Śāstra Vol. III. P. 521.
30. Nīlkaṇṭha's व्यवहारमयूख P. 131.
31. Kane's notes on व्यवहारमयूख P. 220. for the views of दायभाग as given by विश्वरूप.

32. Kane's History of Dharma-Śāstra Vol. V/I P. 147 refers to महाभारत हरिवंश I. 38.36.
33. Ibid History of Dharma-Śāstra- Vol. V/I. P. 560 foot note. 833.
34. Ibid. P. 560.
35. Ibid. P. 557.
36. A.B. Gajendragadkar's notes on शाकुन्तले Act VI. PP. 445-46 (SIXth impression).
37. Kālidāda's विक्रमोर्वशीयम् Act IV. Verse 33b.
38. अहो, कुम्भीलकैः कामुकैश्च परिहरणीया चन्द्रिका। मालविकाग्निमित्रम्। Act. IV.
39. न होढेन विना चौरं घातयेद् धार्मिको नृपः।
सहोढं सोपकरणं घातयेदविचारन्।। मनुस्मृति IX. 270.
40. आपस्तम्ब-धर्मसूत्र I. 25.6.
41. गौतम-धर्मसूत्र XXIV. 12.
42. बौधायन धर्मसूत्र I. 19.18.
43. Mann-Smṛti XI-127, 129, and 130.
44. पराशर-माधव II/I p. 236, वसिष्ठ धर्मसूत्र XXVIII. 18-19 and विष्णुधर्मसूत्र 90.11.
45. Kane's History of Dharam-Śāstra Vol. IV. P. 40.
46. छांदोग्योपनिषद् VI. 16.
47. For फाल दिव्य, History of Dharam-Śāstra Vol.III. P. 375.

V

HOLIDAYS (ANADHYĀYAS) IN ANCIENT EDUCATIONAL SYSTEM

M.M. Dr. P.V. Kane has given a very exhaustive treatment to this topic in his monumental work history of *Dharmaśāstra*, Vol. II/I. pp. 292-402, by consulting Dharma-Sūtras and the Smṛtis and the commentaries on the same. He has also made incidental references to the digest works like the *Smṛticandrikā* and the commetary of Aparārka on the *Yājñavalkya-Smṛti*, which is also of the nature of a digest.

The expression *Anadhyāya* used in the context of the Dharmaśāstra literature is generally translated as 'holiday', or interruption'. I have preferred to translate here as a 'holiday'.

If one seriously considers the discussion introduced by Dr. Kane, one would form the impression that in ancient India, education was primarily concerned with the recitation of the Vedic *mantras*. Hence the holidays were introduced in view of the different situations. For the purpose of a holiday, however, the different grounds such as place, time, smell of bad things, fright, conveyances, musical instruments, natural phenomena, festivals, natural calamities, death of the important persons, the shades of the particularly mentioned trees are considered by the writers on Dharama-śāstra.

It may be mentioned here confidently that Dr. Kane has not consulted the source of the *Gṛhyasūtra* literature, some digest works and the astrological works for th purpose of holidays. Hence by consulting the sources unexplored by Dr. Kane, for the discussion, I would like to bring the discussion nearer to the peak of perfection. In this paper, therefore, the readers will find that matter which has escaped the eagle eye of MM. Dr. Kane or the matter for which he could not give more serious thoughts.

I would like to distribute the matter under three heads - digest works, *Gṛhyasūtra* works and Astrological work.

Before begining with the digest matter, I first mention one important place of *Gautama Dharma-Sūtra* (GDS) 16.34. This *Sūtra* provides that there should be no study particularly in the *Manuṣya-yajñna* and the gathering of friends and the lunch of the brahmins. Here it should be noted that the expression '*Manuṣya-yajña*' in the above *sūtra,* is rendered by Maśkari[1] as *mitramelaka.* i.e. gathering of friends.

Incidentally, the importance of the *Gṛhyasūtra* literature in this context is not ignored by Maśkari who is chronologically later than Haradatta. In his comments on the *Gautama-Dharma-Sūtra* 16.50, Maśkari stressess[2] the views of the *Gṛhyasūtrakāras* and the word ca in the *sūtra* makes the inclusion of other religious creeds.

As regards the material scattered in the digest works, I draw the attention of the readers to the *Brahmacāri-kāṇḍa* of the *Kṛtyakalpataru* of Lakṣmīdhara. He quoted *Vaśiṣṭha Dharam-Sūtra* 13.35 which states[3] that there should not be study at the fall of a mountain, sand, blood from the sky etc. Dr. Kane seems to be quite conscious[4] of this reference since he has mentioned only this exact place of the *Vasiṣṭha Dharma-Sūtra* in the course of his dicussion, only in the bracket. This matter can be included in the portentous phenomena such as rain of blood and stones.

In the *Brahmacāri-kāṇḍa* of the *Kṛtyakalpataru* p. 251, Lakṣmīdhara quotes the view of Baudhāyana.[5] (This is possibly a reference to the *Baudhāyana Śrautra-Sūtra* or *Dharm-sūtra* with the commentary of Govindaswāmī). The view of Baudhāyana is that there should be the holiday for one day on the death of a *deśapati* and *Ekatīrtha*. Here it is interesting to note that Lakṣmīdhara explains[6] '*deśapati*' as a soldier and refers to the Yājñavalkya who declares three days as holidays on the death of a king. Even Hārīta shares this view of Yājñvalkya.

If, however, we consult the *Smṛticandrikā-Saṁskāra-Kāṇḍa* of Devaṇṇbhaṭṭa, we get additional matter on holidays. Devaṇṇabhaṭṭa in his *Smṛticandrikā-Saṁskāra-Kāṇḍa* quotes a passage from the Purāṇa (without disclosing the source) to the effect[7] that one should observe holiday on *Trayodaśi, Saptamī* and the evening of *caturthī,* only if one is desirous of having sufficient growth in his intellegence. From this quotation, it is evident that the concept of holiday is conneted with human intellectual progress and time element. This view has escaped the notice of Dr. Kane.

As regards the place to be avoided for the study of the Veda, Dr. Kane has referred to the *Yājñvalkya-Smṛti* I. 148-151 in the *History of Dharmaśāstra* Vol. II/I p. 396. But he has not considered a reference to the quotation from the text of *Pracetas* quoted by Devṇṇabhaṭṭa. The citation[8] from *Pracetas* simply means that there should be no study at a place where four roads meet, on the high way, on the street, in the garden and near the temple.

Dr. Kane has referred to the view of *Yājñavalkya* that there should be no study on the arrival of a distinguished visitor to the house of a person. Devaṇṇabhṭṭha adds a very important view[9] of Yama that even if a distinguished guest permits, one should not start with the Vedic study.

Coming to the important digest of *Nirṇayasindhu* by Kamalākarabhaṭṭa, one notices that he has laid stress on the *Gautam-Dharma-Sūtra*[10] XVI. 42 (which has escaped the eye of Kane) that there should be no study after a lunch in a festival. Here Maskari in his comments on the *Gautama Dharma-Sūtra* explains that *abhyudaya* has a reference to the all round prosperity and the festival refers[11] to the thread ceremony of a boy. This is certainly a different explanation of the words that have occurred in the *Sūtras*.

Before beginning with the digest matter, I first mention one important place of the *Gautam Dharma-Sūtra (GCS)* 16.34. This *Sūtra* provides that there should be no study particularly in the *Manuṣya-yajña* and the gathering of friends and the lunch of the brahmins. Here it should be noted that the expression' *Manuṣya-yajña*' in the above Sūtra, is rendered by Maśkari[1] as mitramelaka. i.e. the gathering of friends.

Incidentally, the importance of the *Gṛhyasūtra* literature in this context is not ignored by Maśkari who is chronologically later than Haradatta. In his comments on the *Gautama-Dharma-Sūtra 16.50, Maśkari stressesṣ* the view of the Gṛhyasūtrakāras and the word *ca* in the *sūtra* makes the inclusion of other religious creeds.

As regards the material scattered in the digest works, I draw the attention of the readers to the *Bramacāri-Kāṇḍa* of the *Kṛtyakalpataru* of Lakṣmīdhara. He quoted *Vaśiṣtha Dharm Sūtra* 13.35 which states[3] that there should not be study at the fall of a mountain, sand, blood from the sky etc. Dr. Kane seems to be quite conscious[4] of this reference since he has mentioned only this exact place of the *Vasiṣṭha Dharma-Sūtra* in the course of his discussion, only in the bracket. This matter can be included in the portentous phenomena such as rain of blood and stones.

In the *Brahmac1ri-Kaṇḍa* of the *Kṛtyakalpataru* p. 251, Lakṣmīdhara quotes in the view of Baudhāyana.[5] (This is possibly a reference to the *baudhāyana śrautra-Sūtra,* since the passage relied upon by Lakṣmīdhara is not found in the extant *Baudhāyana Dharma-Sūtra* with the commentary of Govindaswāmī). The view of Baudhāyana is that there should be the holiday for one day on the death of a *deśapati, śrotrīya* and *Ekatīrtha.* Here it is interesing to note that Lakṣmīdhara explains[6] '*deśpati*' as a soldief and refers to the Yajñavalkya who declares three days as holidays on the death of a king. Even Hārita shares this view of Yajñvalkya.

If, however, we consult the *Smṛticandrikā-Saṁskāra-Kāṇḍa* of Devaṇṇabhaṭṭta, we get additiona matter on holidays. Devaṇṇabhaṭṭa in his *Smṛticandrikā-Saṁskāra-Kāṇḍa* quotes a passage from the Purāṇa (without disclosing the source) to the effect[7] that one should observe holiday on *Trayodaśī, Saptamī* and evening of *caturthī,* only if one is desirous of having sufficient growth in his intelligence. From this quotation, it is evident that the concept of holiday is conneted with human intellectual progess and time element. This view has escaped the notices of Dr. Kane.

As regards the place to be avoided for the study of the Veda, Dr. Kane has referred to the *Yajñvalkya-Smṛti* I. 148-151 in the *History of Dharmaśāstra* Vol. II/I p. 396. But he has not considered a reference to the quotation from the text of *Pracetas* simply means that there should be no study at a place where four road meet, on the high way, on the street, in the garden and near the temple.

Dr. Kane has referred to the view of Yajñvalkya that there should be no study on the arrival of a distinguished visitor to the house of a person. Devaṇṇabhaṭṭa adds a very important view[9] of Yama that even it a distinguished guest permits, one should not start with the Vedic study.

Coming to the important digest of *Nirṇayasindhu* by Kamalākarabhaṭṭa, one notice that he has laid stress on the *Gautama-Dharma-Sūtra*[10] XVI. 42 (which has escaped the eye of Kane) that there should be no study after a lunch in festival. Here Maskari in his comments on the *Gautama-Dharma-Sūtra* explains that *abhyudaya* has a reference to the all round prosperity and the festival refers[11] to the thread ceremony of a boy. This is certainly a different explanation on the words that have occured in the *Sūtras*.

If, however, we refer to another digest-work known as *Saṁskāra-Kaustubha* of Anantadeva, we have a very important quotation. He quotes a passages[12] which means that when the animals or an ungrateful person passes between the two persons standing on the road, then he should observe a holiday completly. Here it should be noted only incidentally that a mention of an ungrateful person is treated as a sign for the holiday. This point is not at all touched by Dr. Kane. Hence this point deserves mention in this context, there is not expiation laid down by the Dharmaśāstra authors. Here this is further considered as a sign for a holiday, since such a person who is most ungrateful, has become the object of odium in ancient India.

In the *Saṁskārakaustubha*, Ananatadeva refers to the view of Garga[13] who holds that the *dvitīyā*s of four months (Cāturmāsyās) should be treated as holidays. Here he specially point out that the *dvitīyās* of the months Āṣḍha, Kārtika and *Phālguna*. These *devitīyas* should be of the black fornight. This view is further supported by quoting a stanza in this respect.

Now coming to the *Gṛhyasūtra* literature, we have the interesting material in the Pāraskara, Gobhila and *Sāṁkhā-yana-Gṛhya-Sūtra*.

In the *Pāraskara-Gṛhyasūtra* II. 5., it is said[14] that at the sight of a person charged with a crime, a *patīta* person and on the occasions of persperity and woderful events, there should be an occasional holiday. The expression '*Abhyudaya*' in the above *sūtra* is taken by Harihara[15] as having a reference to the birth of a son and marriage. Viśvanātha agrees with Harihara. Gadādhara takes wonderful events[16] as having a reference to the magic play of a magician. It is worth nothing that even the sight of a *patita* and a criminally charged person was disliked by the people.

In the *Pāraskara-Gṛhyaśūtra* II. 11.6, it is held that the particularly described be.aviour of a *śiṣṭa* should be treated as a cause of holiday. The expression *śiṣṭa* is rendered[17] as *śrotriya* by both the commentators Harihara and Gadādhara. This view is also found expressed in the *Gobhila-Gṛhyaśūtra* III. 3.29. The *Saṁskārakaustubha* p. 567 states that when the śiṣṭa has come to the house, there should be no study at all.

There is an identical view expressed in the *Drāhyāyaṇa-Gṛhya Sūtra* with the commentary of Rudraskaṇḍa 2.3 and *Khādira Gṛhya Sūtra* III. 2.3 and III. 2.3031. These two *Sūtras* maintain[18] that according to the *Kaṭhas* and the *Kauthumas*, the study is forbiddn when the rain has fallen and particularly as long as water remains in the ditches. Rudraskanda in his comments on the word *ca* states that by this word, we have to combine the views of other *smṛti* and thereby one should understand other unrevealed occaions.

In the *Saṁkhayāyana-Gṛhya-Sūtra*[19] we have some peculiar views. In IV 27.6, it is stated that the interruption in the Vedic reitation it to be followed on hearing what is forbidden. In IV. 7.34, it is further said that having climbed up a tree, one should observe a holiday. There should be further holiday on the occasions of shaving the hair and beard until the bath, as is clear from IV. 7. 42. It further adds that there should be a holiday, on the occasion of oneself being rubbed. While bathing also this *anadhyāya* is recommended. When, however, one is having sexual intercourse, one should follow a holiday.

Coming to the Astrological literature, one would find that in the *Muhūtra-Mārtaṇḍa* with the commentary known as *Mārtaṇḍa-Vallabhā,* there is a stanza[20] quoted from the *Kūrmapurāṇa* that one should observe the holidays for three nights (i.e. three days) on the death of a person of equal lore, fellow student and a teacher. It is further interesting to note that in the commnentary *Pramitākṣarā* on the Mahūrta-cintāmaṇi V. 164, a stanza[21] is quoted from the Smṛti-Ratnāvalī to the effect that so long as the sun rotates from the constellation Anuradha upto 16 later constellations, there should be no recitation of the Vedic *mantras*. In the commentary known as *Pīyūṣa-dhāarā* on the *Muhūrtacintāmaṇi* V.54, a stanza is quoted from *Jyotiḥsārasāgara* to the effect that according to Purāṇas there should be a holiday on the *dvitīyā* which falls at the end of the four months. It is worth nothing here that these views of the works on *Muhūrta*-Astrology, are not at all considered by Dr. Kane.

In conclusion, it may be stated that the matter presented here in view of the sources unexplored by Dr. Kane is certainly interesting and adding to the matter which is already presented by him.

FOOT NOTES

1. मनुष्ययज्ञे मित्रमेलके। भोजने अनेकब्राह्मणभोजने।
   एतेष्वहोरात्रमनध्यायः। मस्करि on गौतमधर्मसूत्र 16.34. p. 269, (Mysore Edition), 1917.
2. प्रतिवेदं प्रतिशास्त्रं च याननध्यायान् गृह्यकाराः स्मृरन्ति, चकाराद्धर्मान्तरेष्वपि नाधीयेतेति सम्बन्धः Ibid., 16.50, p. 272.
3. दिङ्नादपर्वतप्रपातेषु उपलरुधिर पांसुवर्षेष्वाकालिकम्।।
   –कृत्यकल्पतरु, p.257. Quoted in वसिष्ठ सूत्र 13.35.
4. P.V. Kane- धर्मसूत्र, Vol. II/I p. 399 B.O. R.I. Edition. 1974.
5. देशपति श्रौतियैकतीर्थप्रायेणष्वहोरात्रमनध्यायः। बोधायन I 21.6. is quoted in कृत्यकल्पतरु-ब्रह्मचारिकाण्ड p. 251, (Baroda Edition), 1948.
6. देशपतिः सैनिकादिः। Ibid p. 251.
7. मेधाकाम्यत्रयोदश्यां सप्तम्यां च विशेषतः।
   चतुर्थ्यों च प्रदोषेषु न स्मरेन्न च कीर्तयेत्।। स्मृतिचंद्रिका-संस्कारकाण्ड, p. 154, (Mysore Edition), 1914.
8. Ibid., p. 162.
9. Ibid., p. 164.
10. 16.43, p. 271 p. 276.
11. Ibid., p. 271.
12. गजसारससिंहव्याघ्रमहापातकिकृतघ्नादेरब्दम्। संस्कारकौस्तुभः, p. 568 with Marathi Translation by V.N. Upadhyaya, Śāstrī, Baroda, 1914.
13. शुचावूर्जे तपस्ये च या द्वितीया विधुक्षये।
    चातुर्मास्याद्वितीयास्ताः प्रवदन्ति मनीषिण इति। Ibid. p. 269
14. धावतोऽभिशस्तपतितदर्शनाश्चर्याभ्युदयेषु च तत्कालम्। पारस्कर-गृह्यसूत्र, P. 279.
15. अभ्युदयः पुत्रजन्मविवाहादिः। हरिहर on पा० गृ० सू० पृ० 279.
16. आश्चर्यमद्भुतमिन्द्रजालादि। गदाधर on पा० गृ० सू० पृ०281.
17. शिष्टस्य श्रोत्रियस्य। गदाधर p.283, Also हरिहर p. 283.
18. कार्ष्वं तु कठकौथुमाः। खादिरगृह्यसूत्र III 2.31, p. 112 (Published by Thakar Udayan Narayan Singh, Muzaffarpur, 1934) द्राह्यायण III 2.31. p. 112.

19. Sacred Books of the East Series - Vol. XXIX. सांख्यायन-गृह्यसूत्र Eng Translation, Motilal Banarasidass, 1967, pp. 115-118.
20. समानविद्ये तु मृते तथा सब्रह्मचारिणे।
आचार्ये संस्थिते चापि त्रिरात्रं क्षपणं स्मृतम्।। मार्तण्डवल्लभा Published by Gondhalekar, Bombay, Śaka 1816, p. 137.
21. Nirṇaya Sagar Press, Bombay 1928. p. 162.
मुहूर्तचिन्तामणि।

VI

IMPORTANCE OF VṚDDHA-SAṀYOGA*

The question often arises whether the association of the young generation with the old generation is of any use in life. What is the importance of the persons advanced in age, knowledge, qualities etc. from the point of view of the younger generation. When Bāṇa in his Kādaṁbarī and particularly in the topic of Śukanāsopadeśa remarks that the young prince puffed up with pride by the possession of a good kingdom, looks upon with contempt the advice given by the old people. The point arises as regards the position of the aged persons, their classification, praise of the elderly persons, condemnation of the young generation for not serving the persons advanced in knowledge, age, qualities, etc. and the benefits one gets in every respect. It is, in this direction that the discussion is intended to be made in follwowing pages in the light of the Dharmā-Śāstra literature, Kauṭilīya Arthaśastra and the Mahābhārata. In this very context, it should not go neglected that the importance of the aged persons has not become the centre of the attraction of the sholars who have made the discussion in the Dharma-Śāstra and Kauṭilīya Arthaśāstra[1]. Hence it is hoped that the discussion in respect of the above aspects will not only be important but also instructive.

I. It would be interesting to note the position adopted by the persons praising the assciation or serving the elderly persons or persons advanced in age, qualities, wisdom etc. In the Rāmāyaṇa, Rāma is described[2] as always serving the elderly persons. This is quite clear from the description in the Rāmāyaṇa II.2.22b and II.2.29a. (2) In the Mahābhārata V. 52.11a. Dhṛtarāṣṭra states[3] that Yudhiṣṭhira is always found serving the senior-most persons. (3) Further, Yudhiṣṭhira[4] is seen as describing Dhṛtarāṣṭra as having much heard from the seniors and also serving the aged persons. 4. It is significant to note that Yudhiṣṭhira made the choice of a priest who is rich in intellect and age as the proper envoy to be sent to the Kurus for finding out the via media in a conflicting situation between the Kauravas and Pāṇḍavas in respect of a share in the kingdom. (5) Sañjay has given expression to his view[6] that those persons who are more engaged in carrying out the orders of the seniors in age, knowlege etc. do not disregard their own relatives. (6) In the Mahābhārata X. 2.22-23, Aśvatthāman expressess his own opinion[7] that one who serves the elderly persons and consults them every now and then, gets welfare and also follows their beneficial advice. He further adds that the senior-most persons are to be consulted becuase their opinion is a guiding genius and serves as a root for the success of a man in life. (7) The view point of Nārada is referred to in the Sabhāparva of the Mahābharāta. He States[8] that the physical suffering is to be removed by taking medicines and regular practice. But the mental agony is to be got ride of by serving the elderly persons. In another context[9], Nārada expresses the view that one should hear the speech of the aged persons on the topics conneted with Dharma and Artha. (8) It is further significant to note the opinion[10] of the Lord Kṛṣṇa that by serving the elderly persons, even the juniors become kings. In this context, he cites the case of Puru, the youngest son of Yayāti. Yayāti gaves his kingdom to Puru, for the simple reason that the latter always served him and consulted him. (9) The part played by Vidura[11] on this aspect of the association with the senior-most persons or aged persons is still more important. He points out in the Mahābhārata V. 62.17, that by serving the aged persons, one becomes invulnerable in any situation. He gives an accurate example that by the presence of a lion, a forest becomes protected, likewise by the advice of the advanced persons in age, one becomes almost invulnerable. In another context in the Mahābhārata V. 39.60, Vidura further adds[12] that by serving the aged persons, there is rise in fame, life, glory and strenght of a person. Here the four-fold benefits of serving the aged persons are recorded by Vidura. (10) The Mahābhārata XIII. 149.11a significantly notes[13] that by serving the Vṛddhas, one becomes intelligent. In the ciramarikopadhyanam of the Mahābhārata XII. 258. 72, it is said that one should serve the Vṛddhas for a long time for the success in life. (11) In the Mahābhārata V.165.24, Karṇa gives an expression[14] to his opinion that as per the dictates of the Śāstra, one should always hear the Vṛddhas. He gives a caution that one should not listen to the very old Vṛddhas who are generally treated like children. (12) In the Anuśāsana Parva of the Mahābhārata XIII. 107.105, Bhīṣma gives an important piece of advice[15] to Yudhisthira that under any circumstances, one must maintain the aged relatives, friends and paupers. This comes under the category of Poṣyavargas (persons to be maintained) and it is significant to add that in the later Dharma-Śāstra[16], this list is found enlarged. The above views of the charaters of the Mahābhārata and some opinions expressed in a scatter manner, simply show the importance of the Vṛddhas.

II. It is equally important to note the views of the persons who have blamed the persons for not serving the aged persons. (1) In the Mahābhārata V. 67.9, Gāndhārī[17] is found blaming Duryodhana for not serving and consulting the senior persons. She categorically states that one who goes beyond or crosses the limitation of the advice of the persons who are grown up or advanced in age, Knowledge etc., is sure to lose the prosperity and life and the thereby he makes the other persons as sorrowful. (2) In the Mahābhārata V. 145. 40, Bhīṣma is found blaming the prince Duryodhana and advices him not to doubt the advice of the aged persons and give half of the kingdom to the Pāṇḍavas. (3) In the Mahābhārata III. 146-46-78) Hanumān[18] is found as blaming Bhīma for not serving the elderly persons and causing the destruction of the forest animals without any sense of discrimination.

III. We wil now come to the discussion of the classifiation the grounds of age, Dharma, qualities and rich in wealth. Viddura maintains[19] that one should avoid the Dharma Vṛddhas, if they are destitute of good qualities. This goes to show that he gives preference to the Vṛddhas who are rich in qualities. In another context of the Mahābhārata V. 36.20 Vidura suggests that there are three types of Vṛddhas best, middling and worst. For the good success in life, one should always serve the best Vṛddhas. The middling Vṛddhas are to be served, only if the occation so demands. But he further adds[20] that one should never serve the Vṛddhas who are the worst. He also specifically states that some persons are rich in wealth.

IV. Coming to the banefits recorded by the commentators of the Manu-Smṛti and the Kauṭilīya Arthaśāstra, it would be proper to draw attention to the Manu-Smrti VII. 37 which states[21] that one should always serve the persons who are aged or highly advanced in age.

In his comments on this portion of the Manu-Smṛti, Sarvajñanārāyaṇa[22] states that the aged persons are to be consulted because they know the past history very well and they have the ability to discuss the matter completely that is particularly concerned with the subject proper.

The commentator Govindarāja,[23] gives another reason. He holds that the aged persons are to be consulted or served for creating confidence in them. He further adds that even the demons consult the aged persons in any complicated matter.

It should be stated here that the topic of the association of a person particularly a king with the Vṛddhas has become the subject matter of the Kauṭilīya Arthaśāstra I.5.11 and I.5.16. Kauṭilya specifically asserts[24] that a prince should have constant association with elders in learning for the sake of improving his training, since the training has its root in the association with elders in learning. Kauṭilya further states in clear terms that from continous study, ensues a trained intellect, from intellect comes practical application and from practical application results selfpossession; such is the efficacy of science. In the Kauṭilīya Arthaśāstra I.5.11, there occurs the expression 'Vinaya' which is taken by Prof. R.P. Kangle in the sense of 'trainig or discipline. It must be added here that even Mallinātha, the celebrated commentator of the Raghuvamsa I.23 takes the word 'Vinaya' in the same sense. But Dr. P.V. Kane in his 'History of Dharma-Sastra' Vol. III, p. 52, quotes the view point of the Nītivākyāmṛta p. 162 that Vinaya means an acting with humility towards those who excel in Vratas, Vidyas and are aged.

From the above discussion, it would be proper now to draw the legitimate conclusions :

1. The act of serving the elders in Knowledge, qualities etc is praised by many characters of the Mahābhārata like Yudhiṣṭhira, Dhṛtarāṣṭra, Vidura, Sañjay, Karṇa, Nārada, Kṛṣṇa and Aśvatthāman.
2. The act of non serving the elders and crossing the advice of the elders is condemned by Gāndhārī, Bhīṣma and Hanumān.
3. Vidura has suggested the classification of the Vṛddhas as per qualities, age, knowledge and Dharma and also the three types of Vṛddhas-best, middling and worst.
4. The benefits one gets by consulting the senior in Vidyas, Knowledge, qualities may be stated as giving rise to intellect, cleverness, Knowledge, face, glory, army success, giving correct Knowledge of the past incidents, reliability of the elders in complicated matters, correct advice leading to invulnerableness of a person, and cautioning the warning in the form of destruction of the nation and oneself and making other persons unhappy life, long proper discipline as a source for success and taking pity even upon the wild animals of the forest.

In fine, one may be justified in stating that all these banefies are not mentioned by the scholars while dealing with the topic of serving the elders or consulting the elders in knowledge for the good or grand success in a complicated life. By rich experince of life, one may even add some more benefits such as helping the person to read others correctly, disclosing the secrets of a particular person or intellectual approach to any problem, dangerous nature of our rivals etc., skill in handling any difficult situation etc. But all these other benefits, in fact, fall beyond the scope of the present paper.

In conclusion, one will be constrained to conclude rightly that there is much substance in rightly serving the seniors in knowledge, or consulting them in season and out of season, for the happy journey of our life.

In this paper, references are made to the critical editions of the Mahābhārata brought out by Bhandarkar Oriental Research Institute, Pune, Rāmāyaṇa by the Oriental Institute Baroda, Kaiṭilīya Arthaśāstra by Prof. R.P. Kangle, Published by the university of Bombay in 1969, 1972, and the Manu-Smṛti Vol. IV. part-I, published by the Bhartiya Vidya Bhavan, Bombay, with nine commentaries, 1985 and the Kādambarī published by Nirnaya Sagar Press, Bombay, 1921.

FOOT NOTES

* This paper is sent for Dr. Satya Vrata Shastri Felicitation Volume.

1. जरावैल्लव्यप्रलपितामिव पश्यन्ति वृद्धोपदेशम्। कादंबरी p. 207.
2. प्रियवादी च भूतानां सत्यवादी च राघवः।
   बहुश्रुतानां वृद्धानां ब्राह्मणानामुपासितः।। रामायण II.2.22.
3. बहुश्रुतः कृतात्मा च वृद्धसेवी जितेन्द्रियः।
   तं सर्वगुणसंपन्नं समिद्धमिव पावकम्।। महाभारत V. 52.
4. प्रज्ञाचक्षुर्यः प्रणेता कुरुणां बहुश्रुतो वृद्धसेवी मनीषी।
   तस्मै राज्ञे स्थविरायाभिवाद्य आचक्षीथाः संजय मामरोगम्।
   महाभारत V. 30. 14.5.
5. ततः प्रज्ञावयोवृद्धं पाञ्चाल्यः स्वपुरोहिनम्।
   कुरुभ्यः प्रेषयामास युधिष्ठिरमते तदा।। महाभारत V. 5.18.
6. न ज्ञातिमवमन्यन्ते वृद्धानां शासने रताः। Ibid. VII. 119. 23a.

7. सम्यगिह पुनरियं यो वृद्धानुपसेवते। आपृच्छति च यच्छ्रेयः करोति च हिनं वचः। उत्थायोत्थाय हि सदा प्रष्टव्या वृद्धसंमताः। तेऽस्य योगे परं मूलं तन्मूलासिद्धिरुच्यते।। Ibid. X. 2.22-23.
8. कच्चिच्छारीरमाबाधमौषधैर्मिनियमेन वा।
मानसं वृद्धसेवाभिः सदा पार्थापकर्षसि।। II 5.79.
9. कच्चिचच्छृणोषि वृद्धानां धर्मार्थसहिता गिरः।
नित्यमर्थाविदां तात तथा धर्मानुदर्शिनाम्।। II. 5.105
10. एवं ज्येष्ठोऽप्यथोसिक्तो न राज्यमभिजायते।
यवीयांसोऽभिजायन्ते राज्यं वृद्धोपसेवया।। Ibid, V. 147.13.
11. यस्मिन्काले सुमनसः सर्वे वृद्धानुपासते।
सिंहगुप्तामिवारण्यमप्रधृष्या भवन्ति ते।। V. 72. 17.
12. अभिवादनशलिस्य नित्यं वृद्धोपसेविनः।
चत्वारि संप्रवर्धन्ते कीर्तिरायुर्यशोबलम्।। Ibid. V. 39. 60.
13. दानेन भोगी भवति मेधावी वृद्धसेवया।
अहिंसया च दीर्घायुरिति प्राहुर्मनीर्षणः।। Ibid. XIII. 149. 11.
14. श्रोतव्यं खलु वृद्धानामिति शास्त्रानिदर्शनम्।
न त्वेवाप्यतिवृद्धानां पुनार्बाला हि ते मनाः।। Ibid. V. 165.24.
15. वृद्धो ज्ञातिस्तथा मित्रं दरिद्रो यो भवेदपि।
गृहे वासायितव्यास्ते धन्यमायुष्यमेव च।। Ibid. XIII. 107.105.
16. It may be noted here that the list of the पोष्यवर्ग is extended in the धर्मशास्त्र works cf:- दक्षस्मृति II. 36 and 37 History of Dharma-Śāstra Vol.II/I, p. 569.
17. ऐश्वर्यकाम दुष्टात्मन् वृद्धानां शासनातिग।
ऐश्वर्यजीविते हित्वा पितरं मा च बालिश।।
Ibid. V. 67. 9 and also see St. 10.
18. न त्वं धर्मं विजानासि वृद्धानोपासितास्त्वया।
अल्पबुद्धितया वन्यानुत्सादयसि यन्मृगान्।। Ibid. III. 146. 77.
19. समृद्धा गुणतः केचित् भवन्ति धनतोऽपरे।
धर्मवृद्धान्गुणैर्हीनान् धृतराष्ट्र विवर्जयेत्।। Ibid. V. 39. 6.
20. उत्तमानेव सेवेत प्राप्ते काले तु मध्यमान्।
अधमांस्तु न सेवेन य इच्छेच्छ्रेय आत्मनः।। Ibid. V 36. 20.
21. ब्राह्मणान्पर्युपासीत प्रातरुत्थाय पार्थिवः।
त्रैविद्यवृद्धान् विदुषस्तिष्ठेत्तेषां च शासने।।
मनुस्मृति VII. 37 Also see VII. 38.
22. वृद्धान् वयोवृद्धान् तेषां पुरावृत्तज्ञतयोहापोहशक्तत्वात्। सर्वज्ञनारायण on मनुस्मृति VII. 38. p. 28.

23. वेदज्ञानार्थादिशुद्धान् विश्वसनीयत्वोत्पादनार्थमपि नित्यं सेवेत। गोविन्दराज मनु० II. 38. It may be noted here the मनुस्मृति VII. 41 and VII.42 notes the cases of the kings benefitted and suffered by the presence and absence of विनय respectively.
24. नित्यश्च विद्यावृद्धसंयोगो विनयवृद्धयर्थम् तन्मूलत्वाद्विनयस्य। Kauṭilīya Arthāśātra I. 5.11. It may be noted that सर्वज्ञनारायण on the मनुस्मृति VII. 39. States that विनयमिन्द्रियजयोपायम्। p. 29.

VII

THE BHAGVAD-GĪTĀ AND DHARMA-ŚĀSTRA*

At the very outset it may be noted that the term Dharma-Śāstra is a very wide term and it includes Dharma-Sūtras, smṛtis (running into one hundred), commenaties on the Smṛtis and Dharma-Sūtras, Gṛhya Sūtras and the commentaries on the same, Śrauta Sūtras and their commentaries, and the independent digest works and also purāṇas—both the Mahā-puraṇas and Upa-Purāṇas.

It must be pointed out that the verses of the Manu-Smṛti, Apāstaṁba Dharma Sūtra etc. are utilised by Śaṁkarā-cārya in his commentary on the Bhagvad-Gītā to explain similar ideas or to explain the import of the Gītā. It is thus, clear that Śaṁrkācārya has quoted the Dharma Śāstra authorities on the Bhagvad-Gītā, VI,4,XV,[1] 20, XV IIII.44 and 55 etc. From this it becomes quite clear that there is a good relation between the Gītā and the Dharma Sūtra or the Dharma Śāstra.

It becomes further evident that the writers on the Dharma Śāstra also quote the stanzas from the Bhagvad-Gītā to explain the point. Vaidyanātha Dīṣita in his Smṛti-muktāphalam[2] has quoted the verses from the Gītā about 12 times as is clear from the index clearly prepared by the learned editor

J.R. Gharpure. Mādhavācārya in his Jīvan-mukti-Viveka has also quoted many stanzas from the Gītā as pointed[3] out by Dr. Kane. Haradatta,[4] the commentator of the Dharma Sūtras, has also quoted the stanzas from the Gītā in his Caturveda-Tātaparya-Saṁgraha. Besides, in the Viṣṇu Dharma Sūtra, the stanzas from the Gītā are found quoted.

Incidentally, it may be pointed out that the influence of the Gītā on the Purānas also is an admitted fact. The Agni Purāṇa chapter 381 gives us the summary[5] of the six chapters of the Gītā (2) The Viṣṇu Puarāṇa[6] II.3.25 practically follows the views of the Gītā. (3) If the Bhagvad-Gītā presents the example of the devotion of friendship, the Bhāgvata-Purāṇa present the good examples of the devotion of servant towards the god. (4) In the twelfth chapter of the Bhagvad-Gītā, the saguṇa or vyakta Upāsanā is treated as easier than the Avyakta Upāsanā. But the Purāṇas go the extent of suggesting[7] 11 types of devotion, though the 9 types of devotion are quite well-known.Besides, the Bhakti is based on three guṇas-Sattva, Rajasa and Tamas. (5) In the Gītā, we get the classification of four types of devotees and also the essential qualities of a devotee. But the Purāṇs have suggested the classification of the devotee as first class, second class and also the third class and also named the devotees belonging to these categories. (6) The principle of incarnation of the Lord - for the protection of the good and destruction of the wicked- is fruitfully used in the Purāṇs even by increasing[8] the number of incarnations of the gods as is indicated by Dr. Kane.

In the first chapter of the Gītā, it is said that the intermixture of castes takes place, when the ladies are spoiled. Arjuna has expressed this fear. The Lord Kṛṣṇa further states that he has created the system of casteism based on the qualities and action of the person. It is also further clear that at the time of the Gītā, there was no increase of the castes. Dr.

Kane has significantly shown that the castes arise on account of the professions people adopted, some castes are connected with countries, and even the foreign element has taken an important part in the casteism. In the course of time, however, the number of castes went on increasing. Dr. Kane has given a long list[9] of castes in his History of Dharma-Śāstra, by giving a lengthy discussion on this point. The mixture of castes takes place on account of the Anuloma and Pratiloma forms of marriage and other considerations.

It must be noted that in the XVIIth chapter of the Gītā, we have three types of Dānas-gifts-Sāttvika. Rājasa and Tāmasa. But in the context of Dharma-Śāstra, one notices another division of the gifts such as first class, second class and third class. Further, in the Dharma Śāstra, we notice a good list of works quite independent[10] on the matter of Dāna. They discuss[11] the time, place for dāna, qulifications of a donor and donee, and the persons from whom the donations are not to be accepted. Here one is tempted to remark that the topic of Dāna has received proper justice at the hands of the Dharma-Śāstra authors, though this was only slightly touched in the Gītā. In this context, it should be specifically stated that austerity, sacrifice and donations purify the persons as the special view[12] of the Gītā. Hence it would be proper to say that the topic of the Dāna is common to both the Gītā and Dharma-Śāstra.

In the first chapter of the Gītā, Arjuna has expressed the view[13] that he would incur sin by killing the Kauravas who are incendiaries-i.e. Ātatāyins who give poison to other, burn the houses of others, they take away the lands of others by the force of weapons, property and wives. The topic of killing incendiaries has received full discussion at the hands of the Dharma-Śāstra authors. It must be remembered that the Dharma-Śāstra authors recognise the right of self-defence and allow the incendiaries to kill, when the life of a person is in danger. The question also arises whether killing the incendiaries is a case of injunction or glorifications. The attention of the readers is drawn to the notes of Dr. Kane on the Vyavahāra Mayūkha of Nīlakaṇṭha covering pages 416-417. Devala[14] specially holds that by killing an incendiary, one does not become the killer of Bhrūṇa but by not killing an incendiary, one become a killer of Bhrūṇa.

The second chapter of the Gītā[15] gives full expression to the flowery language of the Mīmaṁsakes who treat that sacrifice is all in all and by doing sacrifices, one is bound toget the fruits that are promised for the acts. The Gītā further holds that by dedicating the sacrifices to the gods, one is not bound by the resultes of the sacrifice. It is further held by the Gītā that for the proper continuation of the circle of the world, the performances of the sacrifices is absolutely necessary. The Gītā is not in favour of the desires that have prompted the persons to perform the sacrifice. In the History of Dharma-Śāstra[16] Vol. II/II Dr. Kane has given full description of the Śrauta sacrifices. It is said that the Kṣatriyas should perform the Rājasūya sacrifices with the intention of establishing their sovereignty over others. The Sautrāmaṇi sacrifice, for example, is recommended for a person who wants to become free from the debt to the mother. The Aśvamedha sacrifice is for becoming free from the sin of killing a brāhmaṇa. One is asked to perform the Paśubandha sacrifice for getting prosperity of wealth and in the increase in the number of cattles. The examples cited here show the attitude of the Mīmāsamkas towards the sacrifices. It must be noted, in passing, that the Gītā is not in favour of the purpose for which these sacrifices are recommended or praised by the Mīmāṁsakas.

In the Bhagvad-Gītā we find references to hells particularly at I.41.42, XVI. 16, and 21 etc. By the intermixture of the castes, it is said that one goes to hell. But at other places, the prominence of anger, strong desire and greedy nature are treated as doors to the hells. From this, it becomes quite evident that the number of hells and the causes for going to hells are stated in the Gītā in a limited manner. In he Mahābhārata[17]—Anuśāsana Parvan, it is pointed out that one who sells his daughter for money, goes to the hell known as Kālasūtra. At the beginning, the number of hells was seven. But later on, it went on increasing. The Smṛtikāra Hārīta admits 21 hells. This view is further accepted in the Nārada Purāṅa. But the Viṣṇu Purāṇa takes the figre to 144. The Brahma Vaivarta Purāṇa has raised the fiture to 86 Narakuṇṇdas. The padma Purāṇa accepts the figure of 140 hells and states several grounds for the separate hells. From this[18], it becomes clear that the authors of the Purāṅas have given elaborate treatment to the hells which are casually referred to in the Gītā.

In the first chapter of the Bhagvad-Gītā, we have a reference to the kurukṣetra which is known as Dharma-kṣetra. In the Dharma-Śāstra, we find different names given to the Kurukṣetra such as brahmasaras, Vinaśana, Sannihati, Samanta-pañcaka. The glorification of the Kurukṣetra is made in the Purāṇas. The Narāda Purāṇa adds taht a person dying at the Kurukṣetra becomes free from the cycle of birth and death. In addition to this, Kurukṣetra or Kurujāngala, is treated as a fit place for the performance of the Śrāddha ceremony by the Dharma Śāstra authors. It may be pointed out here that Dr. Kane has given a good description[19] of the Kuruksetra in the fourth volume of the History of Dharma-Śāstra. The commentator Medhātithi[20] of the Manu Smṛti has given us the etympological explanation of the word Kurukṣetra. This simply means that 'one should quickly perform good deeds which alone would protect a person' (in near future).

In the Bhagvad-Gītā IX.22, there is a reference to the expression 'Yoga-kṣema'[21] with reference to the welfare of a devotee. Yoga means getting a thing not acquired and kṣeme means protecting a thing, which is, thus acquired. But in the Dharma-Śāstra literature, the word Yoga-Kṣema is found used in different senses of a king, a minister, a priest. Some others include umbrella, garment, shoes and a chawari in the word Yoga-Kṣema. Vijañāneśvara in his Mitākṣarā on the Yajñavalkya-Smṛti goes to the extent of expressing the view that the protection one gets by the Śraua and Smārta Agni is intended by the expression 'Yoga-Kṣema.' The Guatama Dharma Sūtra states that the Yoga-Kṣema means a royal road available to a brāhmaṇa to lead a happly life. Caṇḍeśvara in his Vivāda-Ratnākara adds that whatever money one gets by serving a king, as a means of livelihood, is included in the Yoga-Kṣema. Devaṇṇabhaṭṭa in his Smṛti-candrikā adds that whatever wealth a learned brāhmaṇa gets by serving or coming in contact with the rich, is referred to by the term Yoga-kṣema. The above discussion[22] leads one to the legitimate conclusion that the word Yoga-Kṣema has undergone evolution in its sense.

In the Bhagvad-Gītā X.31, the river Ganges is described[23] as the Vibhūti of the lord Kṛṣṇa. But in the Dharma-Śāstra[24], the river Ganges is glorified in several Purāṇas like the Brahma purāṇa, Viṣṇu Purāṇa, Bhaiṣya Purāṇa and the Padma-Purāṇa-Śruṣṭkhaṇḍa. Besides, there are severl independent treatises[25] on the Ganges glorifying the importance. It is further held that if the bones of a dead person fall in the waters of the river Ganges, even then he is said to be benefitted. In the Aṣṭāngayoga it is further held that staying on the bank of the river Ganges, or seeing its water, or touching the same or drinking the same, makes one absolutely free from the sin.

From the aove discussion, it would be fair to infer that there is a good relation between the Gītā and the Dharma-Śāstra works, some topics of the Gītā are properly elbaborated by the Dharma-Śāstra works, in respect of some words, evolution has taken place, disapproval of the sacrifices for personal benefits on the part of the Gītā and approval of the Sacrifices for personal gains by the Mīmāmāskas, increase in the number of hells and the causes for the same and the independent treatises on some topics of the Gītā, and downright condemnation of the acts of incendiearies and their proper killing for the self defence are recommended by the Dharma-Śāstra authors.

FOOT NOTES

1. संकल्पमूल: कामो वै यज्ञा: संकल्पसंभवा:।
   मनुस्मृति II.3. is quoted on गीता XV. 20.
2. स्मृतिमुक्ताफलम् pp. 19, 165, 189, 192, 195 etc.
3. P.V. Kane-History of Dharma-Śāstra vol. I/II. p. 788.
4. Ibid. p. 749.
5. Ibid. Vol. V/II/ p. 967.
6. Ibid. Vol.V./II p. 908.
7. Ibid. Vol.V/II. pp. 966-967.
8. Ibid. Vol. V/II. p.
9. Ibid. Vol. II/I pp. 104.
10. Ibid. Vol.I/II pp. 1041-1044.
11. Ibid. Vol. II/II. pp. 837.888.
12. यज्ञो दानं तपश्चैव पावनानि मनीषिणाम् Gītā XVIII. 5b.
13. पापमेवाश्रयेदस्मान् हत्वैतानाततायिन: Gītā I. 356.
14. उद्यम्य शस्त्रमायान्तं भ्रूणमप्याततायिनम्
    निहाय भ्रूणहा न स्यादहत्वा भ्रूणहा भवेत्।।
    देवलस्मृति passage No. 1514. p. 209.

15. Bhagvad-Gītā II. 42-44.
16. P.V. Kane—History of Dharma-Śāstra Vol.II/II pp. 976 to 1255.
17. Mahābhārata-Anuśāna-Parvan.
18. P.V. Kane—History of Dharma-Śāstra-Vol. IV. pp.162-164.
19. Ibid. pp. 660-686.
20. 'कुरु का सुकृतं क्षिप्रमत्र यत् त्राणं भविष्यतीति। व्युत्पत्तिः। मेधानिधि on मनुस्मृति II.19. 17. 195.
21. तेषां नित्याभियुक्तानां योगेक्षेमं वहाम्यहम्। गीता IX.22b.
22. P.V. Kane-History of Dharma-Śāstra, Vol. III, pp. 588-589, Also see present author's paper in 'सर्वोदय'।
23. स्रोतसामास्मि जाह्नवी। गीता. X. 31b.
24. P.V. Kane-History of Dharma-Śāstra Vol. IV. pp. 552 to 584.
25. Ibid Vol. I/II. pp. 1020.

* This paper is an English version of the paper written in Marathi in the Volume 'Gītā Manthana.' The present paper is contributed to Dr. M.D. Paradkar felicitation Volume.

VIII

RIGHT AND JUSTICE IN INDIA
(WITH PREFERENCE TO DHARMA-ŚĀSTRA AND CLASSICAL SANSKRIT LITERATURE)

In considering the position of this problem in Ancient India in particular, one will have to consider the evidences from the Rāmāyana, Mahābhārata, Dharma-Śāstra, Classical Sanskrit literature, historical evidences and also epigraphic evidances, justice, oaths and ordeals. Whenever in the heart of the heart, a man feels that he has done something wrong, he needs clarification from some senior most persons of the Śāstra itself to nullify the same. This is possible only in the case of those persons who attach more importance to moral values in life. To the simple, morally elavated person, naturally several ways become available from the Śāstra itself. In this paper, therefore, I would like to consider this problem under the above mentioned five heads so as to give proper perspective to the interested readers of this subject.

Confession is regarded as an effective way of reducing the consequences of sin and making the person fit for divine forgiveness and favour. MM. Dr. P.V. Kane in his 'History of Dharma-Śāstra' Vol. IV. p.40 referes to the Tai. Brāhmaṇa I.6.5.2 and the Śatapatha Brāhmaṇa II.5.2.20, for the confession of paramours by the wife in the context of the

Varuṇa-praghāsa. He has, however, not referred to the case from the Mahābhārata. In the Mahābhārata 15.38.20, Vyāsa answers to the point of confession on the part of Kuntī giving birth to a son known as Karṇa, on account of the blessing of the sage Durvāsa. He simply points out that this is not to be treated as a fault[1] on her fault, simply because she was in the state of a Kanyā. He further adds[2] in the Mahābhārata 15.38.23 that whatever is done by a powerful person (particularly a spiritually elevated person) is wholesome, pure, law and the there is nothing wrong in it. He, thereby means to say that there is nothing wrong on the part of Durvāsas to bless her in that way. But, at another contxt, in the Mahābhārata 13.48.32, it is stated[3] that one should not try to hide the sin one has committed. If hidden, the sin goes on increasing. Having committed the sin, one should tell it to a good person (really a sprititually advanced person) who has the power to pacify the effect of the same. It may be noted in passing the importance of Dāna in this context. It is pointed out in the Mahābhārata XIV. 3.5. that the performers[4] of bad deeds get purified by sacrifice, penance and liberal donation. In this context, I refer to other passages from the Mahābhārata XIII.61.52 and XIII.61.57 stressing the importance of the donation of gold, cows, land and earth to become free from the sin. Even the importance of the donation of food is widely praised in the Mahābhārata XII.82.21. From this discussion, it is quite evident that confession of a sin and the remedies for becoming free from the sin have been pointed out in the Mahābhārata.

This problem can be viewed from the angle of expiation. The writers on Dharma-Śāstra firmly believe that even the best sinner can be purified by the expiation. This is also indicative of the attitude of our Dharma-Śāstra towards the crimials. The Dharma-Śāstra authors feel that if a man undergoes an expiation for the serious things he has done in the form of killing a brahmin, theft of the gold of others, sexual intercourse even with the wife of a teacher etc. he becomes purified and acceptable to the society for the social dealings. It is also generally believed that the expiations are meant for the grave sins for which secret punishment by way of an expiation is laid down for a man. The Gautama Dharma-Śastra Chapter 24 and the Vasiṣṭha Dharma-Sūtra Chapter 25 and even the author of the Nirṇaya-sindhu hold that the expitations are to be performed only by the learned brahmins. The performance of expiations could become effective in a society attaching highest importance to the moral values and beliveing in the effects of Karma. Dr. Kane in his 'History of Dharma-Śāstra. Vol. IV. pp. 153-178 has dealt with the consequences of not undergoing expiations. It is said that if one does not undergo any expiation for whatever wrongful acts one has done, one is sure to fall into painful and horrible hails. In the next birth, he will be born as a lower animal, tree and shrub.Besides, disgraceful marks appear on the body in the next birth. It is with the intenion of avoiding such results that the writers on Dharms-Śāstra have prescribed several expiations in view of the nature of the crime one has committed. In this very context, it would be proper to refer to the Uttara-Rāma[5] caritam, Act IV. after verse 3.

Janaka is said to have performed the Parāka-Sāntapana[5] expiation when he heard that sītā was abandoned by Rāmā. The literary reference of this type is important and indicative of the fact that in the eighth century people were actually performing such expiations. This will be the modest conclusion on this point. As held by Dr. R.N. Dandekar[6] in his 'Age of the Guptas', the Yājñavalkya-Smṛti is to be regarded as the product of the Gupta period. Whatever rules were laid down by Manu in the Manu-Smṛti were reoriented by Yājñavalkya and the law was adapted to the changing social condiditons. Here the emphasis was put on the private law and not on the criminal law. Dr. Dandekar further refers to the progressive view of Yājñavalkya-Smṛti III.262 which specifically allows a Śūdra to perform the Cāndrāyaṇa expiation. He further holds that in a way, a legal personality was bestowed upon a Śūdra by the new law-giver. One more intersting point in respect of the expiations deserves notice here. Nīlakaṇṭha in his Prāyaścitta Mayūkha points[7] out that when the expiation is extended from the original case to the extended case, the rate of deduction from the original varies. In the case of Sāmya Atideśa, it becomes half of the original. While in the case of Vācanika and Tādrūpya Atideśa, it becomes therefourth of the original. This is the view propounded by Nīlakaṇṭha who is placed by Dr. Kane in the early part of 17th century.

Coming to the aspect of Inheritance, otherwise known as one's right to the ancestral property, some important observations will have to be made. One important view is that the ownership arises as a birth in a family. Another view is that ownership arises on account of the extinction of the right of the previous owner due to his death. It is further evident that in respect of the kingdom, however, sometines, the right was decided by convention and not by the seniority of the birth of a person. Here a reference to the story of Devāpi and Śantanu of the Kuru family deserves notice. Though Devāpi was elder and Śantanu was younger, yet Śantanu got the kingdom and Devāpi went to the forest to practise penance. As a result of his penance, there was no rain for a period of 12 years in the kingdom of Śantanu, who ultimately became ready to hand over the kingdom to his elder brother Devāpi. Devāpi, however, refused to accept the kingdom and accepted the position of a priest for Śantanu and asked him to perform a sacrifice with the result there was ample rain in his kingdom. This important story becomes available to us from the Nirukta of Yāska referred to by Dr. P.V. kane in his 'History of Dharma-Śāstra' Vol. III. p. 41. (2) In respect of inheritance, it was held that some persons were excluded from the right to the throne on the grounds of physical defects such as blindness, skin disease etc. (3) It was also further held by Jaimini in his Pūrva-Mīmāṁā Sūtra VI. 1.41-42, that the wealth is primarily meant for the sacrificial purpose. Hence some defective persons were not treated as entitled for kingship in view of the glaring example of Dhṛtarāṣṭra. (4) In the context of inheritance, we always come across the expression 'dāyāda.' In the Veṇīsaṁhārā[8] Act V, after Verse 5, this word, 'dāyāda' occurs. Jagaddhara in his comments on this stanza remarks very significantly that 'dāyāda' thus refers to the enemies. It is interesting to remember here that the late Prof. A.B. Gajandra-gadkar in his notes on the Veṇīsaṁhāra confirms the meaning so suggested by Jagaddhara in his comments. Actually it has been our experience that ancestral or throne property gives ample scope for fraternal quarrels in this world.

(5) At the time of Bhāsa, however, it appears that the ancestral right to the throne is very well challenged[9] as it is evident from the famous stanza 'Rājyam nāma nṛpātmajaiḥ sahṛdayaiḥ jitvā ripūn bhujyate' etc (6) Even a right of a daughter to the property of her father was recongniesd at a very later stage. MM. Dr. V.V. Mirashi in his 'History of the Sātavānhanas' refers to the Āpastaṁba[10] Dharma-Sūtra II.6.14.-2 and 4 shows that a daughter is recogniesd as an heir to the property only after a son. It may be remembered in this context, that Dr. Mirashi considers the Manu-Smṛti and Āpastaṁba Dharma-Sūtra as the produts of the Sātvāhana and Śuṅga dynasties. (7) It should be noted here that the

Yājñavalkya-Smṛti II.134-135 has clearly recognised the wife as heir to the property of her husband. But this imperial sanction to the Yājñavalkya-Smṛti seems to have received at a later stage. So far as the Kālidāsian literature is concerned, it is evident from the Dhanamitra episode in the Sixth Act of the Śākuntalam, that the property of a sonless person was generally confiscated and appropriated to the property of a king. But a radical change has taken place. It was held[11] that as the wife of a wealthy merchant Dhanamitra was pregnant, the child in the womb was regarded as entitled for the share in the property of the dead father. (8) In this respect, one more important point deserves to be noted. Nīlkaṇṭha in his Vyavhāra-Mayūkha quotes the Manu-Smṛti IX.217 and points[12] out that even the mother of a sonless person is entitled to the ancestral property but only after the regular order of the heirs laid down by the Yājñavalkya-Smṛti II.134-135 is over. She is made provision in the property, just as we make provision for the uninvited persons only at the end of those persons who come invited. (9) In this respect of inheritance one most important reference form the Mahābhārata XIII.47 deserves to be specially mentioned. Here Bhīṣma points out the mode of the distribution of the ancestral property. He points out that a person belonging to the brahmin commnunity is allowed to marry a brahmin wife. But if he marries the ladies of other commnuities, then the sons of the wives should get the share as follows. A brahmin son would get the best bull and the best vehicle. Out of the remaining property, ten shares are to be made and a brahmin son is entitled to get four shares, a kṣatriya son would get three shares, a vaiśya son would get 2 shares. But if a brahmin is pleased then only he may give only one share to a Śūdra son that also not as a right but also by his grace. The same rate of shares is to be followed in respect of a Kṣatriya person marrying the ladies of different communities. If, however, one marries only a brahmin wife then the sons born of that marriage would be entitled to get equal shares. But if, however, after marrying four ladies of different communities, and the brahmin lady gives birth to a son at last, however, her son gets the maximum share. In this respect, it is the caste of a mother that enables a man to get a share in the property of his father. Bhīṣma makes one more interesting observation. He said that actually a brahmin is not supposed to marry a Śūdra lady. If he marries, he will have to undergo an expiation. If, however, by such a marriage a son is born, then a brahmin should undergo double the expiation. This kind of inheritance is suggested by Bhīṣma to Yudhiṣṭhira in the Mahābhārata. This imporant point of the Mahābhārata has no place in Dr. Kane's History of Dharma-Śāstra Vo. III. (10) MM. Dr. V.V. Mirashi in his History of the Śilāhāra kings of North Kaṅkaṇa, south koṅkaṅa, and kolhapur (Śaka Saṁvat 765 to 1115) very significantly points out that the right of inheritance was by convention.[12] He adds that the king Aparāditya donated to his youngest son Vikramāditya-a portion of the south Koṅkaṇa as is evident from the copper plate of Praṇāl of Vikramāditya. (11) Dr. Mirashi further gives[13] a few examples from the history of Śilāhāras, as regards the quarrels among the brothers for the kingdom. Dr. Mirashi points out on the basis of the copper-plate No.19 from Khārepāṭana that the brother chadvaideva succeeded Vajjaḍa on his death. His name, however, is not found in the line of the dynasty of the śilāhāras. This is further clear from the copper-plate[14] No.4 of chadvaideva, in the Prince of wales Museum, Bombay. He also adds that when the Cālukya king Ist Someśvara attacked, Nāgārjuna died, his younger brother Mummṇi came on the throne, setting aside the legitimate claim of Anantapāla who was very young then.

Here there arose quarrels between Mummuṇi and Anatapāla. The latter was not prepared to give up his right to kingdom. Ultimately Anantapāla succeeded. This becomes particularly clear from the copper-plate[14] No.19 of Anantapāla edited by MM. Mirashi on P. 135. Hence he rightly describes this quarrelssome business as 'dāyādavairivyasana'. Others would call this as 'bhrātṛkalaham' which is also the happy rendering of the Marāṭhī drama 'Bhāūbandakī.'

Coming to the most important aspect of oaths in Dharma-Śāstra, one wil have to trace this point to the Ṛg-Veda VII. 104.15 and 16. Even in the Mahābhārata, XIII.95-13-35 we get a reference to the oaths by the seven sages. In the Dharma-Śāstra and particularly in the Manu-Smṛti VIII.114, it is said that one can oath by touching the heads of the son and wife, son, friend, Guru, father and even by referring to wealth. In the Nārada-Smṛti IV.249, it is said that Oath is to be taken in small matters only. One can employ the water of Ganges, image of god, flowers, Harivāmśa on the head for taking oath. It is further said that for false oath on the part a person, there is a loss of reputation and falling into the hell according to the Manu-Smṛti VIII.111. It is further clear that Yājñavalkya suggests fine for improper and profane oath, particularly at II.236. It is further said that for oath no special procedure is necessary. Only bath is enough for enabling a person to take an oath. (2) Attention may be drawn to the important monograph[15] of Dr. M.A. Mehendala on 'Views of Lüders on Varuṇa, particularly published by Tilak Maharashtra Vidyapitha, Poona, 9 under Pundit Lakṣmaṇa-Śāstri Joshi Murgudkar Memorial Lecture series, in the year 1977.

Dr. Mehendale points[16] out on page 51 that the root Śap is in both the padas (Parasmaipada and Ātmanepada). When it is used in Ātmanpada, it means a curse to oneself. While in the Parasmaipada, it means 'cursing others' What he means to say tht if a person who swears falsely, he thereby curses himself. At the time of swearing, whenever one holds water in one's and, and swears faslely or does not keep up one's promise, then one meets with calamities. It is further[16] said that if the water falls on the ground fron the hands of such a person, then it brings about the destruction of the crops of the land. He further draws our attention to the Rāmāyaṇa in which Vasiṣṭha first cursed saudāsa. When, however, in return Saudāsa became redy to curse Vasiṣṭha, his wife prevented him from doing so. Instead of allowing the water to fall on the ground, he dropped the water (possessing the power of fire) on his own feet, with the result his feet turned black. From that time onwards, he came to be known as 'Kalmsa-ṣapāda.' This is evident from the Rāmāyaṇa VII.65.31-32. It is furthr interesting to remember here that Dr. Mehendale draws our attention to the important practice[16] in Greece. At the time of swearing, people there take the water of the river 'Styx' in the hands. This is the river of the lower-world-nether region. It is said that this river is tobe crossed by the soul of a person while going to the world of Manes. In this very context, it is worthy of notice that Dr. Mehendale also draws[17] upon the Mahābhārata III.281.97 in respect of the swearing of Sāvitrī and III.60.37-38, in respect of the swearing of Damayantī. In the latter case, it is said that when she was separated from the king Nala in the forest, a certain hunter was enchanged by her beauty. By her true swearing, she actually reduced the hunter to ashes by the fire which was produced by the power of her swearing. From this, it is evident that oaths are related to private life or the character of a person. One more evidence[18] is led by Dr. Mehendale from the Sāmajātaka 540. In this story, the parents of Sāma prayed the Sylvan deity to make Sāma free from the effect of poison. It is really a matter of wonder that on account of the sincere swearing and prayer of the parents, the son Sāma became free from the effect of poison. I would like to close this discussion by the remark that the expressions 'satyokti, satyakriyā and Samakriyā (used particularly in the Viṣṇu-Smṛti) are synonymous and are used in the sense of swearing.'

Now I come to the last resort of the Dharma-Śāstra authors to the ordeals. It may be remembered at the very outset that the ordeals can be treated as a religiopsycho-legal test, when any concrete evidence becomes unavailable to decide the case before the judges. Nīlakaṇṭha in his Vyavahāra Mayūkha referes to the several varieties of ordeals such as fire, water, poison, kośa, taṇḍula, taptamāṣa and phāla-divya etc. It should be noted here that for deciding the matter by ordeals, the other factors like time, place, nature of the crime, age of the person who has committed a crime are taken into consideration. Aparārka on the Yājñavalkya-Smṛti II.97 refers to different days and months for undergoing this kind of test. It should be remembered here that the Yājñavalkya-Smṛti II.98 pointed out different ordeals for different castes. Actually this topic has become the topic of the Ph.D. thesis[19] of my friend Dr. S.N. Pendse. This thesis is published by the Oriental Research Institute, Baroda, in the year 1985. (1) Though Kauṭilīya Arthaśāstra makes no reference no the ordeals, yet Rapson in his 'Cambridge History of India Vol. I.p.438, points out that during the Mauryan period, the trials wer held by wager and ordeal. (2) Kalhaṇa in his Rājataraṅgiṇī IV. 102-105 refers to the peculiar ordeal known as 'rice flour[19] ordeal. Here the criminal is asked to walk on the ground near the temple where the flour of rice is spread. If his foot-prints become visible, he was treated as guilty and punished. It may be remembered here that this kind of ordeal is unknown to Dharma-Śāstra literature. (3) Even the epigraphic evidence lends support to this custom of ordeals.

The king Mādhavavarman of Viṣvakundin (575 A.D. to 500 A.D.) is described as well-versed in the knowledge of ordeals. Here the expression used is 'avasitavividhadivyaḥ.' This is particularly clear from Pulomburu[20] plates of Viśvakundin Mādhavavarman particularly published in the Journal of the Andhara Historical Research Society, Vol. VI. pp. 17-24. (4) Even the Gadgaj Insciption[21] of Vikramāditya VI dated 1098 and published in Epigraphica Indica Vol. XV. p.360 supports the usage of ordeals. (5) The Silimpur-Stone[22] Slab Inscription or Jayapāladeva about 1200 A.D. on tulā-divya is well known as is evident from the Epigraphic Indica Vol. XIII.pp. 291-292. (6) The Kuttur[23] Inscription published in the Journal of the Bombay Branch of the Asiatic Society vol. IX pp. 307-309 throws light on the fire ordeal. (7) The Māṇḍya[24] Taluka Inscription No.79 published in the Epigraphica Carnataka Vol.III. 47 and particularly quoted by Dr. P.V. Kane in his History of Dhama-Śāstra Vol. III. p. 377 deserves special mention. (8) Even the literary evidence supported the case of ordeals. Cārrudatta in the Mṛccha-katika IX.43. refers to the water ordeal which may be resorted to if at all he is to be punished for his offence of killing Vasantasenā. (9) Dr. Mehendale has referred to the ordeal of fire performed by Sītā in the Rāmāyaṇa Yuddha-kāṇḍa VI. 116.18-29. We also find references to ordeals in the Kādambari para 47 (Peterson's edition), Naiṣadhīya-Caritam II.27, IV.31, IX,55, XVII, 86,88, and XX.130. In Bāṇa's Harṣsacaritam chapter VI, 'in the expression' nirmulam malava-unmūlanāya-gṛhīta-kośaḥ iva-'. This reference is rather doubtful. There is another reading keśaḥfor kośaḥ. In the commentry[25] of Śaṅkara, the reading kośaḥ is preferred, and explained as an ordeal. Dr. Kane remarks that with this meaning the sentence can not be satisfactrily explained. Even the modern commentator[26] S.D. Gajendragadkar is disinclined to accept the reading koṣaḥ as is clear from his critical remark (10) I would like to close this discussion by noting that Dr. S.N. Pendse has given an appendix I pointing out the oaths and ordeals as practised by some tribes of India, pp. 2451-253. His VIIIth chapter of the thesis 'Social, Anthropological, physicological and legal investigation into the pratice of the ordeal (pp. 218-240) deserves to be mentioned here.

In the light of the above discussion, I am almost tempted to advance the view that in ancient India in the absence of any strong evidence to decide the nature of a crime, the practices,-of confession, expiation, oath, ordeal and law of inheritances-have played very important part in the life of the people as is evident from the literary, historical, epigraphic and Dharma-Śāstra evidences, pariticularly in the case of those who attached supreme importance to moral values in life and also were afraid of the consequences of the effects on the body in the next birth.

FOOT-NOTES

1. अपराधश्च ते नास्ति कन्याभावं गता ह्यसि। महाभारत 15.38.20a.
2. सर्वं बलवतां पथ्यं सर्वं बलवतां शुचिः।
   सर्वं बलवतां धर्मः सर्वं बलवतां स्वकम्।। Ibid. 13.48.32.
3. तस्मात् पापं न गुह्येत गुह्यमानं विवर्धते।
   कृत्वा तु साधुषु आख्येयं ते तत् प्रशमन्त्युत।। Ibid.15.3.8.23.
4. यज्ञेन तपसा चैव दानेन च नराधिप।
   पूयन्ते नरशार्दूल नरा दुष्कृतकर्मिणः।। Ibid. 14.3.5.
5. G.K. Bhat—उत्तररामचरितम्, p. 144.
6. R.N. Dandekar-Age of the guptas and other essays, p. 34.
7. साम्यातिदेशे अर्धं ताद्रूप्यवाचनिकनिकयोस्तु पादोनम्। प्रायश्चित्तमयूख, p.14.

8. A.B. Gajendragadkar—Veṇi-saṁhāra-Noted.1,173.
9. राज्यं नाम नृपात्मजैः सहृदयैर्जित्वा रिपून भुज्यते। तल्लोके न तु याच्यते न तु पुनर्दीनाय वा दीयते।
कांक्षा चेत् नृपतित्वमाप्तुमचिरात् कुर्वन्तु ते साहसम् स्वैरं वा प्रविशन्तु शान्तमतिभिर्जुष्टं शमायाश्रमम्।। दूतवाक्यम्। St. 24.
10. पुत्राभावे यः प्रत्यासन्नः सपिण्डः।............दुहिता वा। आपस्तम्ब धर्मसूत्र II.6.14.2. and 4.
11. गर्भ पित्र्यं रिक्थमर्हति। शाकुन्तल Act.VI.
12. P.V. Kane-व्यवहारमयूख, p. 143.
13. V.V. Mirashi-History of Śilāhāra dynasty, pp.11 and 13.
14. Ibid. p. 135.
15. M.A. Mehendale-Views of Lūders on Varuṇa-p.51.
16. Ibid. p. 52.
17. Ibid. p. 33.
18. सब्बे वना गन्धमया पब्बते गन्धमादने।
एतेन सच्चवज्जेन विसं सामस्स हञ्जतु।। सामजातक-540 quoted in Ibid., p. 35.
19. S.N. Pendse-oaths and ordeals in Dharma-Śāstra, p.199.
20. Ibid. p. 199.
21. Ibid. p. 210.
22. Ibid. p. 202.
23. Ibid. p. 203.
24. Ibid. p. 203.
25. कोषो दिव्यम्। शंकर's संकेत on हर्षचरितम् p. 183.
26. 'न तत् अस्माकं चारु अवभाति।' S.D. Gajendragadkar's बालवोधिनी on हर्षचरितम्। p. 117.

IX

MORE THAN THREE DECADES OF DHARMA-ŚĀSTRA STUDIES

Dr. P.V. Kane completed the last volume of his *History of Dharmaśāstra* (Vol. P. Patt-II) in the year 1962. Thereafter he also revised the first Volume which ultimately resulted into two volumes. These two volumes are pulished by the Bhandarkar Oriental Reaserch Institute in the years 1968 and 1975.

About the importance of the volumimous work of M.M. Dr. Kane, Jan Gojnda of Utrecht, states that it contains innumerable extracts from original sources, quotations from hundreds of texts, references to inscriptions and legislative enactments, thought-provoking theories, sharp observations and conscientious judgements. These erudite surveys of the whole field of Dharma-Śāstra, this gigantic encyclopaedia that embraces far more than the Śāstra itself, will no doubt prove to be an indispensable tool of many generations of scholars in times to come.'

In the light of this observation, it is neccessary to take the survey of the work done during the last three decades and more. It is also necessary to see how far the views and chrono-logical dates proposed by Dr. Kane received modification, addition and corrections. However, I am tempted to do some justice to this topic, knowing full well my own limitations in this field. I do not claim that I have approach to all the books and journals published all over the world on this subject. But whatever works could become available to me in the course of the last thirty years and more, will be found best utilised for the purpose of this paper.

Incidentally, however, it should be noted that so far as the work on this subject is done in the foreign countries, my source is the *Jounal of the Bhandarkar Oriental Research Institute,* and particularly the reviews that have appeared there.

In all humility, I mention here the imporant work *'Bibliography on Dharma and Artha'* published by Ludwik Sternbach, many years ago, though I have no approach to all the books and articles mentioned in that important work.

I must also mention in this very context, that I wrote an article on the contribution MM, Dr. P.V. Kane to the domain of Dharma-Śāstra (pp. 65-82) to MM. Dr. P.V. Kane commemoration Monograph published by the University of Bombay in the year 1974. This article has also appeared in my book '*Studies in the Dharma-śāstra*' published in the year 1991.

Now I propose to discuss in this paper a new matter which has not appeared in my article of 1974.

For the propose of study of Dharma-Śāstra, Dr. Kane has laid down the pattern of the restoration of the lost texts of Dhama-Śāstra, by collecting together the citations of that work from the Dharma-Śāstra works. He has restored the text[1] of '*Saṅkha-Likhita-Dharma-Sūtra*' in the *Annals of the Bhandarkar Oriental Research Institute.* He has also restored the text of the *Kāyāyana Smṛti-Sāroddhāra* and himself published this work. This has certainly influenced the later writers on Dharma-Śāstra. In this very context, it should be noted that I have also restored[2] only after editing the *Vyāghra-Smṛti* with the help of two manuscripts, the portion from the *Vyāghra-Smṛti* covering 142 stanzas from pp. 108-126 which is actually Appendix II to my edition of the *Vyāghra Smṛti* published by the authorities of the Bhandarkar Oriental Research Institute. (2) I have also restored the *ṛṣyaśṛṅga-Smṛti* in the Mysore Oriental Vol. XIV, pp. 65-77 and this has also appeared in my '*Studies in the Dharma-śāstra*' pp. 65.80. Here I have collected about 73 stanzas on the name of *ṛṣyaṛṅga* and have thrown light on his novel view[3] in the Dharma-Śāstra. (3) The text of Pulastya is also restored by Lallanji Gopal and Krishna Kanti Gopal and published in Varanasi in the year 1992, as is further clear from the review of this work at the hands of Prof. M.L. Wadeker in the *Journal of the Oriental Institute,* Vol. XL, March-June 1991, pp. 337-340. (4) It is also evident that the restoration of the Devala Smṛti is done from Baroda by Prof. Wadekar for the Ph. D. Degree in Sanskrti and it is published by Agama Kala Prakashan Delhi, in two volumes. This short survey on the point of restoration of the lost Dharma-Śāstra texts bears testimony to the fact that whatever model is laid down by Dr. Kane is followed verbatim by the later scholars.

In the domain of Dharma-Śāstra, editing of the manuscripts also forms the basis of further research. Dr. Kane himself has edited the text of the *Vyavahāra Mayūkha* published by the Bhandarkar Oriental Research Institute in the year 1925 and *Madana Ratna-Pradīpa* for the Anup Sanskrit Library, Bikaner, in the year 1948. It should be noted here that in Appendix 'E' to his edition of the *Vyavahāra Mayūkha*,

Dr. Kane has quoted passages where Nīlakaṇṭha has expressly quoted Madana-Ratna and either followed or ciritized. (pp. 513-515). This kind of editing of the Dharma-Śāstra texts has largely influenced the scholars both oriental and occidental. Here a reference could be made to the article of Dr. J.D.M. Derrett who edited the rare manuscript of Dharma-Śāstra particularly during the early regime of British India. This manuscript[5] entitled '*Svaśrū-snuṣā-Dhana-Saṁvāda*' is edited by him for Dr. V. Raghavan felicitation and the translation of this manuscripts is also published by him in MM. Dr. Umesh Mishra Commemoration Volume brought out by the Ganganath Jha Research Institute, Allahabad, in the year 1970. (2) Miss. J.H. Dave took ample labours for editing the text of '*śrāddha-Prakāśa of Pṛthī-candra,* a Ph.D. thesis (in an unpublished form) for the University of Bombay, in the year 1959 and particularly guided by Prof. H.D. Velankar. It should be noted here that this thesis is deposited in the libraray of the University of Bombay. (3) The writer of this note i.e. Dr. Moghe has also edited '*The Buddha Smṛti*' with the help of six manuscipts (two from B.O.R.I., Poona, 1 from Benares, 1 from Adyar Library, Madras, 1 from Oriental Insititute, Baroda, and 1 from the India Office Catalogue as noted by Dr. Kane) for the journal of the *Annals of the Bhandarkar Oriental Research. Institute,* Vol. LXIV, 1983, pp. 259-268. It may be noted here that Dr. Moghe has further published the manscript of the *Vyāghra Smṛti* on behalf of the Bhandarkar Oriental Research Instititue, Pune, in 1985. Here one of manuscripts is the one already published by Mansukhalal Mor in the fourth Volume of *Smṛti-Sandarbha* and particularly the manuscript from the Benaras. Dr. Moghe also used the manuscript of the Bhandarkar Oriental Research Institute and edited the text with the help of these two mansucripts and also identified the quotations of the *Vyāghra Smṛti* in the light of the vast Dharma-Śāstra literature. In addition to this, he has also collected about 142 stanzas on the name of Vyāghra particularly given by the writers on Dharma-Śāstra. (5) Dr. Moghe has also published the critical edition of the *śrāddha-Sāgara* of Kullūkabhaṭṭa, on the basis of a solitary manuscript from the Sanskrti college, Calcutta. This work is published in the year 1994 by D.K. Printworld (p) Ltd. Delhi. A very good introduction covering 60 printed pages is added to this work by Dr. Moghe, discussing several problems connected with the *śrāddha-sāgara* of Kullūkabhaṭṭa. (6) The *Divya-tattva* of Raghunandana is published by Richard W. W. Lariviere, with the help of 50 manuscripts, and this is also reviewed by Dr. G.V. Devasthali in the *Journal of A.B.O.R.I.* Vol. LXIV-1983-pp. 272-274. The other important publication in this respect is that of the *Nārada-Smṛti* with English Translatin and Notes by the American scholar Richard Lariviere. (7) The manuscript entitled '*Dāyabhāga-Vyavasthā-Saṁkṣepa*' is edited by Ludo Rocher for Dr. R.N. Dandekar felicitation Volume 1984, pp. 351-385. and (8) Lastly the imporant manscript of the '*Śrāddha-Pradīpa* of Vipramīśra is published by Dr. Braja Kishaore Swain in 1982 with his own commentary in Sanskrit entitled '*Raśmi*'. This book is also reviewed by Dr. Moghe for the *Journal of the A.B.O.R.I.* Vol. IXIX pp.298-301 (1988) and Dr. P.D. Navathe (p. 304). This important survey would reveal that both qualiatively and quantitatively remarkable progress is noticed in respect of editing the rare manuscripts of Dharma-Śāstra.

In the domain of reserach, deciding the chronological dates of the authors and works on Dharma-Śāstra plays very important part. Some of the dates fixes by Dr. Kane are challenged and new dates are suggested for some authors.

Here a short survey would be necessary. (1) Dr. Kane has placed Kullūkabhaṭṭa, the commentator of the *Manu-Smṛti* between 1150 to 1300 A.D. Dr. Moghe has, however, placed him between 1520-1620 A.D. (2) As regards the date of Govindaswāmī, the commentator of the *Baudhāyana Dharma-sūtra*, the two scholars—Dr. Burnel and Dr. Kane differ. Dr. Burnell treats him to be a modern commetator, while Dr. Kane takes him to be a very late writer. Dr. Moghe has placed him between 1650 to 1690 A.D. and has thus treated him to be a mediaeval writer. For the discussion on this point, attention is drawn to discussion in the *Studies in the Dharma-śāstra*, pp. 114-117. (3) As regardds the *Buddha-Smṛti,* Dr. kane has not expessed a definite view. Dr. Kane has fixed the general period of the Smṛti literaure. Dr. Moghe has placed him between 10th and 11th century A.D., in a paper published in the A.B.O.R.I. Vol. LXIV, 1983, pp. 259-268. (4) For the date of the *Vyāghra Smṛti*, there is place in Dr. Kane's *History of Dhama-śāstra* Dr. Moghe has placed him in the 10 century A.D., Particularly in his introduction[7] to the *Vyāghra Smṛti* published by the Bhandarkar Oriental Research Institute in the year 1985. (5) On the date of Ṛṣyāsṛṅga-Smṛti, Dr. Kane is sillent in his work. Dr. Moghe has, how-ever, placed him in the tenth or eleventh century A.D. parti-cularly in a paper[8] '*ṛṣyaśṛṅga Smṛti-restored* ' contributed to Mysore Orientalist. (6) As regards the date of Vaidyanātha Dīkṣita, it must be stated that Dr. Kane has placed him in the 17th century. However, the writer of this note has placed him between 1700 and 1750 A.D. paper[9] on 'Vaidyanātha Dīkṣita' contributed to the *Journal of the Asiatic Society*, Bombay, Volumes 60-61 for 1985 and 1986, pp. 56-61.

Interpretation of Dharma-Śāstra texts also becomes an interesing topic of research. In interpreting the text, it would be worthy of note to mention some difference with the views of Dr. Kane (1) In interpreting the famous line from the *Manu-Smṛti 'Nakṣatariaḥ yaśca jīvati'* III.162, Dr. Kane takes this as a reference to the professional astologer who should not be invited for a lunch at the *śrāddha* ceremony. Dr. Moghe differs from Dr. Kane and points out that this has a reference to the Sham astrologer who does not possess the proper knowledge of astorlogy and goes on foretelling the fortunes of the people. This paper[10] is contributed to the *Journal of the Bharatiya Vidya,* Bombay. (2) In the case of famous Śunaḥśepa, Dr. Kane treats him as a *datrima* son, relying upon the authority of the *Vasiṣtha-Dharma-Sūtra.* Dr. Moghe simply points out in a paper[11] contributed to the *journal of the Ganganatha Jha Kendriya Sanskrit Vidyapitha,* that Śunaḥśepa belongs to the category of a *Kṛtrima* son of Viśvāmitra, if at all the authority of the text of *Aitareya Brāhmaṇa* is respected. He has also shown that in the history of adoption, the case of Śunaḥśpa is, indeed, a unique case. (3) Dr. Kane has not at all considered the interpretation of the Dharma-Śāstra text at the hands of non-Dharma-Śāstra authors lke Abhinavagupta. Dr. Moghe has properly considered[12] the interpretation of the text of the *Gautama Dharma Sūtra* IX. 35 by Abhinavagupta, particularly in comparison with the interpretations of the regular commentators—Haradatta and Maskari and has demonstrated that the interpretation offered by Abhinavagupta is, no doubt, novel; but it suffers from the fault of *Parisṁkhyā,* well-known in the science of Pūrva-Mīmāsā. This paper is publication by the research journal of G.J.K.S.V, Allahabad. Incidentally, it may be added here this paper has found a place in the present author's *'Studies in the Dharma-śāstra',* pp. 172-177. (4) Dr. Moghe has followed the view point of Dr. Kane in interpreting[13] the *Kauṭīlya Arthaśastra* III.5.28, by suggesing that the word *strī* occurring in the *Kauṭilīya Arthaśāstra* has a reference to a kept woman and not to a wife as held by others. This paper is published in the *journal of the Oriental Intititue,* Baroda. (5) For the interpretation of the interesting passages from the *Kauṭilya Arthaśāstra* the attention of the readers is drawn to the present author's book '*Studies in the Dharma-śāstra*' pp. 220-270. All these papers have already appeared in the the research journals and they are brought together in the above book.

In the field of research, it is equally important to know whether there is any real progress in understanding the significance of some concepts or some technical terms that occur in the body of the texts of Dharma-śāstra. (1) In appreciating the significance of the expression. '*ananyapūr-vikām in the Yājñavalkya-Smṛti*' I. 51, the regular commen-tators of the *Yājñavalkya-Smṛti* have simply given faithful rending of the expression. Dr. Moghe has shown the significance of this expression in the light of the *Mahābhārata* evidence with reference to Ambā and Śiśupāla, particularly by applying the rules of the Dharma-Śāstra, pp. 159-164. (2) The concept of Nyāsa is fully explained by Dr. Kane in his *History of Dharma-śāstra*, Vol. III. Dr. Moghe has shown how this concept of Nyāsa has undergone evolution[15] in the Classical Sanskrit literature, even including the evidence from the *Rāmāyaṇa* and the *Mahābhārata*. This is shown by him in a paper contributed to the *journal of the Oriental Institute,* Tirupati, and has found its proper place in the present author's book '*A Peep at Indology*' pp. 35-42. (3) In appreciating the sense of the word *'Bhrūṇa'* in the Dharma-Śāstra, Dr. Kane has done justice from the point of view of Dharma-Śāstra texts. But he has failed to consider the evidence from the

Rāmāyaṇa and the *Mahābhārata*. Even in the modern Sanskrit lexicon prepared by V.S. Apte the and revised by P.K. Gode and others, the meanings given by Dr. Moghe in the light of the above evidence have no place at all. In this article[16] '*Dharmaśāstra Aspects of the Rāmāyaṇna*' which is awaiting publication from the research journal but which has a place in the present author's book *'A Peep at Indology'* pp. 31-32 may be consulted by the serious readers of Dharma-Śāstra. (4) In appreciating the concept of a witness, Dr. Kane has done some justice. But Dr. Moghe has considered this concept[17] in the light of the *Mahābhaṛata* and *Dharma-śāstra* literature in his book '*A Peep at Indology*' pp.19-22. It may be added in passing that this paper is also published by the authorities of the Oriental Journal, Tirupati. (5) As regards the concept of '*Sāpiṇḍya*' i.e. consan-guinity, there is a long of discussion in Kane's *History of Dharma-śāstra*. The generally accepted view is that *Sāpiṇḍya* is accepted upto 5th degrees on mother's side and seven degrees on the side of father. But *Buddhasmṛti* edited by the present author for the *Annals of the Bhandarkar Oriental Journal* for 1983, holds a different view. Buddha accepts *Sāpiṇḍya* unto the tenth degree on father's side. It is further interesing to note that one finds corroboration to this view in the commentary *'Keśava-Vaijayantī'* by Nandapaṇḍita on the Viṣṇu-Smṛti, published by the Adyal Libraray, Madras. It may be noted in passing that this Nandapaṇḍita belongs to the 17th century A.D. This important view[18] of Buddha has just escaped the view of Dr. Kane and this has been pointed out by the present writer. (6) Dr. J.D.M. Derrett has placed his unerring finger on *'An Aspect of the Arranged Marriage in Dharma-śāstra'* in his article contributed to the Diamond Jubliee Volume of the *Annals of the Bhandarkar Oriental Research Institute* published in the year 1978. Here the article covers the pp.

107-120. This aspect has escaped the notice of Dr. Kane. (7) In Dr. Kane's work, one does not find the clarification of the term '*Svayaṁpāka*' used in the context of the *śrāddha* ceremony. Here the attention may be drawn to the significant explanation[19] of Vyāghra who says that when the food for the *śrāddha* ceremony is cooked either by the *Yajamāna* himself,or by his wife or by his son, then that cooked food is called as *Svayaṁpākā*. Dr. Kane has not touched this important point in respect of the *śraddha,* ceremony. The question often arises as to whether some persons are treated as disqulalified from preparing or cooking the *śrāddha* food. Dr. Kane has not touched this point. Here it may be pointed that according to Vyāghra, the food for the *śrāddha* ceremony is not to be prepared by a daughter, a widow, a childless woman, a pregnant woman and a woman with bad appearance. It seems that Dr. Kane could not use this view of Vyāghra for the simple reason that at the time of his writing the volumes of *History of Dharma-śāstra,* the *Vyāghra* Smṛti was not critically edited by any scholar. (8) The concept of a widow needs some explanation. Genarally it is an accepted view that when a husband is dead, his wife is treated as widow. But in the Dharma-Śāstra literature, Kane has not taken any note[20] of *Kapila Smṛti*. This Smṛtikāra holds that a woman is treated as a widow when she has no husband and son alive. This means that when she has a son alive, she is not to be treated as a widow. This revolutionary view of *Kapila-Smṛti* has not attracted the mind of Dr. Kane, for the simple reason that this was published later in the volumes of the *Smṛti-Sandharabha* by Mansukhalal from Calcutta. (9) In Dr. Kane's work, one does not find adequate information in respect of the persons to whom the daughters may not be given in marriage. This aspect has escaped the eagle eye of Dr. Kane. Hemādari quotes on the *Raghuvaṁśa* VI. 23 a stanza[21] from the text of *Vṛddha-Parāśara*. This stanza means that those persons who are always away from home, who are not educated, who have concentrated their mind on getting emancipation, who are brave and who are pauper, should not be given their daughters in marriage by the house-holders.

The readers of Dharma-Śāstra know very well that Dr. Kane has written special chapters in the fifith volume of the *History of Dharma-śāstra* on the relation of the Dhamaśāstra to Sāṁkhya, Yoga, Tarka, Purāṇas and Pūrva- Mīmāmśa. But he has not touched the other topics like Dharma-Śāstra[22] and *Gṛhyaśutras,* Dharma-Śāstra[23] and Kāmaśāstra, Dharma-Śāstra[24] and Āyurveda, and Dharma-Śāstra[25] and and Sanskrit lexicons. Some of these topics are discussed by the writer of this note in the Journals and they are brought together *Studies in the Dharma-śāstra.* Here it must be clarified that Dr. Kane has not written chapter on these topics though he has utilised the matter in these works for the *History of Dharma-śāstra.* So it can be said with reasonable certainly that some of the gaps in the works of Dr. Kane are filled in by the writer of this note, though it is true that his work cannot come up to the level of Dr. Kane. Here inciden-tally, it may be added that Dr. Derrett finds fault with Dr. Kane's work, for not having consulted the sources of Sociology and Anthropology, in his *History of Dharma-śāstra.* In passing, it may also be added that a small gap[26] in the work of Dr. Kane, is filled in by considering the evidence from the Classical Sanskrit literature by connecting it with the *History of Dharma-śāstra* thuoghts. This work has been done by Dr. A.N. Deo for his Ph. D. thesis (now deposited in the library of the Marathwads University and now published) and particularly guided by the writer of this note. In can be said categorically that from the works of the 13th century upto the 19th century, a prospective researcher may consult particularly the classical Sanskrit literature from the point of view of Dharma-Sāstra thought. But this is the topic we reserve for some future scholar.

Some interesing points on the total neglect of Dr. Kane deserve mention. Though it is universally admitted that Dr. Kane's work is a voluminous work, some remaining work aims to be done. Right at the outset it must be pointed out that owing to old age, Dr. Kane could not concentrate on Vaidyanātha Dīkṣita. This is done by Moghe to the *Journal of the Asiatic Society of* Bombay and has thus filled up the gap. The work of Vaidika Sārvabhauma deserves treatment. Besides, it will be admitted by any serious reader of Dharma-Śāstra that some Smṛti works have received only a partial treatment at the hands of Dr. Kane. Some such Smṛti works should be restored by the future research scholars. I make the mention of some such Smṛti[28] works only in the foot-note. Unless such Smṛtis are properly restored, nothing can be said about their contribution to the Dharma-Śāstra thought. In addition to this, Manuskhala Mor from Calcutta has published in 6 volumes of some Smṛtis. There is not a single chapter on these Smṛti in the *History of Dharma-śāstra*. Hence the writer of this note takes this oppertunity to request or appeal to the interested scholars of the Dharma-Śāstra to undertake this kind of work on a grand scale. I prefer to mention[29] some such Smṛtis in the foot-note on which some work deserves to be done.

The importance of the manuscripts in writing the history of any subject is supreme. It must be stated here without any fear of contradiction that though Dr. Kane has consulted some descriptive catalogues of the manuscripts for his monumental history of Dharma-Śāstra and for his section on the *Buddha-Smṛti* alias *Buddha Dharma-Sūtra*. Dr.Kane refers to the two manuscripts on the *Budha Smṛti* in the

Bhandarkar Oriental Research Institute, particularly on page 287. It must be stated here that in the list of the works on Dharma-Śāstra Dr. Kane makes a reference to the manuscript of the *Budha Smṛti* printed in India Office Catalogue Vol. III. 386 (No. 1323) particularly on Page No. 1078. But when the present writer edited this manuscripts for the *Annasls of the Bhandarkar Oriental Research Institute,* for 1983, he found some additional manuscripts which are not at all mentioned by Dr. Kane. Thus, he could secure the manuscript No. TR 690 at tha Adyar Library and Research Centre, Madras. One more manuscript he could get from the Oriental Institute, Baroda. He could also succeed in getting one more manuscript printed in the *Smṛti-Sandharbha* Vol. IV. pp. 2137-2138 particularly from the Royal Asiatic Society of Calcutta. It should be remarked here that in the list of the works on Dharma-Śāstra, prepared by that great scholar, there is no mention of any manuscript on the *Vyāghra Smṛti* (p.1113). But the present author found one manuscript of the *Vyāghra Smṛti* in the Bhandarkar Oriental Research Institute, Pune, bearing No.163 of 1884-86. In addition to this, he found that the manuscript of the *Vyāghra-Smṛti* is published in the *Smṛtisandharbha* Vol. IV. pp. 2491-2528. This manuscript is, however, printed in the volume of the *Smṛtisandarbha* by procuring the same from the Govt. Sanskrti College, Benares.

I am happy to mention here that for critically editing the *Vyāghra-Smṛti,* I made the best use of both the manuscripts. These two illustrations cited above are sufficient to prove my finding that in the matter of editing any manuscript of Dharma-Śāstra, the matter presented by Dr. Kane is insufficient. One thus feels that the importance of the *Catalogus, Catalogorum* prrpared by Dr. V. Raghavan and others from Madras, is indeed, supreme. Every cautious worker on Indology is expected to make the best use of such catalogues for doing the methodical work. Here, incidentally, it may be noted that Dr. Kane also has not made a claim that he has consulted all the catalogues for the purpose of his volumes. Hence there is no point in blaming him as such. I have only casually cited the above illustrations to caution the future readers of Indology and particularly the interested readers of Dharma-Śāstra. (3) The importance of the manuscript is also supreme for filling up the gaps in the previously pointed texts. This point has already been clarified by the present author by contributing a paper[30] on '*Nīlakaṇṭha's Vyavahāra Mayūkha*' and *śavśru-Snuṣā-Dhana-Saṁvāda'* to the *journel of the Asiatic Society of Bombay.* Here in passing, it should be noted that the anonymous Śāstri who wrote the above manuscript supplied some matter which is missing on page 139 of the critical edition of the *Vyavahāra Mayaūkha* so ably brought out by MM. Dr. P.V. Kane. This manuscript presents some new readings which have no place in the *Critical Edition of the Vyavahāra Mayūkha.* Besides, if the portion so supplied by the manuscript is added to the matter of page 139 of the *Vyavahāra Mayūkha,* one gets the important observation of Nīlakaṇṭha that he is rejecting the view point of Madana-ratna. In this way, the importance of the manuscript can be very well stressed. This manuscript is also recorded by Dr. Kane in his *History of Dharma-śāstra* Vol. I/II. p. 1131. In passing. Casually, I would mention a few such cases in the foot-notes to this article.

The next important point is whether the suggestions made by Dr. kane for the codification of the Hindu law are accepted by the modern legislature or not. (1) During the British regime, the Hindu law was based on the Dharma-Śāstra texts of Manu, Yājñavalkya, Nīlakaṇṭha and others. Dr. Kane made the suggestion that the Hindu law should be codified in view of the changing circumstances as a result of which the importance of the Dharma-Śāstra text was decreased. This suggestion of Dr. Kane was favoured by he modern legislature. In this respect, the role of Dr. Kane in the Rājyasabhā of the nation, is indeed noteworthy. (2) For the Hindu Adoptions and Maintenance Act, Dr. Kane made the vital suggestion in respect of the age of the boy to be adopted. Dr. Kane states that no boy is to be adopted after the age of 5 years. If at all, he is to be adopted, he must be adoptd before the *saṁskākara* known as *cūḍā-karma* is performed on him. But it is evident from the provision of the section 10(4) of the Hindu Adoptions and Maintenance Act that the boy or a girl should not have completed the age of 15. If it is borne in mind, one would realise that Dr. Kane's suggestion in respect of the age is turned down by the modern legislature. Besides, Dr. Kane's suggestion that no one can be adopted after the *Upanayana* ceremony is performed on a boy, is not favoured[31] by the modren legislature. (3) Dr. Kane's further suggestion that no one can be adopted after his marriage in the natural family, is also set at naught by the Provision of the section (10) (iii) of the Hindu Adoptions and Maintenance Act of 1956. The modern legislature further held that if a custom in a particular community permits the adoption of the married person, then there is nothing wrong in it. (4) The modern legislature also has not accepted the Mīmāṁsā principle of *Adṛṣṭa* accepted by the ancient Smṛtikāras and their arguments, are not accepted[32] by Jusctice P.B. Gajendragadkar. All these points are already noted by the writer of this note in the research journals. (5) Dr. Kane has made a vital suggestion[33] for the chapter of the *Stridhana* of the Hindu Law. He recommends that woman's sons and daughters should succeed together. *Stridhana* should be the absolute property of the married lady, when there are no heirs. This suggestion is made by the learned doctor in his *History of Dharma-Śāstra*, Vol. III. pp. 801-802. Fortunately this suggestion of the learned doctor is accepted by the modern legislature.

It would be interesting to note the differences with the views of Dr. kane what he has maintained in his *History of Dharma-śāstra*. (1) Dr. Kane has shown that in the matter of sacrifices, a woman is given a subordinate position, that she is not entitled to perform a sacrifice as such. For such views, he has relied on the *Manu-Smṛti* Vol. 155, *Viṣṇu-Dharma-Sūtra* 25.15 and *Āpastamba Dharma-Sūtra* II.6.15.17. Dr. Moghe has shown on the basis of historical evidence, Anantadeva's Mīmāṁsā interpretation and Śabara's important observations, and the views of MM. Ganganatha Jha on the *Mīmāṁsā Sūtra* VI.1.13 and thinks that women are entitled to perform sacrifices. (2) As regards the three rates of donation, Dr.kane has clarified his position relying on Mitākṣarā on the *Yājñavalkya-Smṛti* I. 203. Here Dr. Moghe has combined[35] the sources of the *Rāmāyaṇa* and the *Mahābhārata,* and has suggested a somewhat different rate of the donation in his article on '*Dāna*' section of the DharmaŚāstra (based on the *Mahābhārata*). (3) Dr. Kane thinks that in the *Manuśmṭti* III.162, the professional Astrologer is prohibited for the lunch at the *śrāddha*. Dr. Mough departs[36] from Dr. Kane and holds on the basis of the evidences from the Dharma-Śāstra and Astrology that a Sham astrologer is condemned by Manu for the *śrāddha*-Ceremony. (4) In *ṛṣi-Kalpanyāsa,* Dr. Kane hods[37] that it is not obligatory on women to apply Tilaka mark on the forehead. It is difficult to agree with the learned scholar on this point. One can quote here the stanza[38] No. 192 (of my critical edition) of the *Vyāghra Smṛti* which clearly means tha a brahmin without a *tilaka mark* on his forehead and a pious lady without having the *tilaka* mark on her forehead, these two are condemend among the people and particularly in respect of the matters—*Daiva* and *Pitrya*. This point is already raised by me in my introduction to the *Vyāghra Smṛti*. (5) There is a controversy between Dr. Kane and Dr. Apte V.M. on the point of *Vrata*. This is already referred[39] to by Dr. Kane and his rejoinder in the first part of the fifth Volume of the *History of Dharma-śāstra*. Dr. R.N. Dandekar high-handedly says that the interpretations suggested by both Kane and Apte are unacceptable[40] to him personally. As Dr. Dandekar has not clarified his stand-point with some Vedic evidence so far, his opinion need not be taken seriously.

Now we turn to a few cases of improvement on the part of Dr. Kane. As regards the expression '*ām*ikṣā' Dr. Kane's explanation in his notes on the *Harṣacaritam* p.94 is based on Sanskrit dictionary. The same is the case with the explanation given by Ranganātha on the *Harṣacaritam*. It is MM. Dr. Ganganatha Jha who has given the correct explanation in his Mīmaṁsā-Maṇḍana p. 162. But it must be stated here that if one consults Dr. Kane's *History of Dharma-śāstra* Vol. II/II/ p. 1092 and particularly the foot-note No. 2448, one would be conviced that Dr. Kane has given more correct explanation here. This is a proof of improvement on the part of Dr. Kane Particularly in comparison with the Note on the *Harśacaritam* and correctly explained the word '*Upasangrahaṇam*' when it occurs in the *Harṣcaritam*. In his notes p. 57, he translates it as 'who made a respectful salutation.' Even Rangaṅatha, the commentator of the *Harṣacaritam* explains it. These two explanations, though satisfactory from the point of view of a general reader, will not satisfy the interested readers of Dharma-Śāstra. For a proper explanation, attention may be drawn to the *History of Dharma-śāstra* Vol. II/I, pp. 334-225. This explanation again is a case of improvement in the writings of Dr. Kane. It appears that while writing the *History of Dharma-śāstra,* he has done complete justice to such words as have occurred in his notes on the *Harṣacaritam.* (3) In the collection of papers of Dr. Kane which I presented to the sholarly world in the book, one will notice the tendency in Dr. Kane's writings that he has always made improvement over the matter presented previsously and also added more matter to the previsou articles. Here, in passing, it may be noted that Dr. Kane's note or a chapter in the third Volume of the *History of Dharma-śāstra,* particularly on *Kalivarjyam,* one will notice the addition of respectable amount of matter. Some of his papers will satisfy this requirement. This is a sure proof of his improvement and addition to the subject and when he went on reading and finalising the matter. The same may be said about Asahāya, the commentator of the *Gautama-Dharma-Sūtra.* Dr. Kane has added in his *History of Dharma-śāstra* Vol. I/I, p. 548 that Asahāya probably wrote a commentary on the *Manu-Smṛti* also. This may be treated as a case of addition to his views on Asahāya.

It is always said that the study of the Dharma-Śastra cannot be said to be complete without the study of Pūrva-Mīmāsā. Dr. Kane has written a chapter on *'Mimāṁsā and Dharma-śāstra'* in the fifth volume of the *History of Dharma-śāstra* pp. 1152 to 1351. Here he has explaind the Mīmāṁsā doctrines, theories and clarified the matter with the help of Dharma-Śāstra and Pūrva-Mīmāṁsā. This has influenced Dr. Moghe and others. One may clarify this point by stating that the contribution of the writers on Dharma-Śāstra like Aparārka,[41] Vijñaneśvara,[42] Śūlapāṇi[43] and Mitramiśra[44], the commentators of the *Yājñavalkya-Smṛti,* Kullūkabhaṭṭa[45], the commentator of the *Manu-smṛti,* Haradatta[46] and Maskari[47], the commentators of the *Āpastaṁbha* and

Gautama Dharma Sūtra, digest authors like Nīlakaṇṭha[48] and Śankarabhaṭṭa[49], Devaṇṇabhaṭṭa[50], Raghumaṇi[51], Mādhavācārya, the commen-tator of the *Parāśara Smṛti* (2) In addition to this, Dr. Moghe has also brought to light the contribution of some authors like Medhāatithi for *Anuvāda,* Mitramīsra[52] for *Samuccaya.* He has also guided a thesis[53] on '*Mīmāṁsā in Medhātithi*' for the Ph.D. Degree. (3) Besides, he has evaluated the contribution of Śaṅkarācārya[54], and Sāyaṇācārya[55] for the domain of Pūrva-Mīmāṁsā. (4) Further, he has given a serious consideration to the important topics like Pūrva Mīmāṁsā[56] and Astrological interpretation and Pūrva-Mīmāṁsā[57] and Paurāṇic interpretation (parti-cularly the Dharma-Śāstra material in the Purāṇas intereprted by the Dharma-Śāstra authors from the Mīmāṁsā angle. (5) He has also brought to light some common aspects[58] of the *Paribhāṣās* of Vyākaraṇa and the Mīmaṁsā rules of interpre-tation. (6) He has also made a proper comparison[59] between the two commentaries *Sāvavivecanī* and *Prabhā* on the *Mīmāṁsānyāyaprakāśa* of Āpadeva. (7) He has also made the proper evaluation[60] of the contribution of MM. Dr. P.V. Kane to the domain of Pūrva-Mīmāṁsā, by presentng a special article in MM. Dr. P.V. Kane commemoration Monograph published by the University of Bombay in the year 1974. (8) He has further advocated the evolutionary theory of the science of Pūva-Mīmāṁsā, by writing papers on *Atideśa,*[61] *Punar-vacana.*[62] *Vākyabheda*[63] and *ūha.* (9) His two works *Mīmāṁsā discussions on śrāddha-Srāddha-Sāgara of Kullūka-bhaṭṭha* and Ahaṁkāra śāstra are in progress and wil see the light of the day very soon. (10) Dr. Moghe has also shown how the Mīmāṁsā principles of interpretation are utilised by the writers on classical Sanskrit works and the *Kāmandakīya Nītisāra.* This smal survey will reaveal that there is a good progress in respect of the studies of Dharma-Śāstra and Pūrva-Mīmāṁsā.

It will not be out of place, if only incidentally some important aspects of Dr. Kane's research work are highlighted in the light of the papers which have no place in his volumes of *History of Dharma-śāstra*. In doing this, some times the purpose at the back of the mind of the present author is indicated for the future guidance of the workers on Indology. (1) In a paper on *'Dharma-Sūtras of Saṅkha-Likhita*[65], Dr. Kane has restored the text of the two Dharma-Śāstra authors, Saṅkha and Likhita in the light of the works he has relied upon. It will be an opportunity to the workers of Indology to compare other published works on Dharma-Śāstra and add to the passages which have no place in the collection of the passages by Dr. Kane. (2) In a paper on the '*Arthaśāstra*[66] of Kauṭilya Dr. Kane has experssed his views on the authenticity of the text, its relation to the *Manu-Smṛti, Mīmāṁsā śāstra,* herbs and drugs etc. (3) In a paper on *'The Pārijāta*[67] *and the Madana-Pārijāta,* Dr. Kane has discussed and concluded that the identity of the two works is not possible even chronologically and the two works are totally different from each other. Here the aspects of the identity and chornogloy of the works play very important part. (4) In a paper '*Vedic Mantras*[68] *and Legends in the Purāṇa*. Dr. Kane has shown the relation between the Vedic Mantras and *the Brahma-Purāṇa*. Here he has made two classifications. He first quotes the place of the *mantras* which are actually quoted verbatim in the *Brahma-Purāṇa* and in the second category, he has shown how the stanzas in the *Brahmas-Purāṇa,* contain the good paraphrase of the Vedic *mantras*. This also reveals his knowledge of the Vedic literature along with the Paurāṇic niceties. (5) In an article[69] 'on *Naming a Child or a Person'* Dr. Kane has made elaborate discussion on the pratices in the Gṛhya Sūtras particularly in in comparison with the Vedic literature. Incidentally, he has also considerd the evidences from the *Mahābhāṣya* of Patañjali and the volumious commentary of Aparārka on the *Yājñavalkya-Smṛti*. In fact, the present paper is an addition to the matter presented in the History of *Dharmaśāstra* Vol.II/ I. pp. 238-254. Thus, this paper reveals the aspect of filling up the gap in one's own work by Dr. Kane. (6) In a paper '*The predecessors of Vijñāneśvara*[70] Dr. Kane has considered how Vijñānaneśvara has examined the views of his predecssors like Asahāya, Viśvarūpa, Bhāruci, Śrīkara and Medhātithi.

Here he has explored the vast Dharma-Śāstra literature and noted the similarities and difference of Vijñāneśavara with these authors. Though it is true, that some point from this paper are utilised by Dr. Kane for his *History of Dharma-śāstra* Vol. I/I, yet the elaborateness may be regarded as the special fearture of this paper that is included in this bunch of papers. (7) In a paper of '*The Dvaita-Nirṇaya*'[71] of *śaṅkarabhaṭṭta*, Dr. Kane has considered the manuscript of this work in the Deccan College Collection, Pune. This manuscript was later on published by J.R. Gharpure. In the year 1918, Dr. Kane has shown the importance of this manuscript from the view point of Mīmāṁsā discussions, the Purāṇas quoted by him and the way in which the debatable problems are solved by Śaṅkarabhaṭṭa. He has also placed his unerring finger on the importance of the line '*Dauhitro Bhāgineyaśca śūdrasyā' pi ca dīyate.* It is must be noted here that in the *History of Dharma-śā*stra, there is no chapter on Dvaitanirṇaya, but in some volumes, there are reference to the work. Hence the importance of this paper can hardly be denied. (8) In a paper on '*The Tantravārtika*'[72] *and the Dharma-śāstra literature* Dr. Kane has considered the passages from the Āpastaṁba, and *Gautama-Dhama Sūtras* quoted in the *Tantravārtika* and shown that the *Manu-Smṛti* XI.10 is not to be considered as spurious; it is in fact, a genuine portion on the *Manu-Smṛti*. The importance of this paper lies in the fact that this has no proper place in the *History of Dharma-śāstra* Vol. V/II, but this is of the inter-disciplinary type. (9) Dr. Kane has discussed in a paper entitled '*Asahāya*',[73] *the commentator of the Gautama-Dhama Sūtra and the Nārada-Smṛti,* the contribution of the commentator Asahāya, whose commentary is not now avaibale to us. Here he has collected the information from the commentaries of the Smṛti works like the Manu and the Yājñavalkya and the Hāralatā of Aniruddha. Getting information of an author whose work is not available from other sources forms the important aspect of this paper. (10) Dr. Kane has discussed the actions forbidden in the Kali age particuarly in his paper on '*Kalivarijya.*[74] This paper is properly elaborated by Dr. Kane in his *History of Dharma-śāstra* Vol. III. The importance of this paper lies here in presenting the verses (quoted here in the Appendix) to this paper and which have no place in the monumental work of Dr. Kane. The verses have the bearing on the aspect of the things prohibited in the Kali Age. Herein lies the importance of this paper. (11) In a paper '*The Meaning of ācāryaḥ*'[75] Dr. Kane has refuted the view point of Prof. K.V. Rangaswami Aiyangar, when he held the view by the word 'Ācārya', Kauṭilya refers to his own teacher. Here Dr. Kane has given evidences from the *Nirukta. Mahābhāṣya*, Aparārka etc. to contridict the above view. Hence this article has the research aspect of refutation of the view of others. In addition to this, this paper is only casually mentioned in the *History of Dharma-śāstra* Vol. I/I, p. 209. (12) In a paper '*Passages from the Rājamārtaṇḍa*[76] *on Tithis, Vratas and Utsavas,* Dr. Kane has collected stanzas from the three manuscript and identified the stanzas from the vast Dharma-Śāstra literature. (13) Dr. Kane has discussed in a paper '*Purāṇa-Dharma-*[77] how the Vedic *mantras* and legends are utilised in the paurāṇnic ideas of sacrifies and pilgrimages and bathing in sacred places and has himself filled up the gap of his own work when he dealt with the meaning and sources of *Dharma*. It is thus the important aspect of his research that is revealed here. (14) In a paper on '*king Bhoja*[78] *and His works on Dharma-śāstra and Astrology*' Dr. Kane points out the works of Bhoja such *as Bhīmaparākrama, Bhujabala-nibandha, Rājamārtaṇḍa* and *Vyavahāra-Samuccaya,* and has appreciated importance of the relation of Astrology to Dharma-Śāstra. In this paper, he has further mentioned the places where the manuscripts of these works are there. (15) Dr. Kane has discussed in a paper '*The Kauṭilya*[79] *and the Matsyapurāṇa*' the resemblances between the two works and concluded that the author of the *Matsyapurāṇa* seems to have borrowed the ideas from the Kauṭilya *Arthaśāstra,* though the date of the *Matsyapurāṇa* is said to be uncertain. Here he has actually cited the passages from both the works to enlighten the readers. (16) In a paper on '*Utpala and the Arthaśaśtra of Kauṭilya*'. Dr. Kane has cited some passages from the commentary of Utpala on the *Yoga-yātrā* of Varāhamihira, Particularly from the *Kauṭliya-Arthaśāstra*. basing his discussion on a manuscript in the Bhau Daji Collection of Sanskrit manuscript. (17) *Mahābhārata citations in the śābara-Bhāṣya*' is a paper Dr. Kane wrote to fil up a gap of the paper or a chapter of Dr. V.M. Apte and the Dr. D.V. Garge. Dr. Kane states here that some of the *Sūtras* of Jaimini read like verses or *pādas*.

The writer of this note takes an oppertunity to mention only incidentally some of the interesting papers of Dharma-Śāstra to quench the thirst of the interested readers of Dharma-Śāstra. (1) *The Doctrin of Prāyāscitta in Hindu Law and jains Doctrine of Karma* by Y. Kishanan, in A.B.O.R.I. Vol. LXIV-1983.pp 109-117. (2) *The Doctrine of karma and śrāddha* in A.B.O.R.I Vol. LXVI, 1987, pp. 97-115. (3) *Caṇḍcāvera and His Rājanīti-Ratnākara* by Dr. M.D. Paradkar, in the *Mysore Oriental* Vol. XIV. pp. 83-87. (5) *Position of Wisdom in Early Medieval India in the Light of the Kathāsaritsāgara* by Aparna Chattopadhyaya in JOI, Baroda. Vol. XXIV. Nos. 3-4, 1975, pp. 292-402 (6) *Gotra and Exogamy* by K.C. Mishra in JOI Baroda. Vol. XXIV. Nos. 3-4, 1975, pp. 422 to 427. (7) *Saṁskāras-Their purpose and significance* by Dr. M.D. Paradkar, in *Mysore Oriental* Vol. IV. No.1, 1971. pp. 8-14. (8) *Bṛhaspati on State Patronage to free Bootersm* by Raghavendra Vajpeyi, Kane Centenary Volume issued by Asiatic Society of Bombay, 1977-78. pp. 212-217. (9) *Adoption-Unmarried woman* by H.S. Ursekar, in *Bharatīya Vidyā.* Vol.XXXIX, No. 1. 1979, pp. 55, 68. (10) *Law in Ancient India,* by Prof. R.P. Kangle in *Bhārtīya Vidyā* Vol. L. 1990, Nos. 1-4. pp. 50-57. (11) *Prostitution in Ancient India* by Dr. Krishna Murari, in JGJKSV, Vol. XLI, 1985. pp. 57-65. (12) *śunaḥṣepa and Dattaka-Vidhāna* by S.G. Moghe, in JGJKSV., Vol. JGJKSV. Vol. XXXIV, 1979, pp. 85-96. (13) *Dāsa Varṇa in the Ṛgveda* by Ram Gopal, in JGJKSV. Vol. XXXIV, 1978.pp. 1-12. (14) *Glimpses of ācāra and Vyavahāra in Early India literary and Epigraphic Records* by D.C. Sircar pp. 3-14 of the *Studis in Dharma-śāstra.* (15) *Father Buchet's letter on the Administration of Hindu law* by Ludo Rocher, pp. 15-48 of the above volume. (16) *A Sanskrit jayapatra from 18th Century Mithila by* Richard W. Lariviere pp. 49-80 of the above volume. (17) *Renouncer and Renunciation in the Dharma-śāstra* by Patrick Olivelle, pp. 81-152 of the above volume. (18) *Legat and Symbolic Significance of the Menstrual Pollution of Rivers* by Richard Salomon, pp. 153-178. (19) *What Dharma-śāstra has to say about Dowry* by J.D.M. Derrett pp. 179-193 of the above volume. (It may be noted here that this book is edited by Richard W. Lariviere). (20) *The Origin of the Gotra System in the Ṛgveda by* V.G. Rahurkar, in A.B.O.R.I. Vol. LIII-1972, pp. 95-99. (21) *Mahābhārata and Dharma-śāstras* by M. Bhavana-chari, in J.H. Dave Volume issue by *Bhartiya Vidya,* pp. 253-259. (22) *The Theroy and Practice of Punishment as Recorded in Vardhamāna Upādhayāya's Daṇḍaviveka* by Bhabatosh Bhattacharya, in the proceedings of the A.I.O.C. 26th Session. 1972, pp. 225-244. In passing, it may be noted that the inclusion of the above papers does not mean that other papers are not worth recording. The only important thing is that I have no approach to all the journals in the world, or through oversight, some articles may have escaped my notice.

I would like to close this article by making a specific reference to some of the important books that are published during the last thirty years. (1) *Dharma-śāstra and Juridical literature* by J.D.M. Derrett, pp. 1-75 published by Otto Harrassowits. Wisebaden. (2) *The Socio-legal Position of Women in the Smṛti of Manu and Yājñavalkya* (A Ph. D. thesis deposited in the Poona University, 1971) and an article on the above topic in. Homage to Dr. Mainkar, pp. 1-17. (3) *Oaths and Ordeals in Dharma-śāstra* a published Ph.D. thesis of Dr. S.N. Pendse, and deposited in the M.S. University of Baroda. (4) *Vipramiśra's śrāddha-Pradīpa* with *Raśmi* commentary by Dr. B.K. Swain (5) *The Vyāghra Smṛti* edited by Dr. S.G. Moghe, published by Bhandarkar Oriental Institute, Pune, 1985. (6) *Studies in the Dharma-śāstra* (A collection of 35 papers on Dharma-Śāstra and Kauṭilīya Arthaśāstra) by S.G. Moghe, pubilshed by Ajanta Books International, Delhi, 1991. (7) *A Critical Edition of the śrāddha-Sāgara of Kullūkabhaṭṭa* by Dr. S.G. Moghe, published by D.K. Printworld (P) Ltd. Delhi, 1993. (8)

Mensturation in Ancient India, by Dr. (Smt.) Sarala Srinivasan. (9) Slavery in Ancient India, by Dr. Dev Raj, pubished by people's publication House New Delhi, 1960. (10) *Studies in the Pūva Mīmāṁsā* (a collection of 22 papers) by S.G. Moghe, published by Anajta Books International, Delhi, 1984. (11) *Studies in Applied Pūrva-Mīmāṁsā* (A collection of 22 papers) by S.G. Moghe published by Anjanta Books International, Delhi, 1998. (12) *Dāya-Vibhāga* by I.S.P a Wate, published by Kanatak University. Dharwar, 1979, (13) *The Indian Society in the Mahābhārata* by S.C. Bennerji. (14) *The Sacrament of Marriage in Hindu Society* by Miss. U.M. Apte. (15) *Mīmāṁsā, the Vākyaśāstra in Ancient India* (A Ph. D. thesis partly published) by Dr. G.V. Devasthali. (16) *Smṛti-Material in the Mahābhārata* by Dr. S.C. Bannerji, published at Calcutta.

By writting this very lengthy aritcle, I feel that I have taken a survey of the Dharma-Śāstra literature-articles, Books and Ph.D. theses, indicated the progress in the subject, made suggestions for the future workers of Indology and thereby paid my respectful tribute to the sacred memory of that scholar MM. Dr. Pandurang Vaman Kane, the like of him will not be seen for a long long time to come.

FOOT NOTES

1. A.B.O.R.I. Vols. VII. and VII.
2. The *Vyāghra Smṛti* published by B.O.R.I. Pune, 1985.
3. For the peculiar views of Ṛṣyaśṛṅga, *the Mysore Orientalist* Vol.. XIV. pp. 66-67; Also see Dr. Moghe's *Studies in the Dharma-śāstra,* pp. 67-68.
4. Prof. M.L. Wadekar, Devala-Smṛti. Ph. D. thesis (two volumes) published by Bharatiya Kala Prakashan, Delhi, 1997.
5. P.V. Kane—History of Dharma-Śāstra Vol. I/II. p. 1131 refers to this manuscript of 'Śvaśrū-snuṣā-Dhana-Saṁvāda as per Burnell's catalogue of Tanjore manuscripts p. 143a.

6. Miss Parvati S. Moholar has written a thesis entitled 'A Critical edition of the Vivādacandra of Misrau-Miśra' particularly guided by Dr. Moghe. This thesis is deposited in the library of the University of Bombay, 1984.
7. Dr. S.G. Moghe, The Vyāghra Smṛti Introduction, pp. 18-21.
8. 'Ṛṣyaśṛṅga-Smṛti' restored, Mysore Orientalist, Vol. XIV. p. 67.
9. Also see this paper published in Dr. Moghe's Studies in the Dharma-Śāstra, pp. 165-171.
10. A paper on 'A Fresh Interpretation of the Manu-Smṛti III. 162 published in the Bharatiya Vidya. Vol. XXXXIV-1979, pp. 59-63.
11. Dr. Moghe's paper on 'Śunaḥśepa and Dattaka Vidhāna' published in theJournal of the Ganganatha Jha Kendriya Sanskrit Vidyapitha, Allahabad. Vol. XXXV, Parts, 1-2. 1979, pp. 85-95.
12. Dr. Moghe, 'Studies in the Dharma-Śāstra', consult pp. 172-177 for Abhinvagupta's novel interpretationof the Gautama-Dharma-Sūtra IX. 35.
13. Dr. Moghe's paper on 'Kauṭilya Arthaśāstra III. 5.28-A Reappraisal' in *Studies in the Dharma-śā*stra, pp. 240-244. Also see this paper published in the Journal of the Oriental Institute, Baroda, Vol. XXXVI, Nos. 1-4, 1986-1987, pp. 97-101.
14. Also see the paper '*Significance of Ananyapūrvikā* in the Yājñavalkya-Smṛti' published in the *Studies in the Dharmas-śāstra*, pp. 159-164.
15. For the significance of Nyāsa, see Dr. Moghe's 'A Peep at Indology' pp. 35-42; also see 'Dharma-Śāstra concept of Nyāsya and Sanskrit Literature' published in the *Journal of Oriental Research Institute,* Tirupati, Vol. XXX-1987, pp. 87-94.
16. For the meaning of Bhrūṇa, see Dr.Moghe's paper 'Dharma-Śāstra Aspacts of the Rāmāyaṇa' published in his book '*A Peep at Indology,* pp. 31-32.
17. 'Concept of Witness in the Mahābhārata and Dharma-Śāstra literature' published in a book '*A Peep at Indology*', pp. 19022. Also see Oriental Journal Venkatahvara University, Vols. XXXVIII, XXXXIV, 1989-91, pp. 135-139.
18. A.B.O.R.I Vol. LXIV of 1983, consult p. 263 for the peculiar views of Budha. Also see this paper pulished in the '*Studies in the Dharma-śāstra* p. 56.
19. S.G. Moghe, The Vyāghra-Smṛti 'Introduction pp. 27-28 for the concept of 'Svayaṁpaka' in the context of Śrddha.
20. For the concept of a widow, consult Dr. Moghe's *Studies in the*

Dharma-śāstra, pp. 183-190 and particularly p.184 of the article 'Smṛtis. Smṛtikāras and Digest authors: Retrospect and Prospect.'

21. Hemādari's Darpaṇa p. 132.
22. Ralation of the Gṛhya Sūtra to the Dharma-Śāstra literature' by Dr. S.G. Moghe in Tattvāloka, Vol. No. April 1982, pp. 15-28. Also see this paper in 'Studies in the Dharma-Śāstra, pp. 13-26.
24. Relation of the Indian Medical Science (Āyurveda) to Dharma-Śāstra by Dr. Moghe in Bhāratī-Śodha-Sāra-Saṁgraha, Vol. II, 1973, pp. 51-57. Also see this paper published in the 'Studies in the Dharma-Śāstra' pp. 27-35.
25. Dharma-Śāstra and Sanskrti Lexicons byDr. Moghe published in the book 'Studies in the Dharma-Śāstra, pp. 25-40, Dr. A.N. Deo 'Dharma-Śāstra thoughts in Classical Sanskrit literature (from Bhāsa to Śrī-Harṣa, the author of the Naiṣadhīyancaritam' a Ph. D. thesis in the liberary of the Marathweda University. This thesis written in the Marathi language is deposited in the year 1993 and also published in.
27. Dr. Moghe's paper 'Vaidyanātha Dīkṣita' published in the Journal of the Asiatic Society of Bombay, Vols. 60-61, pp. 56-61. Also see this paper published in 'Studies in Dharma-Śāstra, pp. 165-171.
28. A few smṛtis may be mentioned here. Hārita, Saṁvarta, Laugākṣi, Viśvāmitra, Marīci, Prajāpati, Pracetas, Paithinasi, Dakṣa, Pitāmaha, Karṣṇājini, etc. It may be remarked here that Dr. Kane's treatment on these Smṛtis is meagre.
29. Kapila-Smṛti Vāhūla-Smṛti, Lohita-Smṛti, Nārāyana-Smṛti, Kaṇva-Smṛti, Dalbhya-Smṛti, Bhāradvāja Smṛti, etc. are printed in the volumes of the Smṛti-Sandharbha by Mansukharai Mor, from Calcutta. It is observed that though these smṛtis were published before the revision of the fist volume of History of Dharma-Śāstra; Kane's attention was not drawn to this; otherwise he would have given a thorough treatment of these Smṛtis, in keeping; with his other chapters or sections on the smṛtis. Hence a work on these smṛtis is a desideratum.
30. Dr. Moghe's paper on 'Nīlakaṇṭha's Vyavahāra-Mayūkha and Śvaśru-snuṣā-Dhana-Shaṁvāda' was published in the *Journa of the Asiatic Society of Bombay. Vols. 52-53/ 1977-78 pp. 200-207 (This Volume is treated as MM. Dr. Kane Birth Centenary Volume)*.
31. Dr. Moghe's paper on 'The Hindu Adoption Act-Ancient, Medieval and Modern: A comparison' was published in the Journal of the Oriental Institute, Baroda, Vol. XL. Nos. 3-4, March-June 1991.

pp. 235-242; Also see this paper published in 'Studies in the Dharma-Śāstra', pp. 134-141.

32. This has a reference to 48 Bom. L.R. 196.
33. P.V. Kane's Paper on 'Are women entiled to perform sacrifices?'' is published in 'History Dharma-Śāstra, Vol. III, pp. 801-802.
34. Dr. Mogh's paper on ' Are women entiled to perform sacrifices'? is published in 'Studies in the Dharma-Śāstra, pp. 190-194.
35. Dr. Moghe's paper 'Dāna section of the Dharma-Śāstra (based on the Mahābhārata) published in 'Studies in the Dharma-Śāstra', pp. 196-197 for the rates on donation. Also see 'Prasanna-pārijata' (Datta Mahārāja Kavīśvara Felictation volume in Marathi), 1990. pp. 89-93.
36. Dr. Moghe's paper on 'A Fresh interpretation of the Manu-Smṛti III. 162' is published in the Bharatiya Vidya, Vol. XXXIX No. 1.pp. 59-63; Also see this paper published in 'Studies in the Dharma-Śāstra', pp. 41-46.
37. Dr. P.V. Kane's paper on 'Tilaka Mark' in ṚṢi-Kalpanyāsa, p. 289.
38. *Tilakena Vinā vipro puṇyastrī kunkumam vinā dvau, etau garhitau loke daive pitreye ca karmaṇi St.* 192 of the Vyāghra-Smṛti edited by Dr. S.G. Moghe, p. 69.
39. Dr. P.V. Kane, History of Dharma-Śāstra, Vol. V. Part I pp. 1021 for the controversy between Dr. Kane and Prof. V.M. Apte on the point of Vrata.
40. Dr. R.N.Dandekar's paper in 'Professor P.V. Kane—A Tribute' published in MM. Dr. P.V. Kane Commemoration Monograph published by the University of Bombay. Here particuarly p. 11 may be read with advantage for the above remark of the writer of this note.
41. S.G. Moghe, Aparārka as a Mīmāṁsaka, India Antiquary, Third Series, Vol. V. No. 2, April 1971, pp. 27-92. S.G. Mohge, Nyāyas in the Commentary of Aparārka on the Yājñavlakya Smṛti- G.J.K.S.V. Allahabad, Vol. XXVI part-4, 1970- pp. 47-54.
42. S.G. Mohge, Vijñavalkya and Pūrva-Mīmāsā, Vishvesahvarand Indological Journal, Vol. VII. Parts. I-II, 1969, pp. 89-44. Also see Dr. Moghe's paper published as Vijñāeśvara and Nīlkaṇṭha as the Interpreters of the Yājṇavalkya Smṛti, Oriental Journal. Tirupati, Vol. XII, parts 1&2, 1969, pp. 19-29.
43. S.G. Moghe, On Śūlapāṇi- The interpreter of the Yājṇāvalkya-Smṛti, Oriental Journal, Tirpati, Vol. XVII, parts 1 and 2, pp. 113-121.

44. S.G. Mohge 'A few Observations on Mitramiśra'- The Commentator of the Yāj ñavalkya, *Smṛti-Pratibhanam* (Dr. P.K. Narayana Pillai, Felicitation Volume, 1970 issued by Kerala Institute) pp. 45-46.
45. S.G. Moghe, 'The position of Kullūkabhaṭṭa', Bharatiya Vidya, Vol. XXVIII., Nos-1-4, 1968, pp. 94-102, S.G. Moghe - 'Mīmāṁsaka' Passage in the commentary of Kullūka on the Manu-Smṛti - Journal of the Oriental Intitute and Manuscripts Library, Kerala, Vol. XVIII, Nos. 1&3, pp. 139-150.
46. S.G. Moghe. 'Haradatta as a Mīmāṁsaka' Journal of Oriental Intitute, Baroda. Vol. XX., N0. 3. pp. 208-215.
47. S.G. Moghe, 'Haradatta and Maskari as the Interpreters of Gautam-Dhama-Śāstra- G.J.K.S.V. Allahabad, Vol. XXXIII, part-2, pp. 65-84, 1977.
48. S.G. Moghe, 'Nīlkaṇṭha as a Mīmāṁsaka, - *Umesh Mishra Commemoration Volume* by G.J.K.S.V. Vol. XXIV. parti 1-4, 1968, pp. 87-99. Also see Dr. Moghe's paper on 'a new light on Nīlakaṇṭ ha', *Indian Antiquary,* Third Series, vol. No.3, 1071, pp. 144-153.
49. S.G. Moghe, 'Nīlakaṇṭha's Indebetedness to Sāṅkarabhaṭṭa' - *Journal of the University of Bombay,* No. 80-81, /Vol. XLIV-XLV-October 1975-76, pp. 37-47.
50. S.G. Moghe, The use of the Mīmāṁsā mixims in the Smṛticandrikā of Devaṇṇabhaṭṭa'. (2) and (3) The use of Mīmāṁsā and popular maxims in the Smṛticcandrikā of Devaṇṇabhaṭṭa'. All these three are published in the Journal of the Oriental Research Institute and Manuscripts Library, University of Kerala, Vol. XVII, No.4, Vo. XIX, parṭ, and Vol. XV Part-I.
51. S.G. Moghe, Dattaka-Chadrikā, published in Oriental Journal, Tirupati, Vol. XXI-XXII, 1978-79, pp. 6168.
52. S.G. Moghe, Samuccaya-A Neglected Mīmāṁsā term by Vijñāneśvara. A.B.O.R.I. Vol. L. 1, 1970, pp. 83-92.
53. A.R. Joshi, Mīmāṁsā in Medhātithi'- A. Ph. D. thesis guided by Dr. S.G. Moghe, is deposited in the library of the University of Bombay, 1983.
54. S.G. Moghe, Śaṅkarācārya and Pūrva-Mīmāṁsā'- *Mysore Orientalist,* Vol. IV. No. 2, 1971, pp. 79-89. Also see his paper on 'Śaṅkarācar1ya's approach to Arthavāda'- published in *Journal of the Oriental Insititue* Tirupati, Vol. XXVII, parts 1-2, 1984, pp. 43-56.
55. S.G. Moghe, Sāyaṇācārya's Equipment of Pūrva-Mīṁāsrā- *Journal of the Oriental Institute,* Baroda, Vol. 24, Nos. 3&4, 1975, pp. 257-268.

56. S.G. Moghe, Pūrva-Mīmāṁsā and Paurāṇic Interpretation', Purāṇa Journal, Vol. XIX, No. 2, 1977, pp. 283-291.
58. S.G. Moghe, Paribhāṣās of Vyākaraṇa and the Mīmāṁsā Rules of Interpretation-A Comparative Study, published in ' *Ṛṣi-Kalpa-nay1sa - Rajeshvara Shastri Felicitation Volume,* 1970, pp. 90-100.
59. S.G. Moghe, The Comparative Study of the Commentaries Sāravivecinī and Prabhā on the Mīmāṁsā-nyāya-prakāśa' *Bharatiya Vidya.* Vol. XL. Nos. 203, 1980. pp. 95-100.
60. S.G. Moghe, MM, Dr. P.V. Kane's Contribution to the Domain of Pūrva-Mīmāṁsā in MM, *Dr. Kane Commemoration Monograph* (published by the University of Bombay, 1974) pp. 83-99.
61. S.G. Moghe, The Evolution of the Mīmāṁś technical term Atidesa, A.B.O.R.I. (Diamond Jobilee Volume 1977-78.) ..777-784.
62. S.G. Moghe, Motivations of Punarvacanā, *Journal of the Asiatic of Bombay* Vols. 49-50/1974-75, pp. 128-135.
63. S.G. Moghe, Some Evolutionary Aspects of Vākyabheda J.G.J.K.S.V. Vol. 37, Parts 1-4, 1983, (*Prof. Baladeva Upadhyaya Felicitation Volume*), pp. 169-187.
64. S.G. Moghe, 'Mīmaṁsā Principles as envisaged by Śaṅkarārya, in Jayamaṅgala on the Kāmandakīya Dharma-Śāstra. J.G.J.K.S.V. Allahabad Vol. XI, II pp. 2121-130.
65. P.V. Kane, Śaṅkhalikhita Dharma-Śāstra- A.B. O.R.I., Vols. VII and VIII.
66. P.V. Kane—Arthaśāstra Kauṭilya- A.B. O.R.I., Vol Vol.. VII, 1926, pp. 101-128.
67. P.V. Kane Pārijāta and Mandanapārijāta Procedings of the A.J.O.C. XIIO II pp. 267-272, 1943-44.
68. P.V. Kane, Vedic Mantras and legends in the Purāṇas, Raja Commemoration Volume, pp. 5-14, Madras, 1946.
69. P.V. Kane, Naming a child or a person, Indian Historical quarterly, XIV, 1938, pp. 224-244.
70. P.V. Kane, Prodecessors of Vijñāneśvara- JBBRAS (new Series) 1, 1925, pp. 120-124.
71. P.V. Kane, Dvaitanirṇaya- A.B.O.R.I. Vol. III, 1921, pp. 67-72.
72. P.V. Kane, Tantravāritika and the Dharma-Śāstra literature, JBBRAS (new series) I, 1925.
73. P.V. Kane, Asahāya, the commentator of the Gautama Dharma Sūtra and the Dharma-Smṛti, in JBORC VII. 1922, pp. 120-124.

74. P.V. Kane, Kalivarjaya, in JBBRAS (New series), XII, 1936, pp.,1-18.
75. P.V. Kane, 'Meaning of the Ācāryaḥ', A.B.O.R.I., ZZIII, 1942, pp. 206-214.
76. P.V. Kane, 'Passage from the Rājaṁartaṇḍa on Tithis, Vratas and Utsavas,' A.B.O.R.I., XXXVI, 1956, pp. 306-339.
77. P.V. Kane,s 'Purāṇa-Dharma', *Gode Commemoration Volume, 1960, pp. 70-82.*
78. P.V. Kane,s 'King Bhoja and His works on Dharma-Śāstra and Astrology', JOR, XXIII, 1953-54, pp. 94-127.
79. P.V. Kane,s Kauṭīlya and Matsya Purāṇa' *Law Commemoration Volume*, Poona, 1946, pp. 13-15.
80. P.V. Kane—Utpala and the Arthāśatra of Kauṭilya, A.B.O.R.I., XXVIII, 1948, pp. 136-137.
81. P.V. Kane, Mahābhārata Citations in the Śābara-Bhāṣyā, A.B.O.R.I., XXVIII, 1948, pp. 35-136.

X

THE PROGRESS OF THE STUDIES OF DHARMA-ŚĀSTRA*
(IN THE 20TH CENTURY IN INDIA AND ABROAD)

The Study of the Dharma Śāstra includes the study of the sources of the Dharmaśāstra, Smṛtis, Dharma-Sūtras, commentaries on the Smṛtis and the Dharma-Śūtras, digest works, Purāṇas, Śrauta and Gṛhya Sūtras and the commentaries on the same and the papers on the above subject and the independent monographs on the above topics. At the very outset, I must admit my limitations very frankly in presenting the matter before the learned audience.

1. Search for the manuscripts and the utility of the Descriptive catalogues can hardly be denied by any serious reader. It must be noted that Dr. Bhandarkar's attempt for the search of Sanskrit manuscripts, during the years 1882-83, 1883-84, 1884-87 and 1887-91 which are now deposited in the Bhandarkar Oriental Research Institute. Pune and the descriptive catalogues of the sanskrit manuscripts particularly noted by MM. Dr. P.V. Kane in his monumental History of Dharma Śāstra vol. I/II, p. 987-88. Certainly gave inspiration to the noted scholars like Prof. H.D. Velankar, Dr. G.V. Devasthali, Prof. Haradatta Sharma, Dr. Usha Bhise and

others. Prof. Velankar prepared the descriptive catalogue of the sanskrit manuscripts in the Bombay Branch of the (Royal) Asiatic Society of Bombay in four parts, and classified the manuscripts as per the subject and in the second part, gave us the description of the manuscripts on Dharma-Śāstra, Tantra, and Purāṇa in the second volume. Happily this catalogue of four manuscripts is recently reprinted by the authorities of the Asiatic Society of Bombay, in the year 1998, with 18 colour photographs. (2) Prof. Velankar further prepared the descriptive catalogue of the Sanskrit manuscripts in the Iccharam Suryaram Desai Collection and Classified the Dharma Śāstra manuscripts, giving the numbers 167 to 341 (pp. 34 to 68), for the library of the University of Bombay. Dr. Har Datta Sharma prepared the similar catalogue of sanskrit manuscripts on Dharma Śaśtra for the volumes VII/ I, II and III for the Bhandarkar Oriental Research Institute, Pune. It must also be mentioned here that Dr. G.V. Devasthali, the ardent pupil of Prof. Velankar, also prepared a descriptive catalogue of the Sanskrit manuscripts in 'Prof. H.M. Bhadkamkar collection of the sansirit manuscripts' presented by Prof. Velankar in the memory of his teacher Prof. H.M. Bhadkamkar. Here the manuscripts on the Dharma Śāstra are classified from pages 341 to 449 giving the number to the manuscripts from 140 to 1392. Dr. Miss. Usha Bhise also prepared a descriptive catalogue of the sanskrit manuscripts. In the Tanjore Maharaja Serfoji's Sarasvati Mahal Library, Tanjore and Ganganath Jha Research Institute, Allahabad, Adyar Library and Research Centre, Madras and in the several universities in India similar Descriptive Catalogues are available. The treatment given by Prof. Velankar and Dr. Devasthali, for the preparation of the descriptive catalogue is already noted by the writer of this note in the book 'Academic biography of Prof. Velankar

p. 18 to 19. This treatment or methodology is slightly different from the method that is adopted by Dr. Har Datta Sharma and Dr. P.K. Gode for the Bhandarkar Oriental Research Institute. Here one will have to admit that the considerable progress is made for the study of Dharma Śāstra on the basis of the manuscripts noted in the Descriptive catalogues.

2. As regards the independent works on Dharma Śāstra in the 20th century, it must be mentioned that Śankaraśāstrī Marulakar from Poona wrote independent commentaries on the Dattaka-Mīmāṁsā of Nandapaṇḍita and the Dattaka-Candrikā of Raghumaṇi. These two commentaries Mañjarī on the Dattaka-Mīmāṁsā and Dattaka-candrika are published by Ānandāśrama press poona in the year 1954. The commentary on the Dattaka Candrikā known as Śānkarī was published by the same Institute, in the year 1942 and it was found reprinted recently. One more publication deserves notice here. Dr. Braja Kishore Swain wrote a commentary on the Śrāddha Pradīpa of Vipramiśra. This commentary is known as Raśmi and published in the year 1982. This is the contribution from the Orissa. Incidentally, it should be noted that the valuation of the commentary Śāṅkarī on the Dattaka-Candrika and the review on the Śrāddha pradīpa of Vipramiśra are published by Dr. S.G. Moghe in the research journals.

3. As regards the mere printed editions of the works on the Dharma-Śāstra, it must be mentioned here that Dr. Kane has already taken note of the works of 115 authors in the first two volumes of the History of Dharms-Śāstra. Hence, I take this opportunity of avoiding the fault of repetition. After the publication of the first two volumes of the History of Dharma-Śāstra in the last about 30 years, some printed editions of the works have appeared. Here one must note the publication of the Manu-Smṛti with the help of nine commentaries of Medhātithi, Sarvajñanārāyaṇa, Kullūka,

Rāghavānanda, Nandana, Rāmacandra, Maṇirāma, Govindarāja and Bhāruci. This is published by Dr. J.H. Dave, for the Bhāratīya Vidyā Bhavan, Bombay, making the addition of the two commentaries of Maṇirama and Bhāruci, to the already seven commentaries of the Manu-Smṛti, published by Shri. V.N. Mandalika about 85 years ago i.e., 1887. This is indicative of the progress of bringing to light the new unpublished commentaries. For the completion of this project, it took the long duration of 18 years. (2) It must be pointed out that Dr. J.H. Dave also published for the Bhāratīya Vidyā Bhavan, Bombay, the first part of the Vyavahāra Prakāśa of king Pṛthvīcandra in the year 1962. (3) The Sanskrit Academy Osmania University, Hyderabad also published in three parts the Dāna-Vivekoddyota in the years 1964, 1966 and 1967. These were prepared by Dr. Aryendra Sharma, Shrikhanderao Deshpande and D.G. Padhye, giving the appendix of the works and authors quoted by Madanaratnapradīpa. (4) MM. Kamalakrishna Smṛti Tīrtha published the works of Caṇḍeśvara Ṭhakkura, particularly known as Vivāda-Ratṅakara, Gṛhastharatnākara and other works in the Bibliotheca Indica Series, Calcutta in the years 1926, 1928 and Kṛtya Ratnākara in the year 1925. (5) J.R. Gharpure also published the Mitākṣarā on the Yājñavalkya-Smṛti and the Smṛticandrika of Devaṇṇabhaṭṭa in three parts (containing Ācāra, Vyavahāra and Śrāddha Kāṇḍas). But the Mysore University published the Smṛticandrikā of Devaṇṇabhaṭṭa in six parts (giving us the Āhnika Kāṇḍa, Vyavahāra Kaṇḍa in two parts, Saṁskāra Kāṇḍa, Śrāddha Kāṇḍa and Āśauca Kāṇḍa) during the years 1914 to 1921 6) J.R. Gharpure also published the commentary of Medhātithi on the Manusmṛti in the year 1920. The similar work of this type is also done by MM. Dr. Ganganatha Jha. (7) Gharpure also published in six parts of the Smṛtimuktāphalam of Vaidyanātha Dīkṣita during the years 1937 to 1940 giving at the end the index of the citations in this work. (8) Gharpure also published the twelve parts of the Mayūkhas of Nīlakaṇṭha in the Hindu law Text Series. (9) Gharpure also published in three parts the commentary Bālaṁbhaṭṭī of Bālambhaṭṭa Pāyaguṇḍe on the Mītakṣarā of Vijñāneśvara on the Yājñavalkya Smṛti. This is in three parts and published in the years 1914 and 1924 giving at the end of each volume the index of the works quoted in this work. (10) Gharpure also took pleasure in publishing the commentary of śūlapāṇi on the Yājñavalkya Smṛti in the year 1939. This commentary is known as Dīpakalikā. (11) He also published the Dharma-Dvaita Nirṇaya of Śaṅkarabhaṭṭa, the father of Nīlakaṇṭhabhaṭṭa, the author of twelve Mayūkhras, in the year 1943. (12) one must note here the collection of the sṃrits in two parts by Jīvananda Vidyāsāgara from calcutta, by the Ānandāśram Sanskrit series, and the smṛti Sandarbha in six volumes published by Mansukhalal Mor from Calcutta. The last one is a work containing the text of the Smṛtis published so far. (13) The text of the Parāśara Smṛti with the commentary of Mādhavācārya, first published in the Bombay Sanskrit and Prākṛt series, Pune, went out of print. This was again published in three volumes by the Asiatic Society, Calcutta in the years 1973 and 1974. (14) Besides, the text of the Viṣṇu smṛti with the gloss of Nandapaṇḍita, orginally used by J.Jolly, with some brief extracts, for the Bibliotheca Indica Series No. 91, 1881, was published with the full commentary of Nandapaṇḍita by the Adyar Library and Research Centre, Madras, in the years 1963 and 1964. (15) The text of the Gautama Dharma Sūtra with the commentary of Haradatta and Hindi Translation, was published in the Kashi Sanskrit Series, in the year 1969. (16) One may also add that the text of the Gautama Dharma Sūtra with the commentary of

Maskari, was published by the University of Mysore in the year 1917. The same text with the commentary of Haradatta and Hindi Translation, appeared in the Kashi Sanskrit Series, in the year 1966. (17) In addition to this, the text of the Baudhāyana Dharma Sūtra with the commentary of Govindaswāmī and Hindi Translation was published in the Kashi Sanskrit Series, in the year 1972. (18) The Yājñavalkya Smṛti with the commentaries of Vijñāneśvara and Mitramiśra was published in the Chowkhamba Sanskrit series in the year 1930. The same text is also again reprinted. (19) The text of te Vivāda-Cintāmaṇi of Vācaspatimiśra was published in the last century by Venkatesvara Press, Bombay. In this way, some more works may be added.

4. As regards the critical editions of the smṛtis and digest works, a few works deserve to be mentioned. The text of the Āpastaṁba Dharma Sūtra with the extracts from the commentary Ujjvalā by Haradatta, was published by Bühler in the Bombay Sanskrit and Prākṛt series, Pune, in the year 1932 as the third impression. (2) The text of the Vasiṣṭha Dharma sūtra was edited by Dr. A.A. Fuhrer, as the third impression, in the Bombay Sanskrit and Prākṛt series, Pune, in the year 1830, with the help of five manuscripts. (3) The text of the Vyavahāra Mayūkha of Nīlakaṇṭha with notes was published in the year 1926, by Dr. P.V. Kane, in the Bombay Sanskrit and prākṛt series, with the help of eleven manuscripts. At the end of this work, Dr. Kane has also published the manuscript of the Vyavahāra-Tattva by Nīlakaṇṭha, with the help of two manuscripts, covering the pages from 441 to 473. (4) Kane also published the Madana Ratna Pradīpa (Vyavahāra Portion), for the Anup Sanskrit Library, Bikaner, in the year 1948). The Buddha Smṛti alias Budha Dharma Sūtra was published by Dr. S.G. Moghe, for the Annals of the Bhandarkar Oriental Research Institute, LXIV for 1983,

p. 259-268, with the help of six manuscripts. (6) Moghe also published the manuscript of the Vyāghra Smṛti with the help of two manuscripts, and good introduction and restoration of the other passages of the Vyāghra Smṛti, in the Bhandarkar Oriental Series, in the year 1985. (7) Moghe also concentrated his mind and published the Critical edition of the Śrāddha Sāgara of Kūllūkabhaṭṭa, with the help of a solitary manuscript from the Sanskrit College, Calcutta, in the year 1994. This contains a good introduction covering printed 60 pages and several appendices. Generally for editing the text, the original manuscripts with the commentaries are utilised. But Dr. Moghe has shown that even the secondary source is also useful for this purpose. He showed this aspect for the critical edition of the text of the Vasiṣṭha Dharma Sūtra by contributing a paper on 'Quotations from the Vasiṣṭha Dharma Sūtra' in the commentaries of Haradatta and Maskari on the Gautama Dharma Sūtra for the A.B.O.R.T. Volume LV for 1974, pp. 232-238.

5. As regards the translations of the Dharma Śāstra texts with notes, one may note here the translation[4] of the Manu-Smṛti, by Dr. George Buhler, first published in the year 1886, was published several times, by the Motilal Benarasidas, Delhi. (2) The translations of the Āpastamba Dharma Sūtra, Gautama Dharma Sūtra, by Dr. George Buhler, first published in the year 1882 were reprinted in the years 1965 and 1969 by the Motilal Banarasidas, Delhi. The same is the case with the Baudhāyana Dharma Sūtra and the Vasiṣṭha Dharma Sūtra. (3) The text of the Vyavahāra mayūkha was translated in English, with copious case law and notes by P.V. Kane and S.G. Patwardhan in 1933. (4) The text of the Yājñavalkya Smṛti with the commentary of Mitākṣarā and Vīramitrodaya (Mitramiśra) was translated by J.R. Gharpure in the collection of the Hindu Law texts. These translations were published in the years 1937 to 1940.

6. As regards the restoration of the texts that are now lost to us but their quotations are available in the vast Dharma Śāstra literature, it must be noted that Dr. Kane restored the text of the Kātyāyana Smṛti with English Translation, appendices, in the year 1933. He also restored the text of the Śaṅkha-Likhita Dharma Sūtra for the Annals of the Bhandarkar Oriental Research Institute, Volumes VII. p. 101-128 and Volume VIII, p. 93 to 132 for 1927. This is again published in Prof. Kane's contribution to Dharma Śāstra Literature p. 19 to 89 giving us the total number of 463 prose and verse portions. This is prefaced by a good introduction. (3) The Text of the Ṛṣyaśṛṅga Smṛti is restored by S.G. Moghe, for the Mysore Orientalist Volume XIV, p. 64-77 and this was reprinted in the Studies in the Dharma Śāstra by S.G. Moghe, p. 65-80, in the year 1991. (4) The text of the Vyāghra Smṛti was also restored by S.G. Moghe as the third part of the Vyāghra Smṛti edited by him. This covers pages 108 to 126 giving us the total number of 142 verses not found in the critical edition of the Vyāghra Smṛti which contains only 381 stanzas. This critical edition contains a good introduction of 38 pages discussing several problems connected with the text of the Vyāghra Smṛti. (5) Recently the text of the Devala Smṛti was restored by Dr. M.L. Wadekar, for his Ph.D. thesis. This work is published in the years 1996 and 1997. This contains the collection of about 25,00 passages of Devala in prose and verse and a good introduction and the second part of it is reserved for the critical discussion on the Devala Smṛti. (6) The reconstructed text of the Bṛhaspati Smṛti by Prof. Rangaswami Aiyangar is published in Gaikawad's Oriental Series as No. 85. (7) The text of the Pulastya Smṛti is recently published by Prof. Lalanji Gopal and Krishnakanti Gopal. It must be mentioned here

that Dr. Wadekar also published a paper[5] in the journal of the Oriental Institute, making the addition of the stanzas to the already collected stanzas by Prof. Lalanji Gopal. He has thus filled up the gap in the work of that scholar. (8) The other small collections of Devala Smṛti by S.C. Bannerjee and Pandit Udayavir Shasti are just mentioned here.

7. As regards the chronology of the authors of the Dharma Śāstra, it must be admitted that Dr. Kane has already done this work in the first two volumes of the History of Dharma Śāstra. But some further progress is made by other scholars. (1) Dr. P.K. Gode has fixed the date of the Prāyaścitta[6]-Candrikā of Vishvanātha Bhaṭṭa, the son of Narasīmha Dīxit as before 1543 A.D. It should be noted here that Dr. Kane has not devoted any space for this work in the History of Dharma-Śāstra. (2) Dr. Gode has further fixed the date[7] of Vaidyanātha Dīxit, the author of the Smṛtimuktāphalam, as after 1686 A.D., on which Dr. Kane has made no discussion in the History of Dharma-Śāstra. (3) The Date of Govindaswāmi[8], the commentator of the Baudhāyana DharmaSūtra was doubtful. Kane treated Govindaswāmī as a very later writer and Dr. Burnell treated him to be a modern writer. Dr. Moghe has discussed this problem and showed that Govindaswāmī is to be placed between 1650 A.D., and 1690 A.D. (4) Gode further discussed the date of the Vyavāhara[9] Nirṇaya of Varadarāja as falling between 1100 A.D. and 1450 A.D. Without referring to Gode's article on this point, Dr. Kane places Varadarāja between 1450 and 1495 A.D. He further remarks that Varadarāja must be later than 1300 A.D. (5) Moghe has fixed[10] Kullūkabhaṭṭa between 1520 and 1620 A.D.

8. As regards the interpretations of a line or the significance of some words or some concepts, Dr. Moghe has discussed the line Nakṣatraiḥ yaśca jīvati of the Manu-

Smṛti III. 162 and showed[11] that this line does not refer to a full-fledged astrologer as held by the commentators of the Manu-Smṛti and followed by Kane but it refers to the sham Astrologer who without proper knowledge of Astrology, goes on guiding or misguiding the people. (2) For the significance[12] of the expression 'Ananyapūrvikā' in the Yājñvalkya-Smṛti. Dr. Moghe has shown that the expression becomes significant against the background of the Mahābhārata in respect of Śiśupāla and Aṁbā as narrated in the Ādi parvan and the Udyoga-Parvana of the Mahābhārata. (3) The concept[13] of Nyāsa in the Dharma Śāstra and the classical sanskrit literature is discussed by Moghe to show how the evolution has taken place in the society. (4) The concept[14] of withness in the Mahābhārata and the Dharma Śāstra is also discussed by Moghe to throw further light on this point of witness.

9. As regards the authorship of the works of the Dharma Śāstra works, Dr. Kane has discussed the problem throughout his first two volumes of the History of Dharma-Śāstra. He has also solved the problem of the identity of the authors. P.K. Gode has discussed the authorship[15] of the Sarasvatī-Vilāsa. He ascribed this authorship to Lolla Lakṣmīdhara. Kane disagreed with Gode on this point and clarified his position in the History of Dharma-Śāstra Vol. I/II, p. 875-76 and 878.

10. As regards the interpretation of the Dharma-Śāstra lines by the non Dharma-Śāstra authors, the proper attention, it seems, is not paid by the modern scholars. Here it may be pointed out that Moghe has thrown light on the interpretation of the Manu-Smṛti V.83 by Mallinātha and shown[16] that this interpretation agrees with the view taken by Mādhavācārya on the Parāśara-Smṛti-Ācāra Kāṇḍa p. 577. (2) Abhinava-gupta's novel interpretation[17] of the Gautama Dharma-Sūtra

IX.35, against the interpretation of the commentators Maskari and Haradatta, is further high-lighted by Moghe. This aspect of the studies of the Dharma-Śāstra is open to other texts also, in the opinion of the writer of this paper.

11. Here a reference should also be made to the theories advanced by the foreign scholars in respect of the Dharma-Śāstra works. Here a reference deserves to be made to some such theories which stand rejected at the hands of Kane. (1) Winternitz held the view that the niyoga system is introduced due to the poverty and paucity of women. (2) Max Müller held the view that writing was unknown to India (3) Weber held the view that there is the christian influence on the festival of kṛṣṇāṣṭamī or jayantī and particularly on the life of Kṛṣṇa. (4) Max-Müller followed by Buhler maintains that Mānava Dharma Sūtra existed previously. Kane remarks that the labours of the western scholars are praiseworthy but their conclusions based on slender similarities of facts are not acceptable. Further, they look upon Indian culture as inferior and have no willingness to admit the greatness of Indian Culture. They further take pleasure in showing that the idea of borrowing is from the western culture by the eastern culture.

12. As regards the independent monographs or the collections of the articles of one author or by the several authors, it must be stated that Kane's History of Dharma-Śāstra running into 8 volumes is a 'Gigantic Encyclopaedia' in the words of Jan Gonda. Dr. Kane placed the matter in the historical perspective and consulted all the possible sources of history, epigraphy, grammatical, literary, numismatic, manuscripts and presented the History of Dharma-Śāstra, for which there is no parallel. (2) Dr. Kane's important nineteen papers on Dharma-Śāstra are brought together by Moghe with good introduction and review of the work of

Kane in the book 'Professor Kane's contribution to the Dharma-Śāstra literature' in the year 1997. (3) Moghe has brought out a collection of his 35 papers (26 on Dharma-Śāstra and 9 on the Kauṭilīya Arthaśāstra) in the book 'Studies in the Dharma-Śāstra' in the year 1991 (4) One may also note the work' Studies in the Nibandhas in two volumes) brought out by Bhabatosh Bhattacharya on behalf of Indian Studies – past and present. (5) One may also refer to the Studies in Indian Cultural History Vols. I, II and III published in the years 1961, 1960 and 1969 by P.K. Gode, particularly after his sad demise (6) Some aspects of the Hindu Saṁskāras are brought out by Dr. Heramba Chatterji Shastri of Calcutta, in the light of the Saṁskāra Tattva of Raghunandana in the year 1967. (7) Dr. J.D.M. Derret published the following three books. (1) Introduction to Modern Hindu law. (2) A critique of Modern Hindu law and (3) Essays in Classical and modern Hindu law. (8) Dr. S.C. Banerjee brought out Dharma-Śāstra – A study in their original and development in the year 1962. He also published the 'Smṛti material in the Mahābhārata as the volume I and Indian Society in the Mahābhārata 'as the Volume II'. (9) Dr. Ram Gopal published a book 'India of the Vedic Kalpasūtras in the year 1959 as his Ph.D. thesis. On which Kane has made some important observations in the History of Dharma-Śāstra Vol. I/I. p. (10) Prof. Richard W. Lariviere has edited the work entitled 'Studies in Dharma-Śāstra' containing the learned papers of D.C. Sircar, Ludo Rocher, Richard W. Lariviere, Patrick Olivelle, Richard Saloman and J. Duncan M. Derrett. Dr. Derrett's article on 'what the Dharma-Śāstra has to say about Dowry and Richard Salomon's article on 'Legal and symbolic significance of the 'Menstrual pollution of Rivers' are very interesting. This work is published in Calcutta in the year 1984. (11) One will be pleased to note the other works of

Dr. Derrett such as 'Juridical Studies in Ancient Indian Law, published in 1965 and published by Motilal Banarasidas, Delhi. (2) Religion, Law and the State in India published in London in 1968. (3) Sociology and family law in India and Main Current in Indian Sociology II, Family and social change in modern India, published in 1976, (12) The Several volumes of Dharma-Kośa published at Wai, can be treated as the significant studies of the Dharma-Śāstra for its proper progress.

13. As regards the different approaches to Dharma-Śāstra, Dr. Derrett found fault with Kane's treatment for neglecting the study of anthropology. Recently a Ph.D. thesis is written by Miss. Shrīmathī Madiman on the topic 'Anthropological Approach to the Saṁskārās.' This thesis is accepted for Ph.D. degree by the University of Bombay and it awaits publication. Secondly, the aspect of Dāna or gift is separately dealt with by Kalā Acharya in her Ph.D. thesis on 'Idea of gift in the Purāṇas. Thirdly, there is another Ph.D. thesis in Marāṭhī on the topic' Dharma-Śāstra thoughts in the classical sanskrit literature from Bhāsa to Śrī Harṣa, the author of naiṣadhīyacaritam by A.N. Deo. This is a Ph.D. thesis deposited in the Marathwada University, Aurangabad and published recently in one March 2000. Fourthly, there is also a tendency in the students to edit some rare manuscripts. Miss. Parvàti S. Moholkar edited the manuscript. 'The Vivāda-Candra of Misaru Miśra' for her Ph.D. thesis and one of the two manuscripts was borrowed from the Bhandarkar Oriental Research Institute, Pune and the other one was from Darbhanga.

14. The topics of interdisciplinary subjects have also attracted the mind of the scholars. Moghe has dealt with Dharma-Śāstra[18] and Gṛhya Sūtras, Dharma-Śāstra and Lexicons, Dharma-Śāstra[19] and Āyurveda, Dharma-Śāstra[20]

and Kāmaśāstra. There are many other topics which further deserve consideration such as Śrauta Sūtras, history, numismatic, epigraphy, Vedānta and Tantra-Śāstra and some other topics also deserve further serious study.

15. It would be of interest to mention some important papers on the Dharma-Śāstra that have appeared in the course of some years. Ludwik Sternbach has published some papers. (1) 'Juridical aspects of the Gāndharva form of Marriage' Proceedings of the A.I.O.C. vol. X, Nos. 3-4, p. 69-78, (2) 'Different types of Deposits' in A.B.O.R.I. vol. XXVI, parts 3-4, p. 263-283. (3) 'Law of Deposits' in Bharativiya Vidya vol. VII, Nos. 3-4, p. 1-22, (4) Suretyship–supplement to Bhāratiya Vidyā vol. II, Nos. 3-4, p. 23-50. (5) Legal position of physicians in Ancient India. A.B.O.R.I. Vol. parts 1-4, p. 21-42, (6) Forms of Marriage in Ancient India and their development–Bharatiya Vidya vol. XII, p. 62-138. (7) Mānava Dharma-Śāstra VII.99 and the yājñavalkya Smṛti I.31-317. In Dr. S.K. De felicitation volume p. 82-89. (8) A sociological study of the forms of marriages in Ancient India–A.B.O.R.I. vol. XXII, p. 202-219. I may mention here that I have not mentioned all the papers of that great scholar. I may also refer to the paper of J.D.M. Derrett on 'An aspect of the arranged Marriage in Dharma-Śāstra in the Diamond Jubilee volume of the A.B.O.R.I., p. 107-120. Another important paper is written by V.B. Mishra in the same volume on 'The practice of Niyoga in Ancient literature of India–A Sociological Study p. 773-776.

Another significant paper is written by H.S. Singh on 'Institutions of money lending' in the same volume p. 109-124. In Pandit Baladeva Upadhyaya felicitation Volume, G.C. Tripathi published a paper.' A unique Sale-deed of the 13th Century on copper-plate, p. 263-286. The State of criminal law in the ManuSmṛti is found discussed in the same volume by R.S. Betai p. 279-300. In the volume 'Homage to Dr. Mainkar', Mrs. Vijayalaxmi Deore has written a paper on 'The Socio-legal position of Women in the Smṛtis of Manu and yājñavalkya, p. 1-17 and S.G. Moghe has written a paper on' Significance of the Vyāghra Smṛti in the Dharma-Śāstra, p. 33-40. It may be specifically mentioned here the articles of Ludo Rocher published in the Journal of the Oriental Institute, Baroda. (1) Caṇḍeśvara's Vyavahāra-Ratnākara Vol. 5, p. 249. (2) The Daṇḍaviveka of Vardhamāna Upādhyāya – Notes on textual criticism – Vol. II, p. 71 and 139. He has also published 'Halāyudha Nibandha – A Collection of fragments on the Vivāda padās, volume 3, p. 328 and Volume IV, p. 13. He has also published an article on Halāyudha Nibandha on legal procedure in the volume V, p. 325 and the quotations in Jīmutavāhana's Vyavahāra-Mātṛka vol. III, p. 314. Besides, S.C. Banerji also published an article on 'Flora and Fauna of Dharma-Śāstra, in Volume No. V, page 274, 345, Volume 21, p. 32 and the Reconstruction of some Dharma-Śāstra in other volumes. Another paper on 'Candeśvara and Rājanīti-Ratnākara was published by Upendra Thakur in Vishveshvarananda Indological Journal, Hoshiarpur, vol. VII, pages 56-68.

16. As regards the works on the Gṛhyasūtras, it would be very important to draw the atteniton of the serious readers to the books and papers published during the period of the last 20 years and more and particularly recorded in the Vedic Bibliography Vols. IV and V by Dr. R.N. Dandekar Here a reference could be made to the two papers of Dr. C.G. Kashikar on Trikāṇḍamaṇḍana and the Bhāradvāja School, CASS Study 2, 1974, p. 13-21 and on the Bhāradvāja Gṛhyasūtra and its commentary published in B.D.C.R.I., Volume 35 (1-2), p. 65-75. Besides, H.J.W. Salomons edited

the Bhāradvāja Gṛhya Sūtra and this is published by Mererchand Lacchamandas, Delhi, 1981, pages 25-129. It may be added here that Maya Malaviya edited the Pāraskara Gṛhya Sūtra with the commentaries of Bhāskara and Gaṅgādhara, on behalf of the Ganganatha Jha Kendriya Sanskrit Vidyapitha, Allahabad. The Pāraskara Gṛhya Sūtra is already published with the five commentaries of Karka, Jayarāma, Harihara, Gadādhara and Visvanatha. Hence Maya Malaviya has made improvement on the previously published Pāraskara Gṛhya Sūtra. The Āśvalāyana Gṛhyasūtra is also published with the commentary of Nārāyaṇa. But the Adyar Library and Research Centre, Madras published the Āśvalāyana Gṛhya Sūtra with the commentary of Devasvāmin as edited by Pandit K.P. Aithal with the good introduction of 39 pages. This is reviewed by Frederick M. Smith in Journal of the American Oriental Society, vol. 104. p. 785 and H. Falk in WZKSA volume 30, pages 197-199. Further the Śānkhyāyana Gṛhyasūtra is edited by Sehgal S.R. for the India Books Centre, Delhi, 1987 and it contains pages XVIII+56+203+VIII+XV. This is found reviewed by K.K. Raja in A.LB. volume 53, page 223. Besides, the translations of the Gṛhya Sūtras by Oldenberg H. and Max Muller F. have been reprinted by the Motilal Banarasidas, in the sacred Books of East Vols. XXX and XXXI in the year 1973. Further, the Gṛhyasūtra samgraha is published by Sriram Sharma. It contains the Gṛhya Sūtras of Āśvalāyana, Śānkhyāyaṇa, Gobhila and Pāraskara etc. This is published in the year 1972. Rama Gopal has published a paper on The role of the Gṛhyasūtras in Vedic interpretation. Summary of Paper, Winter Institute, CASS, 1980, pages—4.5. Miss. Jaya Chemburkar has dealt with 'Vāstuparīkṣā, Vāstuśānti and Gṛhapraveśa according to the Āśvalāyana Gṛhya Sūtra in the journal of the Asiatic Society of Bombay, vol. 72 for 1997

p. 42-51. Dr. V.M. Apte has dealt with the social life in the Gṛhyasūtras and the Vedic Mantras in the Gṛhya Sutra setting. These two monographs are very important for the study of the Gṛhyasūtra. In addition to this, Dr. Kane has already explored the source of the Gṛhya Sūtras for his monumental History of Dharma-Śāstra. Moghe has dealt with the relation of the Gṛhyasūtras to the Dharma-Śāstra.

17. Now coming to the works on the Śrauta-Sūtras, it must be mentioned here that Dr. C.G. Kashikar has prepared the first two volumes of the text of the Śrautạ Koṣa and these two volumes are translated by the eminent Vedic scholar R.N. Dandekar. So far the translation volumes of the Śrauta Koṣa as published by the Vedic Samshodhana Mandala, Pune, are vol. I/I, I/II, II/I, II/II, and III (in 1995). The last volume is reviewed by T.N. Dharmādhikārī for the A.B.O.R.I., vol. LXXVIII, 1997, pages 357-350. It should be pointed out that C.G. Kashikar has taken a very comprehensive survey of the entire Śrauta Sūtra literature in the journal of the University of Bombay vol. XXXV (New series), Part 2, Arts Number, September 1966. In his three lectures, Kashikar has given the Genesis of the Śrauta sūtras, in the second lecture, he has given the brief sketches of the Śrauta and other Sūtras and in the third lecture, he has given the glimpses of the Śrāuta-Sūtras, showing the influence of one Śrauta Sūtra over the other, dates of the Śrauta-Sūtras, commentaries on the same and the translations of the same. He has also given us the cultural data in the Śrauta Sūtras from pages 165-173. He has also published in Marathi the book 'Śrauta-Dharmācī Svarūpa-cikitsā'. This last one is reviewed by S.A. Dange in the Journal of the University of Bombay. The survey of the Śrauta Sūtra literature is reviewed by S.A. Dange, for the Vishveshvarananda Indological Journal, Hoshiarpur, Punjab, vol. VII parts 1-2, p. 175-178. If one just consults

the Bibliography of the Books and select articles of Prof. C.G. Kashikar, mentioned in his felicitation volume. One gets the impression that he has persued this topic life long and has done a lot of work, on the Sūtras of Bhāradvāja, hautrika, Vārāha Śrauta Sūtra, Baudhāyana Śrauta Sūtra II—A fresh study, a rare manuscript of the Vārāha School, Baudhāyana Śyenaciti, Agnicayana, yajñapārśve—an unpublished Pariśiṣṭa of the Śukla Yajurveda School. A structural analysis of the Agniṣṭoma sacrifice in India-concept and evolution etc. In fact, he seems to have devoted more than 50 years of his life for the close study of the Śrauta Sūtra literature. It would not be out of place to casually mention here that in his monumental History of Dharma-Śāstra vol. II/II, Kane has devoted about 400 pages for the description of the Śrauta sacrifices. One may also note here the book 'Some women's Rites and Rights in the Vedas by Hanns Peter Schmidt, published in the year, 1987, as P.D. Gune Memorial Lecture, p. VI+134. Besides, the Drāhyāyaṇa Śrauta Sūtra with the commentary of Dhanvin is published by Prof. B.R. Sharma, with the help of 12 manuscripts in the year 1983. This is certainly an improvement upon the matter that is given by C.G. Kashikar, on page 131 of the survey of the Śrauta Sūtra literature. Again, the Baudhāyana Śrauta Sūtra with the Bhāṣya of Sāyaṇa is edited by R.N. Pandya, in the year 1982. This contains pages 345. C.G. Kashikar has recently published a monograph on the Yajñapārśva—important Parisiṣṭas ascribed to Kātyāyana and belonging to the White Yajurveda. This contains the good introduction of pp. XVIII and additional 80 pages. This is reviewed by T.N. Dharmadhikari for the A.B.O.R.I. vol. LXXIX for 1998, pages 288-289. Besides, the Āpastaṁba Śrauta Sūtra with the commentary of Dhūrta-swāmī is edited by Chinnāswāmī and Paṭṭābhirāmaśāstā, in the Gaikawad

Oriental Series, Baroda. This contains two volumes. Further, the Āśvalāyana Sūtra Prayoga dīpikā of Bhattamañjarī is published in the Chowkhamba Sanskrit series. Besides, the Jaiminiya Śrauta Sūtra with the commentary of Bhavatrāta is published by Parpola Asko in the year 1981. The Śānkhyayaṇa Śrauta Sūtra originally published by Caland, has again appeared in the year 1980. The Kauśika Sūtra with the Dārila Bhāṣya is edited by H.R. Diwekar and others. Besides, some important papers on the study of the Śrauta Sūtras are also published by H.G. Ranade.

To conclude, one will have to appreciate the lot of work done by the scholars in the 20th century. For the preparation of the survey of this type, actually, it is necessary to consult the Bibliograies of the learned[21] scholars independently published or published in the felicitation and commemoration volumes of the scholars. The value of the Vedic Bibliography in five volumes prepared by R.N. Dandekar, can hardly be denied. In addition to this, one should also consult the volumes of the Prācī-Jyoti giving us the gist of the papers published in the particular year all over the world. The part played by the reviews of the scholars is also necessary in appreciating the works.

As regards the desideratum, it must be said that there are some smṛtis which are to be restored by the scholars. This becomes evident from Kane's treatment in the first volume of the History of Dharma-Śāstra. The critical editions of most of the Dharma-Śāstra digests and the smṛtis and the commentaries also should be undertaken by the band of scholars. The study of some unpublished works which are only in the manuscript form, but which are deposited in some institutes as mentioned in the Descriptive Catalogues of the manuscripts deserve further study. In addition to this, the importance of the list of works and authors on the

Dharma-Śāstra as given by Kane in the History of Dharma-Śāstra Vol. I/II, p. 989-1242 should be appreciated by undertaking some new works which have escaped the notices of the scholars. Some Purāṇas are there mentioned in the Descriptive catalogues of the Sanskrit manuscripts which should be studied properly for the further progess of the studies.

Lastly the importance of the some institutions like the Kashiraj Trust, Benares, B.O.R.I., Adyar etc. specially devoted to the study of the Purāṇas, deserves approbation at the hands of the scholars. The devoted scholars like P.V. Kane, P.K. Gode, J.R. Gharpure, should be emulated by the young generation. The part played by the universities, Research institutes and private publishers in propagating the studies of the Dharma-Śāstra also should be whole-heartedly appreciated by the scholars who have the desire to make further progress in the subject.

FOOT NOTES

* This paper is presented in 20th Century Sanskrit Seminar, in the year 1999.

1. The commentary Śāṅkarī on the Dattaka-Candrikā-Mysore Orientalist vol. XIII, p. 32-39.
2. Vipramiśra—Śrāddha-Pradīpa is reviewed by S.G. Moghe in A.B.O.R.I., vol. LXIX for 1988, p. 298-301.
3. The manuscript 'Śvaśrū-Snuṣā-Dhana-Saṁvada was edited by Dr. Derrett and translated for Umesh Mishra Commemoration Volume, Allahabad, 1970, p. 26-278 and the manuscript entitled' Dāyabhāga Vyavasthā-Samkṣepa has been edited by Ludo Rocher for R.N. Dandekar felicitation volume 1984, p. 351, 358 and The Divyatattva of Raghunandana was edited by Richard W. Lariviere and this was reviewed by G.V. Devasthali, for A.B.O.R.I., LXIV-1983, p. 272-274.
4. The translation of the Manu-Smṛti with the Bhāṣya of Medhātithi by Ganganatha Jha is again reprinted by the Motilal Banarasidas, in ten volumes, 1999.

5. Addition to the stanzas of Pulastya smṛti by M.L. Wadekar in Journal of Oriental Institute, Baroda, vol. 43, Nos. 3-4, March-June, 1994, p. 195-202.
6. Date of Prāyascitta Candrika by P.K. Gode, in Oriental Research Madras, vol. XVI, I, for 1945, p. 34-36.
7. Date of Vaidyanātha Dīxit is by P.K. Gode, in Mimamsa Prakasa vol. III, p. 39-42.
8. Date of Govindaswāmī is fixed by S.G. Moghe, in the book 'Studies in the Dharma Śāstra,' p. 114-116.
9. Date of Vyavahāra Nirṇaya is fixed by P.K. Gode for Mīmāṁsā Prakāśa vol. III, p. 15-18.
10. For the date of Kullūkabhaṭṭa, See S.G. Moghe's critical edition of the Śrāddha Sāgara of Kullūkabhaṭṭa, p. 39-50, 1994.
11. Bhāratīya Vidyā vol. XXXIX, No. 1, 1979, p. 59-63.
12. 'Significance of Ananyapūrvikā,' See S.G. Moghe's Studies in the Dharma Śāstra, 1991, p. 159-164.
13. For concept of Nyāsa, see Śrī Venkateśvhara University Oriental Journal, Tirupati, Vols. 30-31, 1987-88, p. 87-94.
14. For concept of Witness, Vide, SVUOJ, Tirupati, vols. 32-34, 1989-91, p. 135-140.
15. Authorship of Sarasvatī-Vilāsa by P.K. Gode, Calcutta Oriental Journal Vol. II, p. 233-234.
16. For Mallinātha's interpretation of the Manu Smṛti V.83, Vide Journal of Oriental Institute, Tirupati, vol. XXV, p. 13-16.
17. For Abhinavagupta's novel interpretation of the Gautama Dharma Sūtra IX.35, Vide Journal of the Ganganatha Jha Kendriya Sanskrit Vidyapitha, Allahabad, vol. XLVI, 1990 p. 13-18.
18. Relation of the Gṛhya Sūtras to the Dharma Śāstra, Tattvaloka, vol. V/I, p. 15-28.
19. Relation of Dharma-Śāstra to Indian Medical Science, Journal of the Bharati-Śodha-Sāra Samgraha—Jaipur, vol. III.1-2, p. 51-57.
20. Relation of the Kāmaśāstra to the Dharama Śāstra,' Bharatiya Vidya, vols. XLV, XLVI, XLVII for 1985-1987, p. 126-136.
21. For the Bibliography of the writings of Ludwik Sternbach Consult Journal of the Ganganatha Jha Kendriya Sanskrit Vidyapitha, Allahabad, vol. XXXIII, April-June, Part-2, 1977, p. 1-51, Bibliography of Published writings of Dr. P.K. Gode, Covering, p. 1-28, and C.G. Kashikar's Bibliography Published in his felicitation volume, p. 18-23.

Post Script : MM. Dr. P.V. Kane's 'History of Dharma-Śāstra—In Essence by Dr. Moghe is out in January, 2000.

XI

MM. DR. KANE AND RESTORATION

MM. Dr. P.V. Kane has utilised the technique of restoration in the course of his research activities. The importance and the principles of this technique are brought to the notices of the learned scholars by this paper. It is with this intention in my mind that I am going to make the following discussion.

The importance of this technique of restoration lies in pointing out the views of those authors whose works are not now available to us; but these works were available to our predecessors in the subject, since they have made the best use of such works in the course of their writings. In this respect, a reference could be made to the Śaṅkha-likhita-Dharma-Sūtra restored by MM. Dr. P.V. Kane for the Annals of the Bhandarkar Oriental Research Institute, Poona, Vols. VII (p. 101-128), 1926 and vol. VIII (p. 93-132, 1927). Here in this paper, Dr. Kane has collected together the fragments of the quotations of the Śaṅkha-likhita Dharma-Sūtra becoming avilable in the vast range of Dharma-Śāstra literature. This becomes a case of the restoration of the lost text.

This technique of Restoration is also utilised by MM. Dr. P.V. Kane to present only the views of the commentators of the Manu-Smṛti or the Nārada-Smṛti, whose commentaries are not now available to us but such commentaries were properly utilised by the other commentors and digest authors. Here a reference could be made to the paper of Dr. Kane, entitled 'The Predecessors of Vijñāneśvara' already published in the JBBRAS (New series) I (p. 193-224) 1925.

Dr. Kane has also utilised this technique in respect of restoring the text of the Kātyāyana-Smṛti which is entitled as Kātyāyana-Smṛti-Sāroddhāra, published by him in the year 1933. This restoration is, indeed, an important improvement upon the similar restoration of the Kātyāyana Smṛti by Narayan Chandra Bandopadhyaya from Calcutta. This work contains only 800 verses ascribed to Kātyāyana, without adding any English Translation. Besides, the quotations are collected by him only from five works. Dr. Kane collected from a vast Dharma-Śāstra literature the verses amounting to 973, by adding English Translation, Notes, Introduction and three Appendixes. From this, it is avident that this restoration is really an improvement upon the previous work of the scholar.

Incidentally, a reference can also be made to his magnum Opus 'History of Dharma-Śāstra Vol. I, Parts–I and II in which he has fruitfully employed the technique of restoration to present the views of the authors of Dharma-Śāstra whose works are not now extant. Here it would be proper to mention a few works like Kāmadhenu of Gopāla, p. 616, Prakāśa or Mahāraṇava Prakāśa, p. 652-655, Pārijāta, p. 655-656, Smṛtyarthasāra of Śrīdharācārya, p. 725-727, Harihara on Vyavahāra, p. 735-737, Yogloka, p. 598-599, Bālāka, p. 595, 596, Jitendriya, p. 593, 595, and Devaswāmin, p. 591-593. It must be noted here that presenting the views of these authors was absolutely necessary for him particularly for writing the History of Dharma-Śāstra.

Now the attention of the readers may be drawn to the principles of restoration utilised by that great scholar.

As regards the Śaṅkha-likhita Dharma-Sūtra, it should be remembered that Dr. Kane has settled the date of this work as between 300 B.C. to 100 A.D. By his vast knowledge, he has shown that this work was studied by the students of white Yajurveda and the rules of this author are to be studied in the Dvāpara age according to Parāśara-Mādhava. He also points out that there was a commentator on this Śaṅkhalikhita Dharma-Sūtra whose commentary was available to Lakṣ mīdhara in his Kṛtyakalpataru and Caṇḍeśvara in his Vivāda-Ratnākara. This commentary, however, is not now available to us. Dr. Kane further shows resemblances of this Dharma-Sūtra with the other Dharma-Sūtras like Gautama and Baudhāyana. He has not failed to note the novelty of this Dharma-Sūtra that this work deals with several ordeals on which other Dharma-Sūtras are silent. Dr. kane further adds that in the prose portion and poetry portion (Nos. 64 and 65) ascribed to this author, there is a difference in view. The prose portion allows[2] a brāhamaṇa to have a Śūdra wife. But it is the poetry portion which does not allow[3] him to have such a licence. Incidentally, however, it may be pointed out (though this is not done by Dr. Kane) that this Dharma-Sūtra passage 138 gives the different meanings[4] of the words – iṣṭāpūrta, a good explanation of the persons who spoil[5] the line of Brāhmaṇas at the time of lunch, in para 143, a good explanation of the behaviour of proṣitabhartṛkā in para 341, and the performance of penance for brahmana-killer in para 118. This Dharma-Sūtra pointedly lays down an expitation[6] for making inequality of the distribution of the food in the line of the brāhmaṇas at the time of lunch, in the verse No. 383.

From this discussion, it is evident that for the restoration of any text, a prospective scholar should be in a position to present his peculiar views, his novelty, his resemblances with the other works, his date, his commentator if any. One will observe here that MM. Dr. P.V. Kane has put into practice all these principles in utilising the technique of restoration.

Now coming to the second case of restoration of the Kātyāyana-Smṛti, it is necessary to observe that a highly technical text requires an English Translation with good Notes. This principle, he has followed in the Kātyāyana-Smṛti-Sāroddhāra. Besides, this kind of restoration is to be resorted to only to show the improvement over the work of the predecessor and is to be supplied with good efforts.

Now it would be worthy of note to show the principles he has adopted in the technique of restoration of this text.

1. The comparison of the views of the author with the other works or the modern law as done by Dr. Kane in his notes on stanzas 16, 17 etc.

2. Some times, in explaining the words in the text, the etymology of the word may also be suggested. e.g.st. 69.

3. Sometimes, emendations may be suggested. At the time of presenting the fragments, one goes on copying the portion. But when the question of translation and notes arises, he has to decide whether the reading previously recored is correct or otherwise. Thus on st. 84, he has suggested the emendation in the form of separation of the expression which was originally joined.

4. At times, however, it is observed that one goes on collection of the fragments. But at the time of writing translation and notes, one also consults other sources where the same passage is quoted in other additional works. One may therefore, make a preference of the reading newly available to the old one already recorded. For example, in the stanzas

75-76. The reading 'bodhānīyaḥ śanaiḥ śanaiḥ nṛpaḥ is preferable to 'bodhanīyaḥ as tairnṛpaḥ' particularly in the stanza No. 75. Here three different readings become available and Dr. Kane selects or prefers in the notes the reading dhatadir for vadhadih in view of the context.

5. At times, one has to make a distinction between the two words having similar meanings. Here attention may be drawn to the two expressions Jayapatra and Paścātkāra. In his notes on stanzas 259-265, Dr. Kane notes a distinction between these two words according to Kātyāyana. He points out that the term Paścātkāra refers to a final judgment arrived at after hot contest between the parties. While the expression 'Jayapatra' means a judgment where the claims are cast off without a thorough trial or the suit is declared ex parte.

6. Dr. Kane has expressed his own considered opinions about the views or translations of other scholars like Dr. Jolly and Sham Shastri. In his notes on stanzas 112-113, Dr. Kane points out a mistake in the translation of the Kauṭilīya Arthaśāstra by Sham Shastri. Similarly his comments on the views of Dr. Jolly are also enlightening particularly on stanza No. 437. One may also read a lengthy note of Dr. Kane on stanza No. 560 covering printed three and half pages. This only shows that for clearing the doubts in the mind of the readers, a scholar who wants to restore the text should adopt such techniques.

7. Sometimes, however, it is necessary to know the scope of the stanzas. Dr. Kane's notes on stanza's 398-399, 396-397, 473 etc., are really illuminating from the point of view of the scope of the subject which is covered by the particular stanza.

8. At times, the note written by Dr. Kane throws an altogether different light. For example, in the stanza No.

484, Kātyāyana prescribes proper punishment consisting of fine or corporal injury to a person from the four varṇas, who is not prepared to undergo any expiation for the offences committed. Dr. Kane in his notes on this stanza refers to the Parāśara Mādhava that if the offending brāhmaṇa does not submit to being banished, then he has to be punished just as a kṣatriya would be viz. with fine or imprisonment. He also draws our attention to the other passages in support of the above emplanation.

Now I turn to some interesting points from the paper of Dr. Kane on 'The predecessors of Vijñāneśvara.' Here Dr. Kane points out that the commentary of Asahāya is not available to us. But from the quotations of Asahāya in the Dharma-Śāstra, it becomes clear to us in respect of some of his views. Thus, Vijñāneśvara in his Mitākṣarā on the Yājñavalkya-Smṛti II.24 agrees with Asahāya when he holds that the fourth share of the property may be given to the unmarried sisters, particularly when their brothers are separated.

(2) Bhoja's identity with Dhāreśvara is proved by Dr. Kane. Dhāreśvara seems to have written a commentary on the Yājñavalkya-Smṛti, though this is not now available to us. He points out the peculiar view of Dhāreśvara that ownerwhip is known from the Śāstra. Vijñāneśvara differs from him and holds that it is known from the popular practices. It is laukika. Nīlakaṇṭha, the author of the Vyavahāra-Mayūkha also agrees with Vijñāneśvara on this point.

One more interesting view of Dhāreśvara is that in the expression duhitaraḥ in the Yājñavalkya-Smṛti, he takes it for granted that duhitaraḥ stands for putrikā also. It should be noted here that Vijñāneśvara makes no such distinction between the daughter and adopted daughter.

Dhāreśvara also held on the Yājñavalkya-Smṛti II.121 that a father has no right to give a larger or a small share to any one as he can with his self-acquired property. On this point, Vijñāneśvara construes the same similarly.

Now it would be interesting to know whether the technique of Restoration so fruitfully employed by Dr. Kane is also put into practice by the later scholars or not. Here a few references will not be out of place.

(1) Dr. K. Krishnamoorthy has employed this technique of Restoration to present some views of 'Maṅgala – A neglected name in Sanskrit poetics' particularly in the Journal of the Oriental Institute, Baroda, vol. XX, No. 3, 1971, p. 247-255.

(2) Dr. V.M. Kulkarni has restored the sixth and seventh chapters of the Abhinavabhāratī of Abhinavagupta on the Nāṭyaśāstra, in the journals of the Oriental Institute, Baroda, Vols. 13, 14 and 15 and they are published together in his book 'Studies in Sanskrit Sāhitya Śāstra', published by Bhogilal Leherchand Institute of Indology, Patan, in the year 1983, p. 37 to 60 and 71 to 78.

(3) Incidentally, it may be noted that Dr. Kulkarni has pointed out in a review published in the journal of the Asiatic Society of Bombay, Vols. 60-61, 1985-1986, p. 144-146 on the 'Rasa Theory and Allied problems' by Dr. G.K. Bhatt, that some of his interpretations are wrong on account of accepting corrupt readings of the Abhinavabhāratī.

(4) The writer of this note has also restored the 'Ṛṣya-śṛṅga Smṛti' for the Mysore Orientalist, vol. XIV, p. 65-77, 1987.

(5) The writer of this note has also restored about 142 stanzas from the Vyāghra-Smṛti quoted in the vast Dharma-Śāstra literature and particularly those stanzas which have

no place in the two manuscripts of the Vyāghra Smṛti borrowed by him one from the Bhandarkar Oriental Research Institute, Pune and another from the Govt. College, Banaras particularly published in Smṛtisandarbha vol. IV, p. 2491-2528.

In conclusion, it must be admitted that the employment of the technique of Restoration on the part of MM. Dr. P.V. Kane proved to be inspiring to the later scholars from the point of view of presenting the views of the author, for deciding the date of the work, for writing the history of any work, for improvement upon the work of the predecessor in the field, for presenting the peculiar views of such authors in comparison with the views of the available authors or commentators, for correcting or pointing out the mistakes of the scholars, for bringing the work to the pink of perfection according to the best of the ability of the person, or incidentally expressing one's views for the proper knowledge of the subject even by casual comments upon the translation or the peculiar views of the modern scholar, and giving translation, notes etc. for the real improvement upon the work of the predecessors in the field. In view of these aspects of Restoration brought to the notice of the learned readers, one will be tempted to express the view that as an Indologist, Dr. Kane has indeed made a pioneering and illuminating contribution which would serve as a beacon light for the many many generations to come.

FOOT NOTES

1. A.B.O.R.I. vol. VII, p. 105.
2. ततोऽनुकल्पः चतस्रो ब्राह्मणस्यानुपूर्व्येण तिस्रो राजन्यस्य द्वे वैश्यस्यैका शूद्रस्य। *Ibid.*, p. 47.
3. ब्राह्मणी क्षत्रिया वैश्या ब्राह्मणस्य प्रकीर्तिता। *Ibid.*, p. 47.

4. अग्निष्टोमादिर्भिर्यज्ञैर्यजेत च स इष्टवान्।
अग्निहोत्रं तपः सत्यं वेदानां चैव पालनम्।।
आतिथ्यं वैश्वदेवं च इष्टामित्यभिधीयते।
एकाग्निकादौ यत्कर्म त्रेतायां यच्च हूयते।।
अन्तर्वेद्यां च यद्वानामिष्टं तदभिधीयते।
रोगिणां परिचर्या च पूर्तमित्यभिनिर्दिशेत्।। *Ibid.*, p. 126, passage No. 138.
5. अनध्यायेष्वधीयानाः शौचाचारविवर्जिताः।
शूद्रान्नरसपुष्टाङ्गाः ब्राह्मणाः पङ्क्तिदूषकाः।। *Passage* 143.
6. एकपङ्क्ति उपविष्टानां विषमं यः प्रयच्छाति।
यश्चैवाश्नात्ययं सर्वः कुर्याद् ब्रह्महणि व्रतम्।। *Passage* 383.
7. Etymology of प्राड्विवाकः following the व्यवहारमातृका is 'विचार्य वा जयपराजयरूपं विविधमर्थं वक्तीति विवाकः।' कात्यायन-स्मृति-सारोद्धार, p. 130.
8. कात्यायन-स्मृति-सारोद्धार, p. 167.
9. Kane quotes आपस्तम्ब-धर्मसूत्र II.5.10.15-16 स ब्राह्मणन् नियुञ्ज्यात्। बलविशेषेण वधदास्यवर्जं नियमैरुपशोषयेत्। Also गौतमधर्मसूत्र 12.44.
10. वीरमित्रोदय, p. 528 and 536 (जीवानन्द's edition) Kane refers to this view on p. 223 of his paper. The predecessors of विज्ञानेश्वर।
11. वीरमित्रोदय, p. 658. Also see *Ibid.*, p. 223.

XII

DR. KANE'S VIEWS ON HINDU CODE BILL

In the last chapter 37th of the history of Dharma-Śāstra vol. v/ii, p. 1658 to 1711, Dr. Kane has made a lot of discussion on the Future Trends. We are here primarily concerned with his position in respect of the laws passed after dawn of independence, particularly on the Hindu Law. Kane has slightly discussed this aspect on pages 1672 to 1674 pointing out how the drastic changes have been made in the original position of the Mitākṣarā on the Yājñavalkya-Smṛti by the members of the Rājyasabhā and Lokasabhā. I would like to discuss here the suggestions made by the learned doctor for the codification of the Hindu law for bringing about the solidarity of the Indian Culture. It would be equally interesting to see how far the suggestions made by him have been accepted or rejected by the modern legislature. In this very context, it should be noted that Kane was the member of the Rājyasabhā from 1953 to 1959 and hence his experience as an advocate who was well-experienced in this branch, deserves special mention in this paper.

I. Kane has discussed the topic of Divorce in his History of Dharma-Śāstra vol. II/I, p. 621. He points out that the principle of divorce is unknown to the Dharma-Śāstra. It is only in the Kautilīya Artha-Śāstra that we come across the point that divorce is to be granted on the grounds of mutual hatred and physical danger to each other. Kauṭilya further held that in the approved forms of marriage like Brāhma, Prājāpatya, Ārṣa and Daiva, the question of divorce does not at all arise. But it is only in the case of the unapproved forms of marriage like Rākṣasa, Paiśāca, Gāndharva and Āsura, that the divorce may be granted on the ground of mutual consent. Kane has also shown that other smṛtikāras like Nārada and others have gone to the extent of recommending divorce on the grounds of the impotency of a husband, his becoming samnyasi or an outcast. Against this background in the medieval Hindu law, Kane made the suggestion that there should be some provision for divorce even in the cases of marriages performed under the ancient Śāstric system. Here he relies[2] for the grounds suggested in the English Act of 1937 and particularly A.P. Herbert's Act. In this act, it is suggested that divorce may be granted on the ground of adultery, without having anything more to prove. This suggestion of the learned doctor is accepted in the Hindu Marriage Act section 27, giving the grounds – such as desertion for two years, imprisonment of a husband or a wife, cruelty, incurably unsound mind of a person, mental disorder, leprosy, and unheard of a person for 7 years or more. Any one would be convinced that the suggestion of Kane is accepted adding additional grounds to the grounds mentioned by the writers on Dharma-Śāstra. Here incidentally, it may be noted that Viśvarūpa,[3] the commentator of the Yājñavalkya-Smṛti, holds that adultery is not a ground for divorce. A lady may become pure by performing the penance laid down in that respect. This has been noted by Kane in his History of Dharma-Śāstra.

II. There is no place for widow's marriage in the

Dharma-Śāstra literature. In order to maintain the ideal of chastity and single minded devotion to a husband, it is desired that a widow should not get remarried. It may be pointed out here that Nārada, parāśara and others allowed a widow to remarry, if the husband is dead or is not heard of for some years. Kane further cites the historical evidence to prove that remarriage of a widow was in practice. For this, he relies on the case Dhruvadevī, the wife of Rāmagupta, was married by Candragupta on the death of Rāmagupta. He further gives credit to the Pundit Isvarachandra Vidyasagara for taking interest in passing the widow's marriage act of 1856. Incidentally, it may be added here that some grounds[4] for the remarriage of a widow are given in the work 'Smṛtyarthasāra (between 1150 to 1200 A.D. such as death of a prospective husband before saptapadī, or before consummating the marriage, or before the period of menstruation, or even before the conception of a lady. It is a matter of satisfaction that this suggestion of Kane was accepted by the modern legislature. Incidentally, one may mention that the manuscript[5] entitled. 'punarvivāha-vicāra,' is particularly preserved in the library of the Oriental Institute Baroda.

III. Dr. Kane's suggestion is that for the marriage, there should be the abolition[6] of the bar of sagotra and sapravara in case of a bride and bridegroom. Incidentally, it may be remembered here that the Mīmāṁsā principle of Adṛṣṭa relied upon by Kane on the basis of the Mitākṣarā arguments of sagotra marriage, was rejected[7] by justice P.B. Gajendragadkar in a case of Madhavrao Vs. Raghunatharao as reported in 48 Bom. Law reporter p. 196. From this case onwards, Kane seems to have modified his views and later on supported the Hindu Code Bill for abolishing the bars of sagotra and sapravara in the marriage. However, it may be noted in this very context, that in practice people have not forgotten to apply the principles of asagotra and apravara. There are also some cases where the sagotra marriages take place. One will have to observe here that in the codification of the Modern Hindu law, the very basis of the Dharma-Śāstra, so preserved for centuries together, is attacked so as to solve the social problems.

IV. Kane's suggestion for the Hindu Adoptions Act, should be mentioned here. He states that a boy to be adopted should be within the range of 3 and 5 years. He further states[8] that a married person should not be accepted for adoption. The view of the Vyayavahāra Mayūkha makes room for the adoption of a married person with a son. These two suggestions of Kane are not favoured by the modern legislature. In the section 10 (iii) of the Hindu Adoptions Act., it is said that if a custom permits then one may adopt a married person. Here custom has become the basis of the law. In the Dharma-Śāstra, it is held that a custom in order to achieve the position of a law, should not be repulsive to the test of the Śiṣṭas or Dharmavid persons. Here it may be incidentally remembered that when the law was passed, the members of both the houses, were the representatives of the people but they are not learned in the subject as such. Hence this Provision of the Hindu Adoptions Act., is certainly not appealing to the mind of the good.

(ii) Again it may be noted that the section 10 (iv) lays down that at the time of adoption, he or she has not completed the age of 15. Here also custom plays very important part.

(iii) The modern judges like H.S. Ursekar claim that the introduction of the point of a daughter may be adopted with some restrictions, is a new change that the modern legislature has introduced. But this is accepted only by the illiterate. The good students of Dharma-Śāstra would remember that Anantadeva, the author of the Saṁskāra-

Kaustubha, has introduced the point that a daughter may be adopted. This author Anantadeva belongs to the third quarter of the 17th century A.D., as decided by Kane[9] in his History of Dharma-Śāstra. This adoption of a daughter is permitted by section 7 of the Hindu Adoptions Act.

(iv) There is one more question more debatable in the Dharma-Śāstra known as Vasiṣṭha-Dharma-Sūtra.[10] Can a woman i.e., a married woman accept a son in adoption? This question is decided differently by the different authors by resorting to different Mimamsa principles. The Dattka Mīmāṁsā and Mithila School think that a widow cannot adopt a son. (ii) The Bengal, Madras and Benaras schools think that a widow can adopt a son provided she has secured a permission from her husband during his life-time. (iii) The Madras school further thinks that she can adopt a son with the permission of her father-in-law or other coparceners. (iv) Nīlakaṇṭha and the author of Dattka-Candrikā maintain that in such a case permission is always taken for granted unless she is specifically prohibited by her husband to that effect. The way in which the text is interepreted shows[11] the intelligence of the writers. But this problem is solved by the Hindu Adoptions Act Section 8(a) (b) (c) allowing a female Hindu to adopt a son.

V. Kane's major suggestion[12] lies for the right of a Strīdhana. He states that a Strīdhana is the wealth a woman from male or female. She should become an absolute owner of the estate. (2) He further adds that if a property is inherited from a female, then she should become the owner of the absolute property. (3) On the death of a woman, her sons and daughters should succeed together for the share in the property. (iv) If, however, sons and daughters are not there to claim the share in the property, then a husband can become the owner of a property. (v) He further adds that the estate of a maiden should be given to her brothers, sisters, mother, father or to the person who is nearest to her.

These suggestions of Kane are accepted by modern legislature in the Indian Successtion Act, by vindicating revenge upon the male members of the society as has been rightly shown by Dr. Kane in his History of Dharma-Śāstra Vol. V/II, p. 1672-1673.

VI. Here incidentally, it may be noted that the modern legislature has ignored the importance of the expression 'Ananyapūrvikā'[13] in the Yājñavalkya Smṛti. This is correctly explained by the present author with the evidence of the Mahābhārata. If, however, this principle is not borne in mind, it may given rise to murders, litigations etc.

VII. The present legislature should have taken into account the point of a boy making his own adoption to the other person. Here the point of Svayaṁdatta which is the example of the unique case of adoption of Śunaḥśepa by Viśvāmitra. This point has been adequately discussed by the present author elsewhere[14] for which the attention of the readers is drawn.

VIII. In this other work entitled 'Dharma-Śāstra Vicāra' in Marathi, Kane has made suggestions[15] for the codification of the Hindu law which may be briefly stated here.

1. The extremities in the caste should be avoided.
2. Women should agitate for allowing a man to have one wife only.
3. The sub-castes in a particular caste should be abolished.
4. A superiority of a man is to be decided on the grounds of his character, charity, knowledge and not by caste and birth.
5. He points out the paurāṇic ways for abolishing the principle of untouchability.

6. He further advises asceticism to the people in a different way of removing the tension by rendering service to the people on point of education and lessening selfishness.

It must be stated, in passing that some of these points are noteworthy. These views of Kane have not become acceptable to the people due to their purely selfish behaviour.

IX. The new things introduced by the Hindu Marriage act are the specification of the ages for a bride and a bridegroom and the introduction of the principle of judicial separation. On the age of the marriable girls, there is a lot of discussion in the Dharma-Śāstra. But by specification of the ages, this problem appears to be solved. Here again the custom plays part and the marriages before the prescribed ages do take place and the matters are not appearing in the Court. Besides, by keeping two wives, (openingly or secretly), the principle of one wife for a person, is found defeated. The modern law is abolishing the spirit of casteism and making the people free from the shackles of casteism. We have now become open minded and prepared to give up the narrow-mindedness in the matters which are very complicated.

X. As regards the Maintenance Act, something must be said. The sections 20 and 21 of the Maintenance act, lay down that a person is, by duty, bound to maintain his aged parents, his widow, his son or daughter, unmarried daughter, and others mentioned in the section 21 (iv). But in the Dharma-Śāstra vol. II/I, Kane relies on the poṣyavarga, i.e., the persons to be maintained by a dutiful person particuly on the Dakṣa-Smṛti[16] II.36 and 37 and makes the inclusion of Guru. helpless person who has taken resort to a person and a guest and fire. For the full discussion on the point of Poṣyavarga, attention may be drawn to the discussion in Kane's History of Dharma-Śāstra vol. II/I p. 569.

In Conclusion, some of the suggestions of Kane are accepted by the modern legislature. some other suggestions are rejected outright by the present law. Thirdly there are new changes introduced in the law. Fourthly, there are some interesting points which have no scope or place at all in the law. Fifthly, the significance of some of the expressions is not appreciated by the modern legislature Sixthly, the law is preserved and prepared keeping in mind that the law should be made free from the shackless of casteism as such. Hence whatever were the restrictions laid down previously, they are safely dropped by the modern act. However, some of the practices still prevail and herein lies the root of the old religions and principles ingrained in the blood of the people of India.

FOOT-NOTES

1. Kauṭilīya Arthaśāstra III.3.16-19. (Prof. Kangle's edition)
2. P.V. Kane – History of Dharma-Śāstra vol. II/I, p. 623.
3. Viśvarūpa on the Yājñavalkya-Smṛti III.253-254 quoted in History of Dharma Śāstra vol. II/I, p. 620.
4. *Ibid.*, p. 613-619.
5. The manuscript entitled 'Punar-vivāha-Mīmāṁsā, in Oriental Institute, Baroda. No. 9026 Quoted in *Ibid.*, vol. I/II, p. 1065.
6. Kane – History of Dharma-Śāstra vol. II/I, p. 611.
7. *Ibid.*, vol. III, p. 97/n. and A.S. Ayyar-Mīmāṁsā Jurisprudencepp. 12-13.
8. P.V. Kane – History of Dharma-Śāstra, vol. III., p. 699, foot note No. 1338a.
9. *Ibid.*, vol. I/II, p. 963.
10. Vasiṣṭha Dharma-Śāstra XV-5.
11. S.G. Moghe-Studies in the Pūrva-Mīmāṁsā, p. 249-250.
12. P.V. Kane – History of Dharma-Śāstra vol. III, p. 801-802.
13. S.G. Moghe – Studies in the Dharma-Śāstra for the full significance of Ananyapūrvikā, p. 159-164.

14. *Ibid.*, p. 117-124 for the discussion on the problem of Śunaḥśepa and Dattaka-Vidhāna. Also see Journal of Ganganatha Jha Kendriya Sanskrit Vidyapitha, vol. 35., 1-2, p. 85-95.
15. P.V. Kane – History of Dharma-Śāstra, vol. II/I, p. 439-445. Also see – Dharma-Śāstra-Vicāra, p. 85, 98, 140, 155, 173, 190 etc.
16. *Ibid.*, p. 569.

XIII

MEDIEVAL HINDU LAW AND MODERN LAW – A COMPARISON*

As this seminar is arranged or organised to show the contribution of sanskrit to law. I have particularly chosen to high-light the readers on the above topic, simply because most of the sanskrit literature and particularly the Dharma-Śāstra literature is written in Sanskrit. The relation of this medieval law with the modern law will be more interesting and equally refreshing. As after the dawn of independence, during the period of ten years, more than 450 laws are passed, I have specifically used the expression 'modern law' only to show that Medieval Hindu law is widely spread or divided into several laws specially prepared to meet the needs of Indian people. Here in the comparison shown below, it is expected to reveal the points or the aspects of differences, improvement, acceptance, absence of scope, noted silence, absence of consideration or turning down the particular position or eradicating the particular custom as such.

1. The aspect of the differences in the two laws can be indicated by taking a few examples. (i) As regards the marriagable age of girls, it is said that the age should be from 5 to 10. In this respect, the ratio of age between the marriagable girl and boy is indicated as one to three. The

Dharma Śāstra authors used the expression 'Nagnikā' i.e., a girl who looks pretty when she is naked, is most preferable for marriage. Dr. Kane has contributed an article on this topic in MM. Dr. Ganganatha Jha Felicitation Volume. As compared to this, the modern law lays down the completion of the age of 18 and 21 for a girl and a boy respectively. It is thus, the difference in out-look gets revealed. (ii) The Medieval Hindu law recognises untouchability on the grounds of birth, death, and touching the low class people. In fact, Untouchanility proved a vital role in Indian culture. But by the article 17 of the Indian Constitution, the untouchability is completely eradicated. In fact, to treat any one as untouchable in the public place, is held as a crime. It should be incidentally noted that even B.G. Tilak made an attempt to remove untouchability by presenting articles in the daily news-paper 'Kesarī'. (iii) As regards the share of the adopted son and the natural son born to a person after adoption, the Medieval Hindu Law gives only bare maintenance to the adopted son and the natural son is held as qualified to take the estate of the adoptive father.

On this point of share, it must be stated here that there is a sharp difference of opinion among the judges of the High Courts. The Bombay High Court held the view that one fifth share should be allotted to the adopted son and 4/5th share should be given to the natural son. But the Madras High Court based its decision on the Dattaka-candrikā and held the view that in the case of a Śūdra, both the adopted and natural son take the equal share. This decision is given in the case of Perassu Vs. Subba Royadu in 48 I.A. p. 280.

4. The Medieval Hindu law laid down a condition that there should be no marriage between the two Sagotra persons. If such a marriage takes place, then one will have to perform the Cāndrāyaṇa expiation. The Dharma Śāstra authors, it

may be noted, recommended the asagotra marriage. The Mīmāṁsā principle of Adṛṣṭa is not favoured by Justice P.B. Gajendragadkar in a case of Madhavarao Vs. Raghunatharao, 48 Bom.L.R. 196, and the case particularly argued by Dr. Kane replying on the Mitākṣarā arguments of Sagotra marriage. However, in practice, it must be noted, that many sagotra marriages take place.

The aspect of improvement may be high-lighted by giving another good example. In the Dharma-Śāstra, the idea of divorce is not at all favoured. The Dharma-Śāstra authors treat marriage as a sacrament giving status to the position of a woman. Hence there is no place for divorce. It is only Kauṭilya who favours the idea of divorce in hard cases particularly when, there is likely to be a danger to the life of a person from another partner.

Against this background, Dr. Kane in his History of Dharma-Śāstra, made a useful suggestion that the principle of divorce should be accepted on the basis of the English Law. Now in the Hindu marriage Act, there is a provision for divorce, on the grounds of one leading an immoral life, turning to another faith, suffering from incurable disease of a communicable form etc. It should b further noted that the modern law treats marriage as a contract and as such it can be violated at any time, when the situation stated above arises. Thus, the introduction of the principle of divorce in marriage is really an improvement. It may be incidentally noted that the society severs the connection with a criminal and in this context the expression ghaṭasphoṭa is used. But this expression is not found used in the subject of marriage.

III. It should be significantly pointed out that the positions adopted by the medieval Hindu law are treated as recommendatory and not injunctive. This point can be best illustrated by stating that the Medieval Hindu law does not accept incompatable relations as fit for marriage. In incompatible relations, either husband or woman appear as the father or mother of the another person. But the modern courts took the view that this outlook of the Medieval Hindu law is only recommendatory and need not be followed as injunctive. To put it in other words, even the incompatible relations are also accepted by the courts for marriage. This point can be further justified or illustrated by stating that marriage with one's sister's daughter was held as valid by the Madras High Court.

IV. As regards the point of taxation, the Medieval Hindu law recommends that the taxation should increase bit by bit and it should not be very heavy for the public. In times of distress, however, the king was advised to explore the source of the rich. He should collect money from them and when the time of distress is over, he should try to repay the rich and also confer honours on the rich for helping the nation at the time of difficulty. It further provides concessions to the old persons, pregnant women and invalid persons. Such persons need not pay any tax as such.

Against this background, it must be stated that in the domain of taxation, there is now a wide field. We have to pay several taxes such as income tax, sales tax, gift tax, property tax etc. But as regards the point of concession in taxes, the section 88b of the income tax provides some concession to the senior citizens of the country who are running more than 65th year. Besides, under 80D of the Income tax act, the medical insurance is given concession. There is further rebate in respect of the National Savings Certificate investment, in Life Insurce Corporation and Public Provident fund. It should be further noted that the donations to some educational Institutions and Cultural Institutions doing some social work are given exemption (to some extent) from the tax. Besides, women who are generally treated as the weaker section of the society, are given some special concession in the matter of taxation. Hence it would be correct to state that the principles of taxation and concessions have assumed wider field in the 20th century.

V. As regards the point of punishment, some interesting points deserve mention. For the criminal offences such as theft, murder, kidnapping, assault, battery, etc., the different punishments are laid down in view of the age of the criminal, his financial condition, the time factor etc. The medieval Dharma-Śāstra authors have recommended the punishments of imprisonment, symbolic punishment, fine, expiation, penance, donation of cows, money, field etc, pilgrimage, saving the life of another person in danger of life and recitation of the Vedic Mantras. It seems that the Medieval Hindu Law held that some reformation is possible even in a hardened criminal.

As against the background of the Medieval Hindu Law, it must be admitted that in civil matters, the procedure is very length and one gets the judgments in the matter after spending 10 or 12 years. In the Criminal matters, however, we find the punishments in the form of prison, fine and hanging the person till death or the transportation of life. Besides, the procedure of appeals in the High Court, appeal before division bench, appeal before the bench of five or seven judges and approach to the Supreme Court in such matters takes away the very life of the petitioners. Incidentally, it may be remembered that in the modern criminal law, there is no place for donation, penance, expiation, pilgrimage, saving the life of another in distress, recitation of vedic mantras, feeding the brāhmaṇas for giving freedom from the crimes committed by the criminals. From this position, it would be fair to conclude that the modern criminal law does not accept that any reformation is possible in a criminal. This is perhaps the vital difference in the approach of the Medieval Hindu Law and the modern law.

(2) The Medieval Hindu law also held that the Dattka Homa is absolutely necessary in order that the adoption should become a valid one. In the medieval times, the presence of a king was held as necessary at the time of Dattka-Homa. Śankaraśāstrī Mārulakar in his commentary Śānkarī on the Dattaka-Candrikā, points out that the presence of the officers such as Kulkarni, Patil, Mamlatdar is enogh to serve the presence of a king. But in the Modern Hindu Adoptions Act., there is no place for Dattaka-Homa as such. (3) The Medieval Hindu law is based on the Mīmāṁsā principles of Adṛṣṭa, Kratvartha and Puruṣārtha which are to be strictly followed for valid adoption. It seem that the Modern Hindu Adoptions Act has turned down the above principles. Hence one will have to admit that the modern law has introduced drastic changes or turned down the stand-points of the Medieval Hindu Law.

VI. It would be significant to note that the rule of Dāmdupaṭ which is not favoured by the Medieval Hindu Law is sometimes favoured and sometimes not favoured by the modern law. The principle of the rule of Dāmdupaṭ is that the interest on the principal amount given as loan, should not exceed double of the principal amount. But there is a conflicting situation in respect of the application of the rule of Dāmdupaṭ in the modern courts. Some courts have held that it is applicable in some cases; while the other courts have not followed the same. For the discussion on this interesting and conflicting views taken by the courts, attention of the serious readers is drawn to the discussion in the History of Dharma-Śāstra by Dr. P.V. Kane. In passing, it may be added that the principle of Dāmdpuṭ was followed in some western countries as noted by Dr. Kane in the foot-note.

VII. As regards the system of lawyers in the medieval Hindu Law and modern law, some discussion is necessary. It must be admitted that both the laws have accepted this principle of the system of lawyers. Shri H.S. Ursekar, the retired judge is wrong when he stated that there was no system of lawyers in ancient and medieval Hindu law. It must be mentioned here that the commentary of Asahāya on the Nārada Smṛti (Ṛṇādāna 4) as Kalyāṇabhaṭṭa, reveals that the system of lawyers was accepted in the Medieval Hindu Law. Asahāya states that the persons who are well versed in the Dharma-Śāstra and who help the parties in the court matter by accepting monetary consideration, are to be treated as lawyers holding brief for the parties. Normally no interference was tolerated by the Medieval Courts. But this was allowed only in the case of learned brāhmaṇas well versed in the vedic knowledge, smṛtis and the Dharma-Śāstra, when in particular king or his officer is likely to go wrong or doing injustice to the concerned parties. Hence it would be proper to hold that the roots of the modern system of lawyers are there in the Medieval Sanskrit Hindu Law.

VIII. As regards the point of justice in court matters, it must be said that judiciary has now become highly complicated. In the Medieval Hindu law, the king or his officer was helped by the Sabhyas in giving proper relief to the concerned parties. When the matter appeared before the court, the Sabhyas had the right to bring round the king or the officer when he was likely to go wrong in giving judgment or relief to the concerned parties. If it is noticed that the sabhyas are not giving proper relief, or prompted by hatred, selfish desire or threats of the parties, then they also were fined and removed from the posts and their property was confiscated. Kauṭilya has gone to the extent of holding that if the judges are found bribed, then they also could be fined and removed from the posts.

As compared to the above picture, now a days there is no control over judiciary as such. If the suit was dismissed by the lower court, appeal was allowed in the High Court. Against the High Court decision also, there was a scope for review or appeal or appeal before division bench of judges or the bench of five or seven judges. Against the High Court decision of appeals, the last resort was held as the Supreme Court. Now a days the court of people is established to dispose of the legal suits. As the judiciary has become more complicated, one has to wait for a pretty long time for getting proper justice in the matter. If, however, the Judges of the Supreme court give the decision of hanging the criminal till death, even the criminals are allowed to make the petition of pity to the Rāṣṭrapati (President) of the nation. And in such cases, it was treated as the final one. It is also observed that the judiciary is also dominated by the executives and the transfers of the judges could be effected by the sweet will of the prime minister of the nation. For the disposal of the civil suits, the period of twelve years is taken as normal. It should be noted, in passing that in the Medieval India, there was the control of sabhyas over the king or the officer giving judgment. But there is no control as such over the judiciary. It is due to this aspect of control, even to day, it is observed that the judiciary is under the control or the thumb of the politicians.

IX. As regards some modification in the medieval law by the modern law, it may be pointed out that Anantadeva, the author of the Samskāra-Kaustubha allowed the adoption of a daughter. But this aspect of the medieval law was modified by the Hindu Adoptions Act, by stating that there should be a difference of 21 years between the adoptive father or mother and the daughter or the son to be adopted. It may be said here that this is the important modification the modern Hindu Adoptions Act has made.

Another important modification suggested by the Modern Hindu Adoptions Act is that even a married person can be adopted. In the Medieval Hindu law, a boy to be adopted must be between 5 to 7 years and the adoption was connected with the principles of the Samskāras like the Cūḍā karma and Upanayana. These Samskāras played very important role in deciding the share of the adopted son and the natural son if born to a person after the adoption has taken place.

Incidentally, it may be pointed out that by the section 11(i) and (ii), a person who adopts a son or a daughter, should not have a son or son's son and great grand son at the time of adoption. It appears that the word son in the section or the text of the Dharma-Śāstra is illustrative and it includes grand-son and great grand son.

X. It should be significantly pointed out that the modern law has destroyed the very spirit of Hindu law. In the matter of adoption, the idea of continuation of the family tradition is more important. By giving scope to the adoption of a giri in the Hindu Adoptions Act, the idea of continuation of the family tradition is thrown into background and Dr. Kane is perfectly right when he expressed the opinion that the drastic changes made by the modern law will considerably affect the Hindu Society.

XI. At times, it is observed that the modern law is totally silent on some aspect. The question arises whether one should give the only son in adoption or not. The Medieval Hindu law holds that such an only son is not to be given in adoption. They further hold that out of four brothers, if only one brother has a son, then other brothers need not adopt sons independently. But the modern Hindu Adoptions Act does not state categorically whether the only son can be given in adoption or not.

XII Another good example of the silence of the Medieval digest authors is that they have not dealt with the problem of the disposal of the property by the adoptive father in respect of his adopted son or natural son. But the Indian succession Act provides that an adoptive father can transfer his property by deed of transfer or by the deed of will. But one may notice the similarity in allotting shares to the adopted son and the natural in the Medieval Hindu law and modern law. The Sarasvatī Vilāsa (a noted digest) allows 1/5th share to the adopted son and 4/5th share to the natural son. On this point, the Bombay High Court is in complete agrement with the view of the Sarasvatī Vilāsa.

XIII. As regards the right of a widow or a married woman to spend some portion of her husband's property for visiting the sacred place and perform his sraddha, it is held by the Dharma-Śāstra authors that she should be given this permission. This provision of the Dharma-Śāstra authors is further accepted by the modern court and the widow was allowed to spend some portion of the money for the pilgrimage and Śrāddha at Gayā for the spiritual benefit of her husband.

XIV. The caste system based on the birth and qualitites is the special feature of the Dharma-Śāstra and Indian Culture. The caste system has increased considerably on account of intercaste marriages, influence of the foreign people, countries, customs and manners, professions etc. But the modern law has introduced the new caste system in the form of Prime Minister, State Minister, Members of the Legislative Assembly, Secretaries and other subsidiary or subordinate officers. It should not go unnoticed that the modern method of caste system also has its own demerits and it cannot have the charm of the ancient caste system which has become the part and parcel of the life of people in India.

XV. One important noteworthy point of punishment should not escape from our memory. The abettors who encourage the persons to commit crimes by giving proper guidance, by supplying necessary material or giving shelter or giving food or supplying financial assistance for the crime, deserve punishment. It should be noted here that the Dharma-śāstra Authors of Vyavahāra Prakāśa and Vivāda-Ratnākara and even Kauṭilya make provision for double the punishment or four times punishment for the abettors than the actual perpetrators of crime. But the modern law, however, is bent upon giving lesser punishment to the criminals as compared with the punishment given to the actual criminals. The expression 'prayoktṛ' in the Smṛti text stands for the abettor in the modern criminal law.

XVI. As regards the procedural law, some resemblances may be pointed out. Devaṇṇabhaṭṭa in his Smṛticandrikā quotes the text of Nārada to show that the Plaint may be amended till the reply is filed by the Defendant or the Respondent. This provision suggested by Nārada is in complete agreement with the order XX, rule 13 of the Civil Procedure Code.

Another good point is that the principle of doubt is accepted by the Dharma Sūtrakāras like Āpastamba. He holds that when there is doubt, no judgment is to be given on that point. The point of giving benefit of doubt is generally given to the offender. This provision of giving benefit of doubt is in agreement with the section 3 of the Indian Evidence Act.

In the matter of punishment, generally the principle of tit for tat, tooth for tooth and nail for nail is followed. This principle is found echoed in the Manusmṛti VIII.260 and the Yājñavalkya Smṛti II.215. Incidentally it should be remembered that this principle has its parallel in the sections 196-200 of the code of Hammurabi.

XVII. It would be equally interesting to note the few examples of the Mīmāṁsā rules of interpretation with the Statutes of Maxwell. This is so because in the Medieval Hindu law, the Dharma-Śāstra authors have made abundant use of the Mīmāṁsā rules of intorpretation for resolving the conflict in the mutually contradictory texts of Dharma-Śāstra. (1) The principle of Atideśa (extension) introduced by Jaimini and accepted and followed by the grammarians is also utilised by the Dharma-Śāstra authors. This is also found utilised in Maxwell's interpretations of Statutes, p. 102. This resemblance between two methods of interpretation is already noted by the present author in his article 'Evolution of the Mīmāṁsā Technical Term Atideśa' contributed to the Diamond Jubilee volume of the Annals of the Bhandarkar Oriental Research Institute. (2) The principle of Ūha i.e., substitution, or adaptation introduced by Jaimini in his Pūrva-Mīmāṁsā system is found utilised by the Dharma-Śāstra authors. This principle is utilised in Maxwell's Interpretation of statutes p. 231-248, where it is also shown that the principle of adaptation is used in British law to correct the obvious mistakes in the draft of law particularly framed by the human authors. I have already pointed out that this principle of adaptation is used in English law for the purposes more than one such as (1) to avoid absurd consequences (2) to restrict the scope of jurisprudence, (3) to remove manifest contradiction in the sections of the law. (4) to remove inconvenience to the public in general and particular parties before the Court in particular, (5) to avoid the carelessness of the language in any documents presented before the courts, (6) to correct obvious mistakes in drafting and when the import of the any section of the law appears to have oppossed to the good sense. In passing, it may be casually remarked that though the principle of adaptation is the same in both the systems, yet it is utilised for different purposes in English law.

XVIII. The importance of the Mīmāṁsā principles of interpretation is said to be supreme particularly in deciding the cases of Hindu law before the courts. The Mīmāṁsā principle of Vākyabheda has gone several changes and it has become evolutionary at the hands of the writers of different disciplines of sanskrit learning. Dr. Kane expressed the view in the course of his discussion in the History of Dharma-Śāstra vol. III, p. 694 that the judges do not possess sound knowledge of the Mimamsa principles of interpretation and particularly the principle of Vākyabheda. In interpreting the text of the Manu-Smṛti IX-141-142, the judges during the British regime have incurred the fault of Vākyabheda. Actually, this fault of Vākyabheda arises when in one and the same stanza, the two injunctions are laid down. The text of the Manu Smṛti as interpretated by the judges lays down two injuctions : 1) A person adopted into another family will not take the wealth of his natural father or any one in that family after adoption. (2) A person adopted in another family loses or forfeits on adoption, wealth that he may have already taken absolutely in the natural family as a member of that family before adoption. But after the dawn of independence, the importance of the system of Pūrva-Mīmāṁsā is thrown into oblivion by the modern law and it has just become an academic study now.

In Conclusion, the present paper deals with the aspects of changes in the original Hindu law, addition to the law, abrogating some principles as such, silence of one law and provision by other law, destroying the spirit of Hindu law, method of interpretation of law in both the laws the acceptance of some principles with modifications, completely ignoring the principles of old and medieval Hindu law. Hence we have to admit wholeheartedly that we are standing on the shoulders of the predecessors and thereby suggesting our glorious tradition and desire to make circumstantial improvement as per the needs of the people and law.

FOOT NOTES

* This paper is presented at the Seminar arranged by the Asiatic Society of Bombay, on the Contribution of Sanskrit to Literature, scientific literature and law (for 1000-2000 A.D.) on 30th January, 2000.

1. For Nagnikā, Vide, Kane's History of Dharma-Śāstra, vol. II/I, p. 440 and 444.
2. P.V. Kane—'The Marriagable age of Girls—Ganganatha Jha Commemoration Volume, p. 191-197, 1937.
3. S.G. Moghe—History of Dharma-Śāstra—in Essence, p. 189.
4. *Ibid.*, p. 414.
5. S.G. Moghe—Kane's views on Pūrva-Mīmāṁsā published in Studies in the Pūrva-Mīmāṁsā, p. 244, 1984.
6. Kauṭilīya Arthaśāstra III.4 and S.G. Moghe—History of Dharma-Śāstra—in Essence, p. 241.
7. Gṛhya Parīśiṣṭa II/I, p. 469 quoted in History of Dharma Śāstra, vol. II/I.
8. P.V. Kane—History of Dharma-Śāstra, vol. II/I, p. 469.
9. I.L.R., (43), Madras 830.
10. S.G. Moghe—History of Dharma-Śāstra in Essence, p. 455.
11. S.G. Moghe—The commentary Śāṅkarī on the Dattaka-Candrikā—in Mysore Orientalist.
    Also see this article published in S.G. Moghe's 'Studies in the Dharma-Śāstra', p. 125-133, 1991.
12. P.V. Kane—History of Dharma-Śāstra, vol. III, p. 422-425.
13. H.S. Ursekar—Adoption—Unmarried mother—Bhāratīya Vidyā Bhavana, vol. 39, No. 1, p. 55-58, 1979.
14. P.V. Kane—History of Dharma-Śāstra, vol. III, p. 288-289.
15. S.G. Moghe—History of Dharma-Śāstra in Essence, p. 354-355 for the role of Sabhyas.

16. *Ibid.*, p. 165.
17. Sarasvatī-Vilāsā.
18. P.V. Kane – History of Dharma-Śāstra.
19. 11 Bengal, L.R. 416, in a case of Muteeram Vs Gaopal.
20. Mitramiśra's Vyavahara-Prakāśa, p. 395.
21. Vivāda-Ratnākara, p. 374.
22. S.G. Moghe-Mīmāṁsā Maxims in the Smṛticandrikā of Devaṇṇabhaṭṭa published in Journal of Oriental Research & Manuscripts Library vol. XX, Part – I, p. XIII.
23. Āpastāmba Dharma Sūtra II.5.11.2 reads 'na Ca Sandehe dandam Kuryat'.
24. S.G. Moghe – Evolution of the Mīmāṁsā Technical Term Atideśa – published in diamond Jubilee Volume of A.B.O.R.I., p. 777-784 for 1977-1978. Also See Maxwell's Interpretation of Statutes – 12th paper back edition, p. 102.
25. S.G. Moghe – Studies in the Applied Pūrva-Mīmāṁsā, p. 39 and p. 41.
26. S.G. Moghe – Studies in the Applied Pūrva-Mīmāṁsā, p. 20-29; Also see this paper published in the Baladeo Upadhyaya Felicitation Volume No. 37 for 1981. by Ganganatha Jha Kendriya Sanskrit Vidyapitha, Allahabad, p. 169-188 for some evolutionary aspects of Vākyabheda.

XIV

DR. P.K. GODE'S CONTRIBUTION TO THE DHARMA-ŚĀSTRA

Dr. P.K. Gode's name is known to the scholarly world for his solid contribution to the several branches of Indology. Right from the year 1916 to 1959, Gode contributed 474 research papers to the research journals. These papers have also appeared in book form in six volumes published by different research institutes such as the Bharatiya Vidya Bhavan, Bombay, Bhandarkar Oriental Research Institute, Poona and Vishveshvarananda Vedic Research Institute, Hoshiarpur, Punjab. In this paper, therefore, an attempt is made to highlight his contribution to the domain of Dharma-Śāstra particularly in the context of the monumental *History of Dharma-Śāstra* by MM. Dr. P. V. Kane.

1. Gode published a paper[1] on the *Vyavahāra Mañjarī* by Bhojarāja in the year 1936. This is treated as an unknown work of Bhojarāja. One would be surprised to find that there is no reference to this work in Kane's *History of Dharma-Śāstra*. Besides, there is no entry of this work on the name of Bhojarāja in the indexes prepared by Kane. The first volume of the *History of Dharma-Śāstra* was published in the year 1930. And Gode's article appeared in the year 1936. One may note here that when Kane revised the first volume of

the *History of Dharma-Śāstra,* his attention was not drawn to this unknown work of Bhojarāja. Besides, a question arises whether Bhojarāja is identical with Bhojadeva or not. Anyway the entry of this work in the list of works and authors on the Dharma-Śāstra has become absolutely necessary.

2. It is the practice of Kane to mention the works of the writers on Dharma-Śāstra. Accordingly, Kane has drawn the attention of the readers to the works of Nāgojībhaṭṭa, by quoting the article[2] of P.K. Gode and the probable date of this author. But there is no mention of the article of Gode indicating the chronology[3] of the works of nāgojībhaṭṭa in the *History of Dharma-Śāstra*. Hence this entry has also become necessary in the monumental work of Kane. This is so, because in deciding the chronological position[4] of the works of Nilakaṇṭha, Kane has devoted a special chapter in his introduction to the excellent edition of the *Vyavahāra-Mayūkha* of Nīlakaṇṭha.

3. The date of the manuscripts on the Dharma-Śāstra and of the authors also plays a very important part in the academic study. It would be interesting to see the dates of the manuscripts and the authors suggested by Gode, particularly against the position established by Kane. (1) Gode has fixed the date[5] of the manuscript entitled *Prāyaścitta-Candrikā* of Viśvanātha Bhaṭṭa, the son of Narasimha Dīkṣita, as before 1540 CE. It is worth noting here that Kane has made the entry of the manuscript *Prāyaścitta-Candrikā* of Viśvanātha Bhaṭṭa, in his *History of Dharma-Śāstra,* vol. I/II, p. 1073, but there is no reference to the date of this work, although it was fixed by Gode. This paper was written by Gode in the year 1945 and naturally Kane could not concentrate his mind on many such articles at the time of the revision of the volume. (2) Gode considered that the date[6] of the *Vyavahāra-Nirṇaya*

of Varadarāja falls between 1100 CE and 1350 CE. But Kane in his *History of Dharma-Śāstra,* has accepted the date of Varadarāja as falling between 1450 and 1495 CE. While fixing the date of Varadarāja, it appears that Kane has not made even a passing reference[7] to the article of Gode. This is particularly so because Gode's article appeared in the year 1937 and Kane has not taken any pains to refute the position of Gode at the time of the revision of the volume, because of his old age. (3) In the year 1937, Gode wrote a paper[8] to decide the age of the *Kālikā Purāṇa.* He fixed it as before 1000 CE. But in the fifth volume of the *History of Dharma-Śāstra,* Kane refers to the viewpoint of R.C. Hazra. He held that it falls in the 11th century CE. Kane, however, has placed the *Kālikā Purāṇa* as falling before 1000 CE. It thus becomes clear to the readers that Kane has favoured[9] the viewpoint of Gode against the viewpoint of Prof. R.C. Hazra, though it is true that Kane has quoted the viewpoint or the article of Gode on the point of the date of the *Kālikā-Purāna.* Hence a reference to the entry of Gode's article in the fifth volume of the *History of Dharma-Śāstra* became absolutely necessary. It is further evident that this article of Gode published in the year 1937 has not escaped the eagle eye of Kane. (4) There is no chapter on the *Smṛtimuktāphalam* of Vaidyanātha Dikṣita in the first volume of the *History of Dharma-Śāstra.* This gap is slightly filled up by the writer[10] of this note. In the table[11] of the chronolo-gical dates of the authors, Kane has taken 1600 CE as the probable date of the work entitled *Smṛtimuktāphalam.* In the year 1938, Gode wrote a paper[12] on the 'Date of the *Smṛtimuktāphalam* of Vaidyanātha Dīkṣita' and fixed it as after 1686 CE. As there is no mention of Gode's article in Kane's *History of Dharma-Śāstra*, it is possible to take the view that old age did not permit Kane to refer to this view. (5) Gode has further fixed the date of the commentator[13] of the *Bhāgavata Purāṇa*. He contributed a learned paper on the date of Śridhara Svāmī, the commentator of the *Bhāgavata Purāṇa* and fixed it as 1350-1450 CE. As Kane has not discussed the topic of the dates of the commentators of the *Bhāgavata Purāṇa* in the fifth volume of the *History of Dharma-Śāstra*, it is just natural that Gode's valuable paper on this aspect does not find any place in it.

4. The authorship of the work is also a great problem in the *History of Dharma-Śāstra*. In the year 1935, Gode contributed a paper[14] on the Authorship of the Sarasvatī-Vilāsa. In that article, he held that Lolla Lakṣmīdhara was the author of this work. But Kane in his *History of Dharma-Śāstra* came to the conclusion[15] that Pratāparudradeva is the author of the *Sarasvatī Vilāsa.* Kane further held that Lolla Lakṣmīdhara was a braggart and further held that Gode is wrong in holding such a view.

5. The problem of the identity of the authors is very taxing to the mind of the scholars. Kane has tackled this problem in a very scholarly manner in his monumental *History of Dharma-Śāstra*. But he has failed to make a pointed reference to the paper of Gode which was published in the year 1939. Gode wrote a paper[16] on 'Identification of Dalpat Rāi mentioned in Burhan-i-Masir with Dalapati rāya, the author of the Nṛsiṁhaprasāda.' This paper was read by Gode and it was published in the *Proceedings of the Indian History Congress,* (Allahabad 1938). It is rather surprising that kane has not made any reference[17] to this article of Gode in the section on Nṛsiṁhaprasāda, particularly in the second part of the first volume of the *History of Dharma-Śāstra*. Hence the writer of this note takes the reasonable view that there should be an entry of this article in the *History of Dharma-Śāstra*.

6. Sacrifice is again an interesting topic of the *History of Dharma-Śāstra*. Kane has discussed the nature of the Aśvamedha sacrifice in the *History of Dharma-Śāstra* vol.II/II p. 1228 to 1239. He has also mentioned the kings who performed this sacrifice. There is also a reference to the King Savai Jayasing of Amber (1699-1744 CE). This topic is pursued by Gode by contributing four papers[18] on this sacrifice by consulting different sources for different papers. But there is no reference to these four articles of Gode in Kane's *History of Dharma-Śāstra*. Hence it would be proper to say that there should be a special foot-note for the performance of the Aśvamedha sacrifice, indicating the sources of this actual performance of the sacrifice. Hence the revision of the *History of Dharma-Śāstra* by Kane cannot be said to be adequate. For this, due concession will have to be given to Kane's old age.

7. Kane's treatment of the topics in the Dharma-Śāstra is admitted to be thorough and exhaustive. But this view will have to be slightly modified. In some topics, Kane has not given very exhaustive treatment to the topic as compared with the treatment that is given by Gode in his papers. This point can be best expounded by drawing attention to some of the topics of the *History of Dharma-Śāstra*. (1) The importance of the trees in the context of expiations is an admitted fact. But Kane has not at all touched this aspect. Gode has touched the topic[19] of the history of the Akṣayavaṭa (undecaying Banyan tree) at Prayāga and Gayā as revealed by some Sanskrit texts between the first century CE and 900 CE. This is published in the *Annals of the Bhandarkar Oriental Research Institute*. (2) The Divālī festival is discussed by Kane in his *History of Dharma-Śāstra* Vol. VI, p. 194-210. But for this topic, Gode has spent three valuable articles.[20] He has utilised the sources of the *Nīlamata Purāṇa*

(500-800 CE) and Sukhasuptima of *Ādityapurāṇa* for this purpose. This article covers 12 printed pages. Gode has also discussed the history of the Divālī festival in the *Journal of the Bhandarkar Institute,* covering 50 printed pages. These two cases are enought to prove that Gode has done more justice to the topic of the Divālī festival. (3) Kane has discussed the importance[21] of the river Ganges in the *History of Dharma-Śāstra* vol. IV. But Gode has supplied additional matter[22] on the use of the waters of the river Ganges particularly by the Muslim rulers. Here the qualities of the waters of the river Ganges are mentioned and its medical use is pointed out. For this purpose, Gode has consulted many historical and literary sources and this article covers 26 printed pages. This will indicate that in addition to the spiritual quality of the waters of the river Ganges, there are other noteworthy points which are touched by Gode in his articles. (4) The topic of Bhojana (eating food) is also a topic of practical importance. Kane has dealt with this topic in the *History of Dharma-Śāstra* Vol. II/II p. 755-799. But Gode has consulted the manuscript evidence on this topic. (i) He utilised the manuscript[23] of *Bhojana Kutūhala* by Raghunātha belonging to 1625 C.E. for the article in the *Annals of the Bhandarkar Oriental Institute.* For the second article, Gode made the best use[24] of the contemporary evidence of Śāmjī Nāyaka Puṇḍe's manuscript for the *Journal of the University of Bombay*. For the third[25] article, however, Gode used the evidences of the Dhạrma-Sūtras and Gṛhya Sūtras in respect of the Avarānna. This article, he wrote for the *Poona Orientalist.* From these evidences, it would be just reasonable to hold that whatever sources Kane left untouched are consulted by Gode and importance of these sources can hardly be neglected. Hence the value of the manuscript evidence can be said to be correctly understood by Gode. Here it must be stated that in other respects. Kane has utilised manuscripts but on the point of Bhojana, Gode has certainly made valuable addition to the matter of Kane. Here, incidentally, it should be stated that for Bhojana, Gode used the term 'dietics' of the modern language. (5) The topic of Tāmbūla eating betel leaf is also very interesting in the context of the Dharma-Śāstra. Kane has given meagre treatment to this topic in the *History of Dharma-Śāstra* Vol. II/II, p. 734-735, by discussing the ingredients, guṇas and the persons to whom the tāṁbula should not be given. It must be pointed out in this respect that for this topic of Tāmbūla eating, Gode devoted 18 printed pages and wrote three articles[26] for expounding the importance of Tāmbūla eating. (6) Gode has considered the material of the Dharma-Śāstra from the point of view of medical science. In this respect, it is worth noting that Kane in his *History of Dharma-Śāstra* Vol. II/II, p. 885 refers to Ārogyaśālā (Hospital) and relies upon Aparārka's commentary on the Yājñavalkya-Smṛti I.209. Gode has consulted the Sanskrit and non-Sanskrit sources for this topic (from 500 CE to 1900 CE) in the article contributed to the *New Indian Antiquary*. He further laid stress on the Purāṇic extracts quoted by Aparārka for the point of the Hospital system, appointment of a physician, the care to be taken by the nurses etc. This goes to show that Gode has certainly made a laudable improvement upon the topic which is slightly touched by Kane in the *History of Dharma-Śāstra*. Incidentally, it may be remarked that the introduction of the system of Hospital by the French civilisation cannot be regarded as something foreign to the Indian land.

From the above discussion the following legitimate conclusions can be drawn.

1. Gode has contributed to the dates of the works of the Dharma-Śāstra authors, and the commentator of the Purāṇa work.
2. He has shown the chronological position of the works of Nāgojibhaṭṭa.
3. He has given more exhaustive treatment to the topics which are slightly touched or not touched at all by Kane.
4. References to the important articles of Gode in the *History of Dharma-Śāstra*, would have enhanced the value of the work of Kane.
5. Kane's revision of the first volume of the *History of Dharma-Śāstra*, though excellent cannot be treated as thorough and exhaustive, as is generally held by the scholars and this view needs modification.
6. The present writer takes opportunity to suggest that when the question of the revision of Kane's work would arise again the above interesting points raised in this article should be given proper consideration by the authorities of the Bhandarkar Institute.

FOOT NOTES

1. Gode-Vyavahāra Mañjarī–an unknown work of Bhojarāja-in *Dharma-Śāstra-Mimāmsā Prakāśa*, vol. I, p. 10-11.
2. Gode-Date of Nāgojibhaṭṭa–*Journal of Oriental Institute,* Tirupati, vol. I, part-4, p. 1-16.
3. Gode-Chronology of the works of Nāgojibhaṭṭa–*Oriental Thought*–(Nasik), vol. I, No. 1, October 1954, p. 59-62.
4. P.V. Kane–*Vyavahāra mayūkha*–Introduction, p. XX-XXIV, 1926.
5. P.K. Gode–Date of the Prāyaścitta Candrikā–*Journal of Oriental Research,* Madras, vol. XVI, part 1, September 1945, p. 34-36.
6. Gode–Vyavahāra Nirṇaya of Varadarāja–*Mimāṁsa Prakāśa,* vol. III, p. 15-18, (1938).

7. P.V. Kane—*History of Dharma-Śāstra* Vol. I/II, p. 823.
8. Gode—Date of Kālikā Purāṇa—*Journal of Oriental Research,* Madras, vol. X, p. 289-295, (1937).
9. Kane—*History of Dharma-Śāstra*, Vol. V/II, p. 888.
10. S.G. Moghe—Vaidyanātha Dīkṣita—*Journal of Asiatic Society of Bombay,* vol. 60-61 for 1985-86, p. 56-61.
11. Kane—*History of Dharma-Śāstra*, Vol. III.
12. Gode—Date of the Smṛtimuktāphalam of Vaidyanātha Dīkṣita—*Mīmāṁsā Prakāśa,* vol. III, p. 39-42.
13. Gode—Date of Śrīdhara Svāmī, commentator of the Bhāgavata Purāṇa—*Annals of the Bhandarkar Oriental Research Institute,* Poona (*A.B.O.R.I.*) vol. XXX, p. 277-283, 1950.
14. *Ibid.*, Authorship of the Sarasvatī Vilāsa—*Calcutta Oriental Journal,* Vol. II, p. 233-234.
15. Kane—*History of Dharma-Śāstra,* vol. I/II, p. 877-878.
16. Gode—Identification of Dalpat Rāi with Dalapati-Rāya—*Proceedings of Indian History Congress, Allahabad* (1938), p. 313-318.
17. Kane—*History of Dharma-Śāstra*, Vol. I/II, p. 860-868.
18. Gode's four articles on the Aśvamedha sacrifice by Savai Jayasing of Amber—such as published in following journals :
    (i) Some contemporary evidence regarding the Aśvamedha sacrifice performed by Savai Jaising—*Journal of Indian History* (Madras), vol. XV, p. 364-367.
    (ii) Aśvamedha performed by Savai Jayasing of Amber—*Poona Orientalist*, vol. II, p. 166-180 (1937).
    (iii) Description of Aśvamedha performed by Savai Jayasing Jaipur as given in the *Iīśvaravilāsa Kavya* of Kṛṣṇapati—*Mīmāṁsā Prakāśa* vol. II, p. 44-46.
    (iv) Some contemporary evidence regarding the Aśvamedha of Savai Jaising of Amber in a Hindi work of Dietics of 1739 A.D.—*Proceedings of the Indian History Congress,* Aligarh, 1943, p. 378.
19. Gode—The History of Akṣayavaṭa—*A.B.O.R.I.* vol. 38, p. 82-92.
20. Gode—History of Diwāli festival—*A.B.O.R.I.* vol. 38, 1946, p. 216-262, (ii) *Ganganatha Jha Kendriya Sanskrit Vidyapitha,* vol. III, p. 215-216, (iii) *Journal of the Bhāratīya Vidyā Bhavan,* vol. VIII, New Series, Nos. 3-4, p. 53-73. It may be noted here that this last article is based on the evidence of Purāṇa relied upon by Hemādri, in *Caturvargacintāmaṇi.*
21. Kane—*History of Dharma-Śāstra*, vol. IV, p. 585-617.

22. Gode – Use of the Ganges water by Muslim Rulers (from 1300 to 1800), *Annals of the Tirupati Oriental Institute,* vol. I, part 3, p. 1-15.
23. Gode – A topical analysis of Bhojanakutūhala, a work on Dietics composed by Raghunātha between 1675 and 1709 *A.B.O.R.I.* vol. XXII, 1942, p. 254-263.
24. Gode – A contemporary manuscript of Bhojanakutūhala of Raghunātha, belonging to Śāmji Nāyak Puṇḍe between 1650 and 1685 – *Journal of Bombay University,* New Series), vol. XIII, part-2, (September), 1944, p. 40-45.
25. Gode – Studies in the History of Indian Dietics – *Poona Orientalist,* vol. XII, Nos. 1-4 (1948), p. 1-9.
26. For the use of Tāmbūla – (i) Gode – *Poona Orientalist,* vol. XIII, parts 3-4, 1948. p. 10-14. It may be added here that this paper is based on Purāṇic extracts quoted by Aparārka in his commentary on the *Yajñavalkya-Smṛti* 1-209.
   For Tāmbūla (ii) Gode – *Journal of Oriental Institute,* Baroda – vol. 1, p. 275-277. (1952).
   for Tāmbūla – (iii) Gode's paper in *New Indian Antiquary*, vol. VIII, p. 76-79 (1946).

* It may be mentioned here that for this paper, adequate use of the Bibilography of the published writings of P.K. Gode from P.K. Gode's Commemoration Volume brought out in 1960 is made.

This paper is published in the Journal of the Asiatic Society of Bombay, vol. 76 for 2001, p. 78-85.

XV

CONTRIBUTION OF V.N. MANDALIK TO DHARMA-ŚĀTRA

Among the authors who made significant contribution to the studies of the Dharma-Śāstra, a reference will have to be made to the works of Rao Saheb V.N. Mandalik who flourished in the 19th century A.D. Incidentally, it would be worth nothing the progress on the work of Mandalik by the later writers or scholars of Dharma-Śāstra.

V.N. Mandalik deserves the credit of publishing the Manu-Smṛti with seven commentaries of Medhātithi, Kullūka, Rāmcandra, Rāghavānanda, Nandana and others in the year 1886. The text published here is rather corrupt at some places and the printing also is not atrractive to the eyes of the readers. A good improvement upon the work of Mandalik is made by Prof. J.H. Dave, by bringing out the Manu-Smṛti with nine commentaries, adding the commentaries of Bhāruci and Maṇirāma to the seven commentaries published by Mandalik. The twelve chapters of the Manu-Smṛti with nine commentaries become available to the scholars in seven volumes. This is published by the Bhāratīya Vidyā Bhavan, Bombay. Incidentally, it is worth remarking that the edition brought out by Prof. Dave can not be regarded as a critical edition for the simple reason that there is no attempt on the part of the editor to identify the quotations and to note the various readings of the text and the commentaries. However, it must be said that the edition is a good one from the point of view of excellent printing. Hence one will be justified in holding that Prof. Dave's edition is really an improvement upon the edition of Mandalik. Incidentally, it must be noted here that according to Mandalik, the Manu-Smṛti borrowed verses from the Mahābhārata. MM. Dr. P.V. Kane has clarified his standpoint[1] in the History of Dharma-Śāstra vol. I/I, and held that the extant Mahābhārata is later than the extant Manu-Smṛti. It is likely that the Manu Smṛti was recast between 200 B.C. and 200 A.D.

Mandalik also has published the edition of the Vyavahāra Mayūkha of Nīlakaṇṭha for which there is the basis of the Benares lithographed edition of 1879 printed at Kashi Sanskrit yantrālaya. He brought out the edition of the Vyavahāra mayūkha with English translation and critical notes. This is a scholarly edition based on six manuscripts and two printed editions. This edition was not available at the time when Kane decided to bring out the edition of the Vyavahāra Mayūkha in 1926.

In this edition, Mandalik published the pedigree of the Bhaṭṭa family prepared by Kantānātha Bhaṭṭa, the descendant of Kamalākarabhaṭṭa, the famous author of the Nirṇaya Sindhu. This information is supplied to Mandalik by the modern Śāstrins. On this pedigree of the family of Nīlakaṇṭha Bhaṭṭa, given by Mandalik, Kane observes[2] in his introduction to the Vyavahāra Mayūkha that this information is not quite accurate. He adds that MM. Dr. Ganganath Jha was not able to find recently any living descendant of Nīlakaṇṭha in Benares. Mandalik's information suggests that there is no descendant of Gāgābhaṭṭa, Rāmabhaṭṭa lived at Benares near 'Ratnaphātak'.

The English Translation of the Vyavahāra Mayūkha was first published by Borradaile in the year, 1827. On this translation, Mandalik made considerable improvement[3] on the points of accuracy of translation and the presentation. It is said that Mandalik published this translation in the year, 1883.

The interesting point to be noted is that in this English translation of the Vyavahāra-Mayūkha, Mandalik has omitted the translation of the chapter on ordeals. Besides, there is no place for the cases decided during the British regime in the High Courts.

It must also be pointed out here that J.R. Gharpure brought out the English Translation of the Vyavahāra Mayūkha by omitting the translation of the chapter on the ordeals. His translation is regarded as an improvement upon the English Translation by Mandalik. But the point to be noted in connection with the Translation of Gharpure is that it did not give proper consideration[4] to the body of decisions of the High Courts, though this was published in the year 1924.

Kane, therefore, brought out the translation of the Vyavahāra-Mayūkha in the year 1933 by giving due consideration to the decisions on the cases by the High Courts. This translation by Kane is really an improvement upon the earlier editions of Borradaile, Mandalik and Gharpure, not only on the points of accuracy, Mīmāṁsā knowledge, scholarship but also on the point of table of cases decided in the High Courts.

Kane further points out that the translation given by Mandalik is defective at some places. In his notes on the Vyavahāra-Mayūkha, Kane has pointed out the places where Mandalik's translation is obviously wrong and does not carry the proper sense. Mandalik's explanation of the famous

'Daṇḍāpūpikā-Nyāya' is entirely wrong. The Mīmāṁsā term 'Vākyabheda' is not correctly translated by Mandalik. Kane further adds that Mandalik's translation of the word 'Vadha' is not correct. It should be translated as 'Corporal punishment.' In addition to this, the word 'Saundika' translated by Mandalik as 'drunkard' is wrong and it should be translated as a 'liquor seller'. I draw the attention of the readers to the pages of the notes[5] on Vyavahāra Mayūkha and also the pages of the English Translation[6] of the Vyavahāra Mayūkha for the places where Mandalik is proved to be wrong or unconvincing.

Mandalik will be remembered for his book on 'Hindu Law'. The utility of this book is appreciated by Kane in his monumental 'History of Dharma-Śāstra' vol. I/II, p. 923-924. In his 'Book on Hindu Law,' Mandalik has supplied the information of Nandapaṇḍita alias Vināyakapaṇḍita on page No. LXXII. The founder of the family of Nandapaṇḍita was Lakṣmīdhara who was a resident of Bidar and who went to Benares. This information supplied by Mandalik is confirmed by Dr. Jolly and the persons who were ninth in descent from Nandapaṇḍita. Mandalik also gives a detailed generological tree of Nandapaṇḍita. He also gives information about the works of this author. Nandapaṇḍita was described[7] as Dharmādhikārī and was patronised by three kings in different periods of his life. Mandalik further mentions 13 works of Nandapaṇḍita and on page LXXII points out that the Mādhavānanda Kāvya was also written by Nandapaṇḍita. One fails to understand the reason why the geneological tree of Nandapaṇḍita was not given by Kane in his work, when in particular he has given the pedigree of the family of Nāgojibhaṭṭa on Vol. I/II, p. 966 and of Nārāyaṇabhaṭṭa on page 906. From the point of view of symmetrical treatment to the authors, this is rather pinching.

In conclusion, one will have to admit that Mandalik took initiative in publishing the Manu-Smṛti with seven commentaries, brought out the edition of Vyavhāra-Mayūkha of Nīlakaṇṭha, made improvement upon the earlier edition of Borradaile, on the points of accuracy of translation and presentation, took pains in supplying the personal history of Bhaṭṭa family and Nandapaṇḍita, though on the points of translation and spirit of the Dharma-Śāstra passages, technical terms and Mīmāṁsā and popular maxims, his explanation is said to be wrong in the eyes of Kane. His name will be continued to be remembered for his solid contribution to the studies of Dharma-Śāstra and for the progress of his on earlier works and progress on his works by later scholars.

FOOT NOTES

1. This conclusion of Dr. P.V. Kane is noted by Dr. S.G. Moghe-See-Dharma-Śāstra – In Essence, p. 51.
2. P.V. Kane – Vyavahāra-Mayūkha – Introduction p. III-IV. (Published by B.O.R.I., Poona, 1926).
3. P.V. Kane – Vyavahāra-Mayūkha – English Translation – Introduction, p. IX, and preface, p. V.
4. *Ibid.*, P.V.
5. P.V. Kane – Vyavahāra-Mayūkha – Notes, p. 2, 117, 125, 139, 142, 185, 193, 202, 221 and 371.
6. P.V. Kane – Vyavahāra – Mayūkha – English Translation, p. 15, 31, 35, 36, 40, etc.
7. P.V. Kane – History of Dharma-Śāstra, vol. I/II, p. 923-924.

XVI

PRINCIPAL J.R. GHARPURE'S CONTRIBUTION TO THE DOMAIN OF DHARMA-ŚĀSTRA

The probable period of Shri Jagannatha Raghunatha Gharpure is regarded as 1870 to 1962 A.D. He was the Principal of the Law College, Poona. He also practised in the Court for many years. In this paper, therefore, an attempt is made to determine the nature of his contribution. In doing this, care is also taken to show how his work proved to be a tool for the works of later scholars on Dharma-Śāstra.

Before determining the nature of his contribution, it becomes absolutely necessary to know the circumstances in which he worked. It was beginning of the British regime. In the courts, naturally, the importance was given to the Sanskrit texts on Dharma-Śāstra workers such as Vijñāneśvara, Devaṇṇabhaṭṭa, Viśveśvarabhaṭṭa, Bālaṁbhaṭṭa Pāyaguṇḍe and others. The judges during the British regime were quite innocent of the knowledge of the Dharma-Śāstra texts and their translation. This need of the judges and the then practising lawyers was fulfilled by the scholars like V.N. Mandalik, P.V. Kane, J.R. Gharpure and others. Gharpure brought out the critical editions of the old Dharma-Śāstra texts and also introduced English translation of the texts with the addition of the case law and also delivered Memorial lectures in the University of Bombay and Lucknow and rendered good services to the cause of the ancient and Medieval Hindu Law.

Bālaṁbhaṭṭa Pāyagunda has written an exhaustive commentary on the Mitākṣarā of Vijñāneśvara on the Yājñavalkya Smṛti. Gharpure brought out the critical edition of three parts of Bālaṁbhaṭṭa – known as Ācāra, Vyavahāra and the Prāyāscitta Adhyāyas. These three parts, he published under the Hindu Law Text Series as Nos. 5, 6 and 8. For the preparation of these editions, he utilised five manuscripts and these three parts together constitute pages 1275. He wrote a very lengthy introduction for the Ācara Adhyāya covering 37 pages. Further, at the end of each volume, he added the index of the works quoted and also the Mīmāṁsā principles utilised in these works. Kane informs us that Gharpure has also translated the Vyavahāra portion of the Bālaṁbhaṭṭī into English. It must be stated here that this material of Bālaṁbhaṭṭi supplied by Gharpure proved to be very useful to Kane in his History of Dharma-Śāstra not only for contributing a chapter on Bālaṁbhaṭṭa but he also consulted these parts time and again and remarks that this work has given a wider interpretation of the Mitākṣarā of Vijñāneśvarī.

He further edited in the Hindu Law text Series No. 28, the Dvaita Nirṇaya of Śaṅkarabhaṭṭa. When Kane wrote an article on 'The Dvaita Nirṇaya' for the journal of the Annals of the Bhandarkar Oriental Institute, vol. III, p. 67-72 for 1921, he utilised a single manuscript from the Deccan College Collection of Manuscripts No. 109 for 1895-190. Later on Gharpure published the Dvaita Nirṇaya of Śaṅkarabhaṭṭa with the help of 8 manuscripts borrowed from the different quarters of India and also noted the various readings in the foot-notes. In passing, it may be noted that this edition of Gharpure is utilised by the writer of this note for an article on 'Nīla-kaṇṭha's indebtedness to Śaṅkarabhaṭṭa' contributed to the journal of the University of Bombay Nos. 80-81 for 1975-76, p. 37-47. The novel point of this edition is that Gharpure has written an excellent introduction to this work in sanskrit. He has also reproduced here the complete pedigree of the family of Bhaṭṭa from the edition of the Vyavahāra-Mayūkha brought out by V-N. Mandalik. Kane elsewhere points out that this information is not reliable and states the grounds for the same.

Gharpure also took interest in bringing out the critical edition of the Dīpakalikā of Śulapāṇi, a commentary on the Yājñavalkya-Smṛti. This book is published under the Hindu Law Text Series as No. 29, in the year 1939. Here the text covers printed pages 1-110 and the index at the end covers pages 111-120. It may be mentioned here that Gharpure borrowed a copy of the manuscript from the India office catalogue and the other copy of the manuscript he borrowed from the collection of the manuscripts of Mandalik in the Forgusson College. It is further clear that Mandalik borrowed the copy of this manuscript from the collection of Sadashiv Bhataji of Indore and Dhondo Shamrao Garuda copied it for him in the Śake 1801. Gharpure has placed Śūlapāṇi in the latter part of the 14th century and the former part of the 15th century A.D. Kane held in his History of Dharma-Śāstra vol. I/II, that Śūlapāṇi flourished between 1365 and 1445 A.D. The writer of this note has utilised this edition of Śūlapāṇi's commentary for a paper contributed to the Journal of the Oriental Institute, Tirupati, Particularly from the Mīmāṁsā angle.

Gharpure further published the Bhāṣya of Medhātithi

on the Manu-Smṛti, under the Hindu Law Text series as No. 9 in the year 1920. For this edition, he utilised seven manuscripts and gave the text covering pages 1-938 and the index of the authors and quotations covers, p. 101-117. This work just comes to printed 1091 pages. Medhātithi's Bhāṣya is further translated into English by MM. Dr. Ganganath Jha in several volumes. It may be noted here that the copies of these translation are available in the library of the University of Bombay and Khalsa College, Bombay. I am happy to mention here that I have contributed a paper on 'Medhātithi's Contribution to Anuvāda and published this paper in the book'. Studies in Applied Pūrva-Mīmāṁsā. Published by Ajanta Books International, Delhi in 1997. Dr. A.R. Joshi has written a thesis for the Ph.D. Degree on the problem 'Mīmāṁsā in Medhātithi' under the guidance of Dr. S.G. Moghe and is preserved in the library of the University of Bombay in the year 1983. Mr. J.H. Dave also published the Bhāṣya of Medhātithi on the Manu-Smṛti in the nine commentaries on the Manu-Smṛti in seven volumes. Kane utilised Gharpure's edition of medhātithi's Bhāṣya on the Manu-Smṛti for his purpose.

Gharpure deserves credit for publishing the Smṛti-candrikā of Devaṇṇabhaṭṭa under the Hindu Law Text series No. 11 in the year 1918. Here he has published four Kāṇḍas known as Ācara, Vyavahāra, Saṁskāra, and Śrāddha. Here the text including the indexes of the authors covers 918 printed pages. It may be noted here that Āśauca Kāṇḍa of the Smṛticandrikā is not published by Gharpure. But the University of Mysore published this Āśauca Kāṇḍa in the year 1921. Kane utilised Gharpure's edition of the Smṛticandrikā for other Kāṇḍas and for the Āśauca Kāṇḍa, he relied on the Mysore edition. In passing, it may be noted that the writer of this note utilised the edition of Gharpure for discussing the popular and the Mīmāṁsā maxims in the journal of the University of Kerala.

Gharpure developed his interest in the book 'A General Introduction to the Yājñavalkya-Smṛti and the Mitākṣarā under the Hindu Law Text series No. 29 and published it in the year 1944. This scholarly introduction covers 190 pages and this is followed the Sāpiṇḍya by Nāgojibhaṭṭa and Sapiṇḍya Nirṇaya Dīpikā by Śrīdharabhaṭṭa. This work covers pages 68. For writing this section, he has also utilised the other extracts from the works of Madanapārijāta, Smṛti-candrikā, Saṁskāra Mayūkha, Nirṇaya-Sindhu, Dharma-Sindhu, Mitākṣarā, and the commentary of Bālaṁbhaṭṭa on the Mitākṣarā, Dāyabhāga of Jīmutavāhana, Dattaka-Mīmāṁsā by Nandapaṇdita, Dattka-Candrikā by Raghumaṇi and Dvaita-Nirṇaya by Śaṅkarabhaṭṭa. In this part, there is also a general note on the Sāpiṇḍya in English. This note is important and consists of the remarks and also the discussions accompanied by the translation of the portions which are in sanskrit and which have been incorporated in the part two. It is also worthy of note that at the end Gharpure has also added the index indicating the cases under the law. It is tragic that at the time of the revision of the first volume of the History of Dharma-Śāstra, Kane passed over this introduction of Gharpure in silence.

Another big digest publication to the credit of Gharpure is the Smṛtimuktāphalam by Vaidyanātha Dīkṣita. This is in six parts. It deals with Varnāśrama dharma kāṇḍa, Āhnika Kāṇda, Āśauca Kāṇda, Śrāddha Kāṇḍa, Kāla-Kāṇḍa and the Prāyaścitta Kāṇḍa. These six parts together constitute printed 944 pages and this is followed by the lengthy index of the works quoted in this work and this covers pages 945 to 1027. It must be mentioned here that for preparing this edition, he consulted the manuscripts of the India office, Madras, collection of Shri Dravid at Satpura and the copy secured by Raobahaddur Bhikaji Vyankatesha Dravid and one that is already printed at Chidambaram in the year 1908 and Kumbhakoṇam as noted by Kane in his History of Dharma-Śāstra, vol. I/II, p. 1152-53. Gharpure has noted the various readings in the foot-notes. Kane takes this work as belonging to the 1600 A.D. P.K. Gode, however, has fixed the date of this work as 1680 A.D. The writer of this note also agrees with Gode on this point. It must be incidentally mentioned here that there is no chapter on this digest in Kane's History of Dharma-Śāstra, inspite of the review on Kane's work at the hands of Kuppuswami Śāstri of Madras. Possibly old age might be the reason for the omission of this work. Though it is true that Kane has not written a chapter on this digest, Kane has made ample use of this digest in his volumes of History of Dharma-Śāstras, as alredy noted by the writer of this note. In passing, it may be added that right from the year 1937 to 1940, Gharpure published the six parts of this digest.

The commentary entitled 'Subodhinī' written by Viśveśvarabhaṭṭa on the Mitākṣarā of Vijñāneśvara on the Yajñavalkya-Smṛti, was also published by Gharpure in the years 1912-1914. This is published under the Hindu Law Text Series No. 3. This printed edition contains 110 pages and index of two pages. Kane in his History of Dharma-Śāstras, vol. I/II, p. 799 observes that the commentary Subodhinī is not a word to word commentary on the Mitākṣarā but it is very learned and explains the important passages. Kane further informs us that this portion on the Vyavahāra aspect of the Mitākṣarā is translated into English by Gharpure and the same is also translated by S.S. Setlur. The writer of this note is very happy to mention here that he wrote a learned paper on Subodhinī for the Journal of the Bhāratīya Vidyā Bhavan, Bombay. Hence the importance of this work of

Viśveśvarabhaṭṭa can hardly be gainsaid. In the History of Dharma-Śāstras, Kane mentions five works bearing the name 'Subodhinī' which have nothing to do with the present work as such.

Gharpure's role as the translator of the three Adhyāyas of the Yājñavalkya-Smṛti with the commentaries of Mitākṣarā, Vīramitrodaya and Dīpakalikā is indeed very great. The translation of all these Adhyāyas, in all, covers printed pages 2030. All these translations are published by Gharpure under the Hindu Law Text Series. In passing, it may also be noted that the commentary of Vīramitrodaya and Śūlapāṇi is also utilised by the writer of this note from the point of view of Mīmāṁsā angle.

Gharpure also brought out the edition of the twelve Mayūkhas of Nīlakaṇṭha. This is a big digest and for every edition he consulted several manuscripts and noted the various readings in the foot-note. It is further worthy of mention that Gharpure has also translated the Vyavahāra-Mayūkha of Nīlakaṇṭha into English. Kane states that generally he follows the translation of V.N. Mandalik. But from the point of quality he (Gharpure) has certainly made a good improvement upon the translation of the Vyavahāra Mayūkha by Mandalik. But the only deficiency in Gharpure's edition of the translation is that it has not covered the case law during the British regime.

Another significant contribution of Gharpure lies in his extension lectures. He delivered lecturers under Sir Lallubhai A. Shah lecture series in the year 1949 under the auspices of the University of Bombay on the problem 'Rights of widows under Hindu Law'. These lectures are also published by the University of Bombay. These lectures are now out of print.

He also brought out a book on 'Hindu Law' which went through the fourth impression. In this book, he has revised and enlarged with a map of India, indicating several territorial jurisdictions of the different schools of Hindu Law and also added at the end the index of the Mīmāṁsā rules of interpretation and the doctrine of Sāpiṇḍya.

Gharpure's contribution to the comparative study of the Hindu Law with Roman Law is indeed supreme. Here he has given comparative references to the parallel provisions in the Hindu law and other systems of law. In comparison with the treatment given by Gharpure, Kane's treatment to the introduction of the Kātyāyana-Smṛti-Sāroddhāra, will have to be treated as very meagre.

It must be mentioned in this context that Gharpure also delivered a series of lectures in the University of Lucknow under Dr. Mukerjee lecture series No. 4.

Now I take this opportunity to bring to light some important points of the writings of Gharpure with a particular reference to his translation of the Smṛticandrikā of Devaṇṇa-bhaṭṭa in English. The importance of this contribution seems to have been ignored by Kane in his monumental work. Hence some important observations on his treatment will not be out of place in this place.

It should be noted that though Gharpure has rendered English rendering of the Smṛticandrikā, he has also supplied some portion to his book from the Mysore edition of the Smṛti and also added the translation of the same in his English rendering. Secondly, his notes on mythological personalities or the technical terms of the Dharma-Śāstras like Aṇi Māṇḍavya and Vipra are at once illuminating. Thirdly, in his foot-note to the translation of the Smṛticandrika, he brings to light the different interpretations of the manu-Smṛti VIII-153. Fourthly, he cleverly notes the difference between yajña and Sattra in his notes on the Smṛticandrikā. Fifthly, he takes care to explain the Mīmāṁsā rules of Interpretation and also the Sūtras of Pāṇini in his notes to the translation of the work. Sixthly, for the interpretation of the stananzas in the Nārada-Smṛti, Gharpure utilised the source of the commen-tary of Asahāya at some places. He also notes the difference of opinion between the author of the Smṛticandrīka and the author of the Mitākṣarā, and Nīlakaṇṭha. He has not failed to note the misinterpretation of the passage offered by Devaṇṇabhaṭṭa. He has taken care to point out how the a word in the Vedic source is differently interpreted by Devaṇṇa-bhaṭṭa and Sāyaṇācārya. In his foot-notes, he has also high-lighted the court decisions passed on the basis of the text of the Smṛticandrikā of Devaṇṇabhaṭṭa. He has also pointed out the novel view of the Smṛti-Candrikā in the interpretation of the text. He takes care to suggest better reading of the stanza so as to improve the meaning of the text. In his foot-notes, he has given at some places, the translation of the passages as offered by Dr. Jolly. At one place, he has noted the similarities between the Hindu law and Burmese law, and Roman law. He has consulted a lot of authorities for this edition like the works of Medhātithi, Jīmūtavāhana, Viśveśvarabhaṭṭa, Bhāruci, Pratāparudra'ṣ Sarasvatī vilāsa. One is here tempted to say that Gharpure has moved no stone unturned to make the work as best as he could and for which no praise would be too high.

In conclusion, Gharpure's contribution to the Dharma-Śāstra lies in his attempt at producing the critical editions of the several Dharma-Śāstra texts in consultation with several manuscripts, translations of the scientific texts of Dharma-Śāstra like Yājñavalkya-Smṛti with commentaries, Smṛti-candrikā, Vyvahāra Portion of the Bālaṁbhaṭṭi and Subodhinī, his independent lecture series at different places on the different aspects of Hindu law, comparative study of the Hindu law with other systems of law, his improvement upon the work of Kane on the point of Dvaita Nirṇaya of Śaṅkara-bhaṭṭa, his excellent sanskrit introduction to some works and other important points brought to light by the writer of this note, will have to be regarded as his enduring contribution to Dharma-Śāstra, particularly during the British regime. One will have to admit that he was indeed an indefatiguable scholar of Dharma-Śāstra in the words of Dr. P.V. Kane and it is he who provided food to the judges, lawyers and scholars like Kane and others for the further studies of the Dharma-Śāstra texts. This fact can hardly be gainsaid in the case of Gharpure and herein lies his true greatness.

FOOT NOTES

1. S.G. Moghe – Śūlapāṇi – as the Interpreter of the Yājñavalkya-Smṛti in Journal of Oriental Institute, Tirupati vol.
2. S.G. Moghe – Studies in Applied Pūrva – Mīmāṁsā, p. 42-48 published by Ajanta Books International, Delhi – 1998.
3. S.G. Moghe – The use of the Mimāṁsā Maxims in the Smṛti-Candrikā of Devaṇṇabhaṭṭa – Journal of the Oriental Institute and Manuscripts Library, Kerala, vol. XVIII, No. 4.

   (2) The use of the Mīmāṁsā maxims in the Smṛticandrika of Devaṇṇabhaṭṭa – *Ibid*, vol. XIX, Part – II, p. I-XIII.

   (3) The use of the Mīmāṁsā and Popular Maxims in the Smṛticandrikā of Devaṇṇabhaṭṭa, vol. XX, part-I, p. I-XIV.
4. P.K. Gode – Mīmāṁsa Prakāśa, vol. III, p. 39-42.
5. S.G. Moghe – A few observations on Subodhinī of Viśveśvara-bhaṭṭa on the Mitākṣarā of Vijñāneśvara – Bhāratīya Vidyā, vol. XXXVIII, Nos. 1-4 for 1978, p. 36-41.
6. J.R. Gharpure – Smṛti-Candrikā—English Translation, p. 267, ft. No. 1, and also p. 312 foot No. 3.
7. *Ibid.*, p. 44, for Aṇi Māṇḍavya and p. 26 for the term Vipra in the light of the Atri Saṁhitā verses 373-384.
8. *Ibid.*, p. 293.
9. *Ibid.*, p. 355.

10. *Ibid.*, p. 378, 500, 590, 25, 29 and 72.
11. *Ibid.*, p. 57, 94, 179, 228, 241, 322, 518 etc.
12. *Ibid.*, p. 536, 563.
13. *Ibid.*, p. 546, foot note No. 4.
14. *Ibid.*, p. 552.
15. *Ibid.*, p. 591, 600, 605, 606, 608, 609 and 612.
16. Devaṇṇabhaṭṭa rules out Marriage as a Saṁskāra-See, *Ibid.*, p. 576, foot note No. 4.
17. *Ibid.*, p. 81.
18. *Ibid.*, p. 228, 241, 1 and 26, 375, 507 etc.

XVII

A NOTE ON VIPRA*

Among the Smṛtikāras, it is Atri who has contributed a novel thought to this term Vipra and has shown connection with other castes rather significantly. Devala also has introduced somewhat similar types of Brāhmaṇas and it would be worth our while to compare the thoughts presented by these two smṛtikāras with the background of the castes presented by Kane in his monumental History of Dharma-Śāstra.

Generally it is held that a person, when born, is treated as a Śūdra, by the Saṁskāras on him, he becomes a Vipra and when he acquires the knowledge of the lores, he is known as Śrotriya.

In dealing with these two smṛtikāras and the picture presented by Kane, the discussion will pertain to the particular type of a brahman immediately.

In the Atri Saṁhitā, we have the stanza Nos. 373 to 382 describing the ten varieties. Devala Smṛti quoted by Aparārka on the Yājñavalkya-Smṛti also gives the similar description on page 284 in particular, and also introdcues some novel thought as compared with Atri.

There are ten types of brāhmaṇas (Vipras) like a god,

muni, dvija, king, vaiśya, śūdra, niṣadaka, paśu, mleccha and a cāṇḍāla.

Among the ten varieties of Vipras, Atri holds that one who daily performs sandhyā, bath, offers oblations into fire, worships the gods, worships a guest and performs the Vaiśvadeva rite is known as Deva-brāhmaṇa. The Vaikhānasa Gṛhya Sūtra I.1 (quoted by Kane in History of Dharma-Śāstra vol. II/I, p. 131) states that he is known as Brāhmaṇa who is initiated and who studies the Gāyatrī mantra. Here in calling a Vipra as brahmana, the details mentioned by Atri, are dropped.

In the stanza No. 375, Atri states[1] that one who is well engaged in Śāka, patra (leaves), fruits, roots and always interested in staying in the forest, and busily engaged in daily performing the Śrāddha, such a Vipra is known as Muni. As opposed to this, Devala holds that he is known as muni who has withdrawn his interest from the worldly matters, who knows all the philosophical truth, who is devoid of desires and anger, who is bent upon meditation, who is passive in doing any activity, who is well controlled and who looks upon the clod of clay and gold with an eye of equality, is known as Muni. If these two descriptions offered by the two smṛtikāras are read together, one would notice that these descriptions are complementary to each and in this respect, one will have to admit that both the smṛtikāras have contributed differently to the thought development of the term muni as such.

In the Stanza No. 376, Atri states that a vipra is known as dvija who always studies vedānta, gives up all the attachment, and engages himself in the thought of the Sāmkhya and yoga (path of knowledge and yoga). But in the stanza No. 141 of the Atri Saṁhitā, the thought that is generally connected with dvija is expressed. From this, it is further clear that Atri has slightly modified the concept of dvija in the own writing.

In the Stanza No. 377, Atri states that a Vipra is known as a Kṣatriya Vipra who has killed archers at the front of the battle-field and who has, at the beginning, also conquerred all the persons. Against this view of Atri, it may be pointed out that the Āpastaṁba Dharma-Śāstra I.10.29.7, does not allow a brāhmaṇa to become a kṣatriya. The Gautama Dharma-Sūtra VII.6 takes the moderate view that at the time of distress, a brāhmaṇa can become a kṣatriya i.e., he can take the weapon in his hands. Kane relies[2] on the Pāṇini's Sūtra V.2.71 and the bhāṣya of Patañjali on the same and states that a brāhmaṇa who takes up the weapon in his hands is known as Brāhmaṇaka. In the Mahābhārata, we have the famous example of Droṇa (a brāhmaṇa) who takes the weapon in his hand and fights on the battle-field. It may be noted in passing that only at the time of distress, a brāhmaṇa is allowed to change the profession but when the circumstances become normal, he should assume the duties of his original caste.

In the stanza No. 378, Atri points out that a brāhmaṇa is known as a Vaiśya who is engaged in the act of agriculture, guards the cows, and who has undertaken the activity of the commercial nature. Here it may be pointed out that the Manusmṛti III.152 disallows a brāhmaṇa living his livelihood by the commercial activities.

In the Stanza No. 379, Atri specifically states that a brāhmaṇa is known as a Śūdra who makes the sale of wine and meat and kusuṁbha mixed with the juice of lak and milk and sarpiṣ. As against this stand-point of Atri, the Manu Smṛti X.92 states that by selling the meat, salt and other things, a brahmana falls from his caste and is reduced to the position of a Śūdra. Here the stress is given on the activity for selling the forbidden things for three days. As a result, the immediate fall of a brāhmaṇa takes place. This view of the Manu-Smṛti is in agreement with the view of the Baudhāyana Dharma-Śutra I.5.95. The Manu-Smṛti VIII.102 further holds that such brāhmaṇas should be given the treatment of the Śūdras.

The stanza No. 380 of Atri states[3] that a vipra known as Niṣāda who behaves like a thief, commits robbery, who is a back-biter, who troubles others and who is always of the greedy nature with respect to the fish and meat. Here it should be noted that in the History of Dharma-Śāstra vol. II/I, p. 86-87, Kane states that Niṣāda is the offspring of a brāhmaṇa husband and a Śūdra wife. Besides Niṣāda is treated as equal to Pāraśava. In the Manu-Smṛti X.8, it is said that Niṣāda is also known as Pāraśava. From this, it becomes clear that Atri treats a Vipra as a niṣāda not on the basis of his marriage activity but on the basis of his vices or bad activities and this is certainly a different view from the Manu-Smṛti.

In the Stanza No. 381, Atri points out that one who does not know the nature of brahman, but who is simply proud of his sacred thread, is known as a beast. Devala holds[4] that he is a nominal brahmana (mātra) who is only born in the family of a brāhmaṇa, but has not studied any part of the Veda nor does he perform any actions suitable to the brāhmaṇas. One will be right in inferring that Atri's concept of a brāhmaṇa being a beast comes near to Devala's concept of a nominal brāhmaṇa.

In the stanza No. 382, Atri expresses[5] the view that a Vipra who obstructs the functioning of the wells, tanks and gardens meant for the pleasure of public, without any feeling of any anvil of doubt, is to be known as Mleccha. Kane in his History of Dharma-Śāstra, vol. II/I, refers to the Sūta Saṁhitā, according to which, the Mleccha is nothing but the offspring of the clandestine union of a brāhmaṇa woman and a Kṣatriya male. It may be noted here that the other Smṛtikāras like the Manu-Smṛti IX.280 and the Yājñavalkya-Smṛti II.240, 245 and 228 lay down punishment for the obstructive activities of this kind. From these other references, it becomes evident that Atri has treated a Vipra as a Mleccha on the ground of his obstructive activities and not on the basis of the clandestine union of a brāhmaṇa woman and a Vaiśya male.

Atri treats that Vipra as a Cāṇḍāla particularly in the stanza No. 382 by showing[6] that he is a fool, devoid of prescribed rites, and beyond the pale of all Dharma and particularly cruel. This behaviour of a Vipra reduces him to the position of a Cāṇḍāla. From Kane's History of Dharma-Śāstra, vol. II/I, p. 81-82, it is clear that a reference to the Cāṇḍala also occurs in the Mahābhārata – Anuśāsana Parvan 29.17. It is a case of Pratiloma marriage. Mātanga is actually a son born of a brāhmaṇa woman and a barber husband. Secondly, it is also held that it is a case of offspring of a Śūdra from the Brāhmaṇa woman. Thirdly, it is held that it is an offspring of a union with a sagotra girl.

Devala, However, has introduced[7] the categories of Anūcāna, bhrūṇa, ṛṣikalpa and ṛṣi on the basis of different qualities. As Kane has discussed the nature of these in the History of Dharma-Śāstra, vol. II/I, p. 1312, it is better to pass over this point in Silence.

In conclusion, one will be right in holding that Atri has made a significant contribution to the thought of the Dharma-Śāstra literature that a brāhmaṇa is reduced to the different castes in view of his particular activities and particular vices and this thought has nothing to do with the intermixture of castes which gave rise to the other castes. Secondly, some thoughts of Atri also agree with the views of Devala. Thirdly,

Atri here does not refer to the punishments imposed on the brāhmaṇas for these activities but these are laid down by other Smṛtikāras. Devala has also contributed to the categories of brāhmaṇas mentioned above and these are certainly different from the categories indicated by Atri.

FOOT NOTES

* For the present paper, the Atri Saṁhitā as published in the collection of the Smṛtis by the Ānandāśrama Sanskrit Series as No. 48, in the year 1929 is utilised.

1. शाके पत्रे फले मूले वनवासे सदा रत:।
   निरतोऽहरह: श्राद्धे स विप्रो मुनिरुच्यते।।
   Atri-Saṁhitā, St.No. 375.
2. P.V. Kane – History of Dharma-Śāstra, vol. II/I, p. 122.
3. चोरश्च तस्करश्चैव सूचको दंशकस्तथा।
   मत्स्यमांसे सदा लुब्धो स विप्रो निषाद उच्यते।।
   Atri Saṁhitā stanza No. 380.
4. Aparārka on the Yājñavalkya-Smṛti p. 284.
5. वापीकूपतडागानामारामस्य सर:सुच।
   नि:शंकं रोधकश्चैव स विप्रो म्लेच्छ उच्यते।।
   Atri Saṁhitā stanza No. 382.
6. क्रियाहीनश्च मूर्खश्च सर्वधर्मविपर्जित:।
   निर्दय: सर्वभूतेषु विप्रश्चांडाल उच्यते।।
   Atri Saṁhitā stanza, No. 383.
7. Aparārka on the Yajñavalkya-Smṛti, pp. 284-285.

XVIII

CONTRIBUTION OF MAHARASHTRA TO DHARMA-ŚĀSTRA-I

This paper is based on the descriptive catalogue of the sanskrit manuscripts under Bhadkamkar Collection of manuscripts presented by Prof. H.D. Velankar, to the University of Bombay. This catalogue is prepared by Prof. G.V. Devasthali, under the supervision of Prof. Velankar and published in the year, 1944. It may be noted here that this collection of the manuscripts was presented by Prof. Velankar, in the memory of his teacher professor H.M. Bhadkamkar of the Wilson College, Bombay.

It is an admitted fact that for writing the history of any language, it is absolutely necessary to consult the Descriptive Catalogues of the manuscripts prepared by the scholars like Eggeling, Winternitz, Jacobi, Dr. Jolly, Dr. Stein and the modern scholars like Prof. Velankar, Prof, Devasthali and Hara Datta Sharma and others.

In presenting this matter to the scholarly world, I have kept in mind the view that the authors whose names are less known and whose works have not seen the light of the day, should be given preference in this article. In this respect also, I have to restrict myself to the contribution of the writers on Dharma-Śāstra, particularly from the Mahārāshtra.

Incidentally, an attempt is also made in this paper to point out if there is any other copy of the manuscript in the other research Institute in Mahārāshtra or not. Besides, it is also necessary to note in this context whether MM. Dr. P.V. Kane has mentioned the particular manuscript in his list of the works and authors of Dharma-Śāstra particularly published in the History of Dharma-Śāstra, vol. I/II.

In the Bhadkamkar collection of manuscripts, there is a manuscript entitled 'Antyeṣṭipaddhati by Keśava Ananta-bhaṭṭa Laugākṣi of Puṇyastaṁbha. Punyastambha is identified with Puṇatambe in the state of Maharashtra. This manuscript bears No. 963. It may be added here that another copy of this manuscript is available in the Bhandarkar Oriental Research Institute, Poona. In the catalogue of the manuscripts of Dharma-Śāstra prepared by H.D. Sharma in the vol. VII/I, this manuscript bears No. 34. This manuscript discusses at length the funeral rites to be performed in the case of a dead person. Kane has mentioned this manuscript in his History of Dharma-Śāstra, vol. I/II, p. 991.

There is a manuscript entitled 'Āhnika' by the author Lakṣmīdhara Lālibhaṭṭa of Kauṇḍinya Gotra. This manuscript gives information about the daily duties of a person. This work is written on the confluence of the rivers Kṛṣṇā and Veṇī, near Pavanī in Nagpur. This manuscript bears No. 994. Incidentally, it may be noted that Kane has not given entry to this manuscript in his work.

We have further the benefit of a good manuscript called 'Gotrapravara-nirṇaya' by Jīvadeva, the son of Āpadeva. This manuscript bears No. 1025. This work seems to have been written at about 1690 A.D. The special view of this manuscript is that the gotra of a mother is to be avoided by the Mādhyandinas for the marriage ceremony. This manuscript describes at good length the nature of Gotra and Pravara which is important for the purpose of marriage. The Dharma-Śāstra authors generally favour the view that the marriage should be settled between the two persons who do not belong to the same Gotra. However, this view is neglected in the regular practice of the people in Maharashtra particularly in the 20th century. Kane has made an entry of this manuscript on p. 1023 of his above mentioned work.

We have here a case of the manuscript written by the author and copied by another person for him. Rāmacandra-bhaṭṭa Mālavaṇakar wrote the manuscript known as 'Dānakhaṇḍa and this was copied by Rāmacandra Lele. The two names 'Mālavaṇakar and Lele suggest that they have come from the region of Mahārāshtra. This manuscript bears no. 1073. There is no entry of this manuscript in Kane's work. It may be noted only incidentally that there is a lot of literature on the Dāna aspect of Dharma-Śāstra. Hemādri has written the Dana-Khaṇḍa and Nīlakaṇṭha has written the Dāna-Mayūkha.

Mr. Vasudeo Chitale is another person from Chiplon, who is the author of Prayoga-Ratnamālā. In this work, he quotes the Nirṇaya-Sindhu of Kamalākarabhaṭṭa who wrote it in the year 1612 A.D. as pointed out by Kane. He is a Chitpāvana Brāhmaṇa but Peterson made a mistake in taking Chitpāvana as the surname of the author as noted by Devasthali. Since Mr. Chitale quotes kamalākarabhaṭṭa, the probable date of this manuscript falls between 1680 and 1760 A.D. Kane States[2] that this work is also known as Vāsudevī. This work deals with the establishment of the images of the gods like Viṣṇu and others.

It is further evident that some digest works and the

Purāṇas have also given inspiration to the other authors to present the subjeet. Nṛhari Paṇḍharapūra has written Prasāda-Pratiṣṭhā. This is particularly based on the Pratiṣṭhā Mayūkha of Nīlakaṇṭha and the Matsya Purāṇa as noted by the compiler Devasthali. Kane in his work, p. 1077 states that this manuscript is copied in the sake 1714 i.e., 1792-93 A.D. In the history of Dharma-Śāstra, there is a good deal of literature on the Pratiṣṭhā aspect of the Dharma-Śāstra.

It is further clear that some persons were bent upon preparing the abridged edition of the larger works on the Dharma-Śāstra. There is a famous work entitled 'Puruṣārtha-Cintāmaṇi' written by Viṣṇubhaṭṭa Āṭhavale. Kane points out that this work is printed by Nirṇaya Sagara press, Bombay and there is a manuscript of this work in the library of the Oriental Institute, Baroda and this bears No. 1666. This manuscript is dated sake 1706, i.e., 1784-85 A.D. Vīreśvara-bhaṭṭa Godbole prepared the manuscript 'Laghucintāmaṇi' which is an abridged edition of the larger work Puruṣārtha-Cintāmani. The original work deals with Kāla, Saṁskāra and other aspects of Dharma-Śāstra. This is particularly based on the works of Hemādri and Mādhavācārya who is the author of Kāla-Mādhava. Hence the small edition of Godbole is meant for the simplification of the subject for the common run of people. The Laghucintāmaṇi manuscript bears No. 1140.

The tonsure ceremony in the case of a widow is a hotly discussed topic in the 20th century. In a court matter, the matter was argued on the basis of the Mīmāṁsā rules of interpretation, and Kane succeeded in the matter and the tonsue ceremony was avoided in the case of a widow. Mr. Vināyaka Mangeśa Devulkar wrote a manuscript on the topic 'Tonsure ceremony' for a widow. It is worth noting that he has quoted the work 'Vrata-Rāja' and states that a widow should first perform the Arundhatī Vrati[3] for the destruction of the sins of a birth and then perform this Vrata as such. This manuscript bears No. 1144. Kane seems to have neglected this manuscript. Incidentally, it may be added here that MM. Vasudeoshastri Abhaynkar, the learned Sanskrit Pundit of Poona, held the view that a widow must undergo the tonsue ceremony, because the sins committed by a person stick to his hair. This view he has expressed in the Sanskrit digest work 'Dharma-Tattva-Nirṇaya Pariśiṣṭam.

In conclusion, one will have to admit that the contribution to the Dharma-Śāstra thoughts and topics is made by the writers of Maharashtra either by bringing out an abridged edition of the larger work, or writing under the influence of established writers or for helping the people to solve the problems of tongure ceremony or Gotra-pravarana etc. It is further evident that Kane generally mentions the manuscripts on the subject but at times some manuscripts have escaped his eagle eye.

FOOT NOTES

1. P.V. Kane–History of Dharma-Śāstra, vol. I/II, p. 104.
2. *Ibid.*, p. 1071
3. P.V. Kane–History of Dharma-Śāstra, vol. V/I, p. 261 gives us information of Arundhatī Vrata.
4. Vasudeoshatri Abhyankar-Dharma-Tattva-Nirṇaya-Pariśiṣṭam, pp. 51-54.
   (Anandāśrama Sanskrit Series No. 98, Poona, 1935)

XIX

CONTRIBUTION OF MAHARASHTRA TO DHARMA-ŚĀSTRA-II

This is the second instalment on the above topic. This is based on the Descriptive Catalogue of the Sanskrit Manuscripts particularly Dharma-Śāstra manuscripts preserved in the Bhandarkar Oriental Institute, Pune, and prepared by Dr. Haradatta Sharma, and published in the year 1975. For the purpose of this paper in this volume, I have concentrated on the vol. VII/I prepared by Dr. Har Datta Sharma.

There is a manuscript entitled 'Dattārka' written by Dādā Karajgī, the son of Mādhava Nṛsiṁha Karajgī. In this work, the author quotes Nirṇaya-sindhu and Mayūkhas of Nilakaṇṭha. He was a pupil of Kṛṣṇācārya and stayed at Nasik on the bank of the river Godāvarī. This manuscript is copied in Sake 1691 i.e., 1769 A.D. This author belongs to the Vasiṣṭha Gotra and this manuscript bears No. 550. It must be stated here that the subject matter of this manuscript is adoption.

Bāḷakṛṣṇa Devabhaṭṭa Dīkṣita of Paḷaniṭakar family wrote a manuscript entitled 'Datta-Siddhānta mañjarī'. This manuscript bears No. 549. The author was the Guru of Advaitānanda. Kane in his History of Dharma-Śāstra, vol. III has noted that Bāḷakṛṣṇa held that when any person is having the sons who are dumb, blind or lame, then he can adopt a son. This is a novel view contributed by the author of this manuscript to the thought development of the Dharma-Śāstra aspect of Adoption.

Rāghavabhaṭṭa wrote the work 'Tithinirṇayoddhāra' and this was copied by R.G. Thombare from Koparagrama i.e., karpūragrāma in Sanskrit. This author specifically makes a mention of Kamalākarabhaṭṭa and Nīlakaṇṭha and hence this work must be placed later than 1640 A.D. There are two copies of this manuscript. This work is also printed at Bombay as noted by Kane on page 1034 of his History of Dharma-Śāstra vol. I/II. Further, this manuscript is copied in the Śake 1681 i.e., 1759 A.D. This work is also known as Tithinirṇaya or Tithisāra – Saṁgraha.

There is a manuscript known as Kuṇḍamārtaṇḍa with the commentary by Govinda Gadādhara i.e., Govinda Daivajña. This author belongs to the Mādhyandina branch of the Veda. This author wrote the work at Pallīpattana otherwise known as Pālī in the Bhora State. This manuscript is copied by Raghunātha Somaṇa in 1693 A.D. and bears the No. 313.

There is another work 'Kuṇḍamaṅḍapasiddhi with the Vivṛtti commentary by Viṭṭhala Dīkṣita of Kṛṣṇātri-gotra from Saṅgameśvara in the Ahamedanagar district. This manuscript is copied in the Śake 1541 i.e., 1619-20 A.D. This manuscript bears No. 311.

One will also come across the manuscript of the Kuṇḍamaṅḍapasiddhi with the commentary by Mahadeva Pathaka Saptarṣi. This manuscript bears No. 310. He seems to be the resident of Khetakagrama. Kane is silent about this manuscript in his monumental work of the History of Dharma-Śāstra.

There is further a good manuscript on the topic of satī i.e., Anumaraṇapradīpa by Gauriśa, the son of Nāyaka-Paṇḍit. His grand-father Damodarabhaṭṭa was born in maharashtra, on the bank of a holy river in Yajñabhūmi. But later on he settled at Benares. In this work of Anumaraṇa-pradīpa, there are references to Śūlapāṇi, Madanapārijāta and Anumaraṇaviveka. As this work is written 67 years after the death of Akbar the muslim king, the probable date of this work comes to 1609 A.D. which is apparently a Printing mistake on the part of Sharma. It may be noted here that there are two copies of this manuscript in the library.

On the Ācāra aspect of the Dharma-Śāstra, Sadāśiva-Śarmā Daśaputra (Dasaputre?) seems to have written the Ācāra-Smṛti candrikā. This manuscript bears No. 73 and Kane has also mentioned this work in his work at p. 995.

On the Dharma-Śāstra aspect of impurity due to birth and death, there is a manuscript named 'Āśauca-Nirṇaya by Mr. Tryambaka Raghunātha son of Nārāyaṇa. He belongs to the Āngirasa Gotra. As he has mentioned the works Nirṇaya-Sindhu and quoted the author Nāgojibhaṭṭa, it is probable that he belongs to about 1760 A.D. This manuscript bears No. 108. Incidentally, it may be added that there are six manuscripts of this work in the library of the Bhandarkar Institute. Kane mentions that this work is printed by the Nirṇaya-Sāgara Press, Bombay.

On the daily duties of a man, there is another manuscript known as Āhnika-Paddhati by Śivarāma Viśrāma Śukla. This work is concerned with the daily duties of the Chāndogas. Kane in his History of Dharma-Śāstra, vol. I/II. p. 1003 points out that this work Āhnika-Saṁksepa by Śivarāma is actually an abridged edition of Vaidyanātha's Āhnika. In passing, it may be stated here that in the Dharma-Śāstra, there are three works bearing the title Āhnika Paddhati. The present work bears No. 166.

On the thread ceremony, there is a manuscript Upanayana-Paddhati written by Ṛṣibhaṭṭa. This is copied by Rāmacandra Ganesh Thombare of Karpūra-grama i.e. Koparagaon. This manuscript is copied in Śake 1698 and bear No. 185. It is surprising that Kane is silent about this manuscript. Incidentally, attention may be drawn to the two works – Upanayana-paddhati written by Rāmadatta for the followers of Vājasaneyi Saṁhitā and another by Viśvanātha Dīkṣita. Kane has made these two entries on page 1004 of his work.

The above discussion will lead one to the pointed conclusion that the writers from the Maharashtra have made contribution to the different aspects of Dharma-Śāstra by writing commentaries or copying the manuscript or making the abridged edition of the bigger works or dealing with the smallest topic of the Dharma-Śāstra. Kane has also helped for identifying the places.

XX

A NOTE ON USHA JAIN'S ARTICLE THE CUSTOM OF BITING GRASS IN RETOSPECT

I have read with keen interest the above aritcle of the said volume and have to make following important observations :

(i) It seems that Usha Jain has copied verbatim (with perhaps some changes here and there in language) the contents of the article on 'References to the custom of holding grass in the mouth as a token of surrender in Indian and foreign sources' written by Dr. P.K. Gode, the then curator of the Bhandarkar Oriental Research Institute, Poona-4 and particularly published in *Indian Culture,* Volume XV for July 1948 – July 1949 which is regarded as *Prof. B.M. Barua felicitation volume*. Here the article of Dr. P.K. Gode covers p. 60-65.

(ii) Usha Jain seems to have deliberately dropped the name of Dr. Gode and also the source from the Marathi language and the *Dūta-Vākya* of Bhāsa (possibly on account of her total ignorance of correctly understanting these evidences) or has made an attempt to show that her article partakes of originality.

(iii) As compared with the exhaustive article of Dr. Gode, there is no novelty in the article of Usha Jain.

(iv) Usha Jain should have written an article of this kind either to support the contentions of Dr. Gode or to controvert the same with some more reliable evidence. One also wonders why Usha jain has observed studied silence on the article of Dr. Gode, whose material she has borrowed without any acknowledgment.

(v) If at all, any novelty is to be traced in Usha Jain's article in the matter of contents not available in Dr. Gode's article, a reference could be made to the incident of Sakiyas mentioned by her with the help of Hiuen-Tsang's account (p. 244-245) and the custom among the Punjabis and Himachalis (p. 248). But these points are very miner.

(vi) So far as the sources other than those mentioned in V. are concerned one will find that most of the sources she has taken from Dr. Gode's article.

(vii) The writer of this note personally feels that Usha Jain's article is a good case of plagiarism and not a contribution to the subject proper and she should stop, in near future, writing the articles of this type and take proper care to disclose the sources of her article without fighting shy for the same.

FOOT NOTES

1. JGJKSV. Vol. No. XV Parts 1-4, pp. 283-284, 1984.

XXI

DEVALA SMṚTI RECONSTRUCTION AND A CRITICAL STUDY*

Dr. Wadekar's attempt at reconstruction of the lost Devala Smṛti is certainly laudable particularly against the background of the incomplete and futile attempts of other scholars like S.C. Banerji and Pandita Udaya Vira Śāstrī. In the matter of reconstruction of the lost text. Dr. Wadekar has followed the model laid down by P.V. Kane and K.V. Rangaswami Aiyangar and others.

As regards the contents of the first Volume, it must be stated here that Wadekar has exhaustively discussed the bio-data of the Smṛtikāra Devala, necessity of reconstruction of the text of the Devala Smṛti, General information of the Smṛtis and the causes for the extinction of the smṛtis and the methodology of reconstruction. Further, the text of the Devala Smṛti is arranged under the four heads of Acāra – Adhyāya, p. 1-207, Vyavahāra Adhyāya, p. 208-214, Prāyaścitta Adhyāya, p. 223-294 and Pariśiṣṭam – Devaloktam Jyotiṣam – including the Saṁskārāḥ, Kṛṣiḥ, Grahācāra and Ariṣṭahāni, p. 320-329 and the Bibliography, p. 331-357.

So far as the second volume is concerned, Wadekar has

discussed in all seven chapters, reconstructed text-out-line. reconstructed text-date, reconstructed text-region of its origin, text summary of the reconstructed text, the distinctive features of the text under the religious features, sacramental features, ritualistic features, expiatory features, social features and legal features. He has further discussed Devala's philosophical speculations, his indebtedness to Sāṁkhya and Yoga and the Relevance of the present text in the modern age. He has devoted one more section as an appendix for Authors and Works mentioned in the text, Mantras quoted and indicated in the text, place names occurring in the text, three more articles on Devala–A forgotten Authority on Jyotiṣa, the unnoticed Devala exposition of comets and additional verses ascribed to Devala in the Yatidharmasamuccaya of Yādava Prakāśa, and lastly the index of verses. At the end, he has given General Index to both the volumes and Bibliography.

As regards the treatment given by Wadekar to the subject. it must be stated here that it is very exhaustive, thorough and systematic. He has also adopted the comparative outlook in respect of the views of Manu. Yājñāvalkya and Devala.

Wadekar has fixed the probable date of the Devala Smṛti as not later than 200 A.D. He has also thrown light on the personality of Devala as a Brahmavādin; philosopher, Yogin, Jyotiṣī and his acquaintance with the Caraka and Śilpa Śāstra. He has also added that the present reconstructed text indicates three different strata from the 1st century B.C. to the 12th century A.D. In these strata, there is the inclusion of matter of Sūtras, Smṛtis and Vratas from the Purāṇa. Wadekar has also explained the ten impediments in the Yoga p. 163, shown 11 respectable persons according to Devala p. 29-30 and simple and practical explanations of Yogic terms on the part of Devala. He has also brought to light the priority of Devala to the Sāṁkhyakārikā, p. 172 and the Vedānta influence on Devala, p. 171.

Some of the novel views of Devala particularly in comparison with the views of the other Smṛtikāras deserve special notice here :

(1) When, however, the adequate number of brāhmaṇas is not available, and it is impossible for a person to perform the Śrāddha in its fullness, Devala has given seven substitutes for which attention may be drawn to the volume II, p. 50. But it may be noted in this context that in Kane's *History of Dharma-Śāstra,* there is no place for this point.

(2) As regards the number of Yajñopavītas to be used by a person, Devala goes to the extent of suggesting the number from 1 to 5, as is clear from the discussion in the Devala Smṛti vol. II, p. 61.

(3) Devala gives consolation to a sonless person. He does not agree with other Smṛtikāras that a person, without having a son, goes to hell. From the discussion in the Devala Smṛti, vol. II, p. 37-38, it becomes clear that if a person properly brings up his daughter and gives her in marriage, he does not go to hell.

(4) As regards the consanguinty (sāpiṇḍya), the general view is that one should not marry a girl falling within 5 degrees on mother's side and 7 degrees on father's side. Devala has a special view. If a girl of proximate relation is to be married, at least she should be beyound three degrees from father's and mother's side.

(5) On theft, Devala has a novel view. Devala holds that the stealing of the books, manuscripts, cover, holder, wrapper etc., becomes very sinful. Such a person committing the theft of the writing material becomes completely dumb on this earth. (vol. II, p. 99)

(6) As regards Bhrūṇa, Devala has a special view that is reflected in the passage No. 1541 quoted on p. 209 of the first volume. When a small child, holding a weapon in the hands, comes to attack a person, one who kills such a child does not become a killer of a child but by not killing such a child, he becomes a killer of a child. For the different meanings of Bhrūṇa, attention is drawn to the discussion of the present reviewer in 'A peep at Indology,' p. 32, D.K. printworld, Delhi, 1994.

(7) The Dharma-Śāstra authors accept *gurutalpagamana* as a great sin. By the word Guru, Devala includes 11 persons such as Upādhyāya, father, eldest brother, king, maternal uncle, father-in-law, protector, maternal grand-father and paternal grand-father, senior-most in the caste and uncle. Devala holds, (vol. 1 passage No. 10, page No. 2) that cohabiting with the wife of the above mentioned 11 persons is a great sin. Devala's interpretation of the word 'Guru' as inclusive of eleven persons is perhaps the widest interpretation of the term.

(8) The Devala Smṛti is composed in Northern India and probably in the Sindha country as pointed out by Wadekar. The Social importance of this smṛti lies in re-admitting into the Hindu fold the persons who are converted to other faiths. Compared to Kane's treatment of this point Wadekar's treatment is rather meagre. But he has done more justice to this topic by contributing a paper on this aspect of re-admittance to the Journal of the Oriental Studies of Aligarh University , vol. V, Nos. 1-2, 1988, p. 159-161. Here he has given the chart of the expiations as per duration of stay and act. This will have to be considered as an improvement upon Dr. Kane's treatment in the History of Dharma-Śāstra.

Coming to the identification of the places mentioned in the Devala Smṛti vol. 1, p. 210-218, one will have to say that

Wadekar has shown his interest in the Geography of India. Though Dr. Wadekar has made the best use of the material available in the fourth volume of Kane's monumental *History of Dharma-Śāstra*, he has not stated the chapters and verses given by Kane. Here one is almost tempted to say that he had an opportunity to use those figures. He could have compressed the matter from it. At one place his information on Malahārī, vol. II, p. 213 is not found in Kane's work. But his treatment of the place Pṛthūdaka is complementary to the matter of Kane. Here one will have to remember that Kane's treatment of this topic is very exhaustive, methodical and systematic. Further, for the Aditya Tirthas and Lohita, Wadekar has, not at all utilised the matter from Kane's work.

As regards the Bibliography given in both the volumes, it must be stated that Dr. Wadekar has consulted a large number of books and naturally one will not be justified in expecting him to consult more works. The nove feature of the bibliography is that he has consulted the manuscripts in the Oriental Institute of Baroda, for the purpose of reconstruction of the Devala Smṛti.

Dr. Wadekar deserves credit for collecting about 2,500 passages ascribed to Devala scattered in the vast Dharma-Śāstra literature. The present reviewer, however has come across one place which is not found in collection of the quotations from Devala in the reconstructed text.

In the Vidyāmādhavīya vol. III, p. 65, there is stanza quoted from the astrological work of Devala on the point of bad *tithis* on which one should not undertake any journey. This stanza runs as follows :

"शुक्लपक्षे प्रतिपदि पञ्चदश्यां तथैव च।
न याति यात: स्वगृह्यं वित्तनाशं तथाऽश्नुते।"

This work is published by Mysore University – 1926. It

would be out of place in this review to draw Dr. Wadekar's attention to the two learned papers of Prof. Lallanji Gopal on 'Asita Devala in the Śānti Parva of the *Mahābhārata*' published in the Journal of the A.B.O.R., vol. No. LXVIII for 1987 (150th Birth anniversary volume of R.G. Bhandarkar), p. 245-267 and his another paper in the Ganganath Jha Kendriya Sanskrit Vidyapitha, vol. XXXVII, p. 189-197. One would like to know his reactions on these two papers of Lallanji Gopal.

Finally, I close this review by congratulating Dr. Wadekar from the bottom of my heart, for his excellent presentation of the reconstructed text of Devala-Smṛti and his treatment to the Dharma-Śāstra. Students of Dharma-Śāstra will remain indebted to Dr. Wadekar for his sincere service to the cause of Sanskrit learning in general and Dharma-Śāstra in particular.

FOOT NOTES

* This review is published in JAS, Bombay, Vol. No. 74 for 1999, pp. 284-287.

AUTHOR/BOOK INDEX

TOPICAL INDEX